# FRANK AYDELOTTE AND THE OXFORD APPROACH TO ENGLISH STUDIES IN AMERICA, 1908-1940

### Michael G. Moran

University Press of America,® Inc.
Lanham · Boulder · New York · Toronto · Oxford

Copyright © 2006 by
University Press of America,® Inc.
4501 Forbes Boulevard
Suite 200
Lanham, Maryland 20706
UPA Acquisitions Department (301) 459-3366

PO Box 317
Oxford
OX2 9RU, UK

All rights reserved
Printed in the United States of America
British Library Cataloging in Publication Information Available

Library of Congress Control Number: 2006923756
ISBN-13: 978-0-7618-3477-9 (clothbound : alk. paper)
ISBN-10: 0-7618-3477-X (clothbound : alk. paper)
ISBN-13: 978-0-7618-3478-6 (paperback : alk. paper)
ISBN-10: 0-7618-3478-8 (paperback : alk. paper)

∞™ The paper used in this publication meets the minimum
requirements of American National Standard for Information
Sciences—Permanence of Paper for Printed Library Materials,
ANSI Z39.48—1984

To Alison, with love

# Contents

| | |
|---|---|
| Preface | vii |
| **Chapter I** | |
| Introduction | 1 |
| **Chapter II** | |
| Education in America and Britain | 29 |
| **Chapter III** | |
| Developing the Thought Approach at Indiana, 1908-1915 | 53 |
| **Chapter IV** | |
| The Oxford Approach at MIT, 1915-1921 | 91 |
| **Chapter V** | |
| The Oxford Approach and Honors Education at Swarthmore, 1921-1940 | 123 |
| **Chapter VI** | |
| Conclusion | 159 |
| Bibliography | 165 |
| Index | 177 |
| About the Author | 185 |

# Preface

I first came across the name Frank Aydelotte in James A. Berlin's *Rhetoric and Reality* when that book appeared many years ago. Since I was then directing writing programs, and looking for ways to combine reading and writing into a coherent program of study, I was drawn to Aydelotte's work on the thought approach to composition as a general model. As I delved deeper into Aydelotte's writings, I found other connections with him. Like me, he had also been interested in technical communication, and, like me, he was interested in honors education. I felt a real confluence between my interests and his, even though he had begun working as a teacher and administrator more than half a century before I did.

As I read his extensive body of work, I came to see Aydelotte as a centrally-important figure in a number of areas of English studies during a time when English was defining itself as a discipline. His seminal experience was becoming a Rhodes Scholar from Indiana in 1904. While at Oxford University, he experienced a curriculum that he considered superior to the American methods then in general use. Oxford's undergraduate honors schools stimulated students to do their best work by means of weekly tutorials, extensive reading lists, and comprehensive examinations. When he returned to America to take a position in the English Department of Indiana University, he developed the thought approach to composition, which challenged students to work out their best thought in writing. Like many innovators, however, he drew the ire of more traditional colleagues and left IU under a cloud. Upon moving to MIT, he applied the principles of the thought approach there, publishing *English and Engineering* (1917), the first anthology of essays for the technical writing course. After a successful six years in Cambridge, he moved to Swarthmore College, where, as president, he modified his Oxford principles to develop that college's influential Honors Program. This program was based on the honors seminar, which made writing and presenting essays the center of his educational method. Under his leadership, Swarthmore became one of the most influential small colleges in the nation.

My work, I hope, contributes to the on-going attempt to understand the development of English studies in the United States. My method of approach deserves some comment. It is biographical because I wanted to accomplish two broad goals. First, I wanted to do more than discuss Aydelotte's ideas. I also wanted to examine in various social, cultural, educational, and personal forces that shaped Aydelotte's work. As I read and thought about his life and work, I came to appreciate the degree to which he committed himself to the ideas he experienced at Oxford. Even though his rejection of formal instruction in rhetoric is a notable weakness in all of his curriculums, his emphasis on the importance of encouraging original thought was a notable achievement at a time when much American higher education emphasized the social over the intellectual life, and rhetoric was limited largely to the concepts of Harvard formalism.

*Preface*

The biographical approach had a second advantage: it allowed me to present Aydelotte's work in its entirety. Some work had been done on parts of Aydelotte's extensive contributions to English studies. His thought approach had been discussed by historians of composition studies, his work on engineering writing had been discussed by historians of technical communication, and his Swarthmore honors program had been discussed by historians of education. But no scholar had presented Aydelotte's work in English studies as a whole. The biographical approach allowed me to do this, and I hope the book helps readers understand better Aydelotte's work in its complexity.

I also hope this book makes clear both Aydelotte's strengths and weaknesses, but I especially hope it elucidates his many efforts over a long career to use writing to make students better thinkers.

This book does not replace Frances Blanshard's *Frank Aydelotte of Swarthmore*, the standard biography, but I hope it supplements it in useful ways. Blanshard's book is a fuller study, which discusses Aydelotte's entire career, including several important areas that my book does not address, including, for instance, Aydelotte's significant work on the Rhodes Trust and the Guggenheim Fellowships. My book concentrates almost entirely on Aydelotte's contributions to English studies, especially composition and technical communication, areas that Blanshard touches on but does not fully explore. My book is also more critical of Aydelotte and his work in an attempt to present a more balanced assessment. Blanshard was a close associate of Aydelotte's at Swarthmore, his Dean of Women for a time, and her biography, which resulted from a collaboration with the subject, has some of the weaknesses of such a work.

There are many people who helped me research and write this book. I would like to thank especially the archives of the three libraries that hold collections of Aydelotte material. At the Indiana University archives, Heather Munro, Faye E. Mark, and Elizabeth Andrews were specially helpful as was Elizabeth Andrews (a different Elizabeth Andrews!), the Reference Archivist at the Libraries of the Massachusetts Institute of Technology. Special thanks go to Swarthmore, which holds the majority of Aydelotte's papers. Alfred H. Bloom, President of the college, took time out of his busy schedule to meet with me and give me permission to use the archives, and Mary Ellen Chijioke, then Curator of the Friends Historical Library of Swarthmore College, kindly made her facilities available to me. Without access to the manuscript material, I could not have written the book.

I also want to thank Professors John C. Brereton and Charles Bazerman for reading an early version of my manuscript and providing suggestions for revisions. Their suggestions made the book better than it would have been. I, of course, take responsibility for all remaining weaknesses.

I would also like to thank Baywood for allowing me to use in chapter 4 a revised version of "Frank Aydelotte: AT&T's First Writing Consultant" originally published in the *Journal of Technical Writing and Communication*.

*Preface*

I would also like to thank Maureen Hardegree, who served ably as my Assistant Director of First-Year Composition at Georgia, co-authored the Aydelotte bibliography with me, and wrote a strong thesis under my direction on the early work of Aydelotte and Harrison Steeves.

Thanks also go to Hugh Ruppersburg, then Head of English at Georgia, for providing me with a travel grant to work at Swarthmore, to my colleagues Simon Gatrell, who discussed the Oxford system with me, Jonathan Evans, who gave key advice about formatting the book, and Michelle Ballif and Christy Desmet, who offered support through the years..

Special thanks go to Michael Simon, who encouraged me during the dark days.

As usual, I wish to thank my wife, Molly Hurley Moran, for all her support during the long process of researching and writing this book. Without her, nothing else makes sense.

This book is lovingly dedicated to my daughter, Alison Emily Moran, who has taught me the meaning of courage.

Michael G. Moran

# 1: Introduction

In June 5, 1933, Frank Aydelotte's face appeared on the cover of *Time* magazine as a tribute to his many significant contributions to American higher education. He was, in fact, at the height of his influence as an educator. As the American Secretary to the Rhodes Trust, he had been the driving force behind making the Rhodes Scholarship the most prestigious academic scholarship that an American student could win (Blanshard 239-43; "Rhodesmen at Swarthmore" 47-48). In 1925 he had been instrumental in establishing the distinguished Guggenheim Fellowships and, in 1933, continued to serve as the organization's Educational Advisor (Blanshard 246-54). Since 1921 he had been President of Swarthmore, a 500-student Quaker college that he had formed into one of the nation's best small liberal arts schools (Beardsley et al. 3; Clark 186; "Rhodesmen" 48; Embree "Order" 662). He accomplished this goal by establishing Swarthmore's influential Honors Program, which he, with the help of the Swarthmore faculty and its Board of Managers, had designed to stimulate bright students to work to their full potential free from the distractions of daily preparation for conventional classes. By 1933, the Swarthmore program had become the national model of its kind, and the academic community considered Aydelotte the leading expert on honors education. The editors of the June 5, 1933, issue of *Time* recognized his influence by commenting on the cover that "He would reprieve democracy from mediocrity," a statement that expressed a growing belief at the time that American higher education catered to the average and neglected the superior student. It also expressed a growing sense of elitism that began to permeate American higher education–the belief, which Aydelotte embraced, that at least some American colleges should prepare a select group of leaders to exert American influence on the world stage.

While Aydelotte has been recognized for his many accomplishments as an administrator, he has not been as widely recognized for his contributions to the development of English studies during the first half of the 20th century. Before accepting Swarthmore's presidency, he was in fact one of the most innovative English professors in the United States, developing nationally important English courses and curriculums at Indiana University (1908-1915) and the Massachusetts Institute of Technology (1915-1921) before revamping Swarthmore's traditional small college curriculum (1921-1940). He attempted to apply to all of his curriculums some of the methods that he had experienced as a Rhodes scholar at Oxford from 1905-07 and 1912-13. This experience convinced him that Oxford had established educational methods, such as the tutorial system and the honors schools, that produced a better-trained undergraduate than did the American system. Oxford graduates, in his opinion, were prepared to function as leaders in their fields and thereby expand the influence of England throughout the world. He believed that the Oxford system could be modified to meet American needs (*Breaking* 20) and produce an equivalent cadre of leaders who would extend the prestige and power of the United States. Aydelotte's primary contribution to higher education, then, was to modify the Oxford method of English instruction to make it workable in the very different climate of the American college and university. Because of his commitment to the personalized methods of British instruction, Aydelotte brought to the American college a progressive spirit of flexibility and individuality and, to use one of his favorite words, "thoroughness" that American higher education, according to historian Frederick Rudolph, at the time largely lacked. As *Time* noted in 1933, Oxford instilled "scholarliness" in the American Rhodes scholars like Aydelotte, and the Rhodes scholars, upon returning home, "spread scholarliness among their [American] fellows" and students ("Rhodesmen" 47).

The purpose of my study is to establish the critical role that Aydelotte's work played in shaping the development of American education, English studies, and composition theory and instruction during the first half of the 20th century. His body of work should be better known than it is because this work sheds light on issues and problems that university and college English departments and writing programs continue to grapple with today. These issues include the relationship between literature and writing, the humanistic basis of technical communication, and the need to develop curriculums and programs that use writing to stimulate students, especially above-average students, to work to their full potential. As one of the important progressive educators during the first half of the 20th century, he changed the face of American English instruction in particular and higher education in general.

## Historical Contexts

## Education

When Aydelotte began his college teaching career at IU in 1908, many American institutions of higher learning were nearing the end of an evolution from the small, often denominational college to the large, complex university (Adams *History* ch 1; Veysey ch 1). The old college, an institution only occasionally challenged before the Civil War, was typically a small, intimate, religious school that based its set curriculum on the classical languages, rhetoric, and mathematics with some attention to history, science, and moral philosophy. While restricted, this curriculum prepared an elite social group for a few gentlemanly professions, primarily the ministry, politics, and law. The college rejected a wider vocationalism in favor of liberal studies which produced gentlemen who had the right, the colleges assumed, to ascend to leadership positions in American democracy because of their class. In such positions, the elite, due to its cultured background, could control other elements of society, including "the twin excesses of grasping businessmen and unruly industrial proletarians" (Graff 21).

To prepare this elite, the old college emphasized discipline, both moral and mental (Russell 36). As a quasi-religious institution, the college inculcated its student body with the moral principles of its sect. Mental discipline was ensured by rigid instructional methods, the primary mode of which was recitation. Teachers required students to recite orally from memory the particulars of the textbook for the course. This process, the argument went, developed mental discipline, the assumption, based on faculty psychology, that the "mind and character are strengthened by strenuous, repetitive exercise on disagreeably difficult tasks" (Graff 30). In actuality, in the hands of a less than gifted teacher, the method privileged memorization of factual minutiae over the mastery of deeper knowledge. The goal of the college was not to educate broadly but narrowly--to form students into an educated elite sharing the same values and prescribed body of knowledge.

After the Civil War, the American public demanded that the traditional college expand its curriculum to reflect the changed realities of the second half of 19th-century America. As historian Frederick Rudolph put it, "the evidence abounded that Latin and Greek did not have much to do with the directions in which American society appeared to be headed" (*Curriculum* 57). The American college was now expected to serve a new clientele composed of students from middle class families. This group expected training for careers in the new worlds of business, industry, and government service (Berlin *Writing* 58; Veysey 4-5). These worlds were vastly different from the antebellum agricultural society based on rural and small town life. The new realities were structured by urban manufacturing, industrialization, and the science on which they were based. The Civil War had been won by the North's industrial and technological superiority as well as its army (Earnest 138), a fact that might have been lost on the old college traditionalist but not on the public at large.

The old college in reality was becoming irrelevant as other avenues to wealth and prestige opened (Russell 36), and many young men preferred a business career in the city to being a college-educated small-town lawyer or clergyman (Veysey 4-5). Practical people of the time, many of them financially successful men of the world who had not attended college, recognized that if the United States hoped to compete on the world stage, it needed to encourage the growth of new fields, especially science, technology, and agriculture. In order to flourish, these fields needed to be based on scientific research. To ensure the development of such research fields, powerful industrialists and manufacturers bequeathed fortunes to specific universities to create vocational curriculums for science, technology, and business. Such men included Ezra Cornell (Cornell University), J.S. Pillsbury (University of Michigan), and Johns Hopkins (Johns Hopkins University), to name but three. These gifts worked toward the same end as did the Morrill Act, which Abraham Lincoln signed in 1862. The act took effect gradually over the following decades and encouraged vocational and technical studies by donating public lands in states and territories to build land-grant universities required to teach agriculture and engineering. By 1900, because of these various changes, college students studied the liberal arts only during their first two years and then, during their last two, could specialize in various courses of studies such as engineering, agriculture, business, and the humanities (Adams *History* 1).

To create the new university, some of the more innovative American colleges turned to the German university for a new model of higher education, one based not on the old college's dissemination of received wisdom but on specialized research and the development of new knowledge (Rudolph *American College* 274-75). While a handful of Americans had studied in German universities in the early years of the 19th century, by mid-century there was intense interest in those institutions, which many reformers saw as appropriate models for American education (Veysey 10). Unlike the American professor, who as a generalist could teach a variety of subjects, the German professor was a specialist in his field who lectured to his undergraduates in his area of expertise. Specialization led to a new division of labor, replacing the old college generalist with the new university specialist (Higham 3).

The rise of specialization therefore drastically changed the purpose and structure of the college and university. As John Higham argues, "the rampant growth of specialization," with its emphasis on the development of specialized knowledge, changed the objective of 19th-century education (3-4). This new objective became to certify specialists to enter occupations that controlled esoteric information not available to the outsider. A college degree became the credential that admitted a graduate into a profession just as the lack of that credential excluded the non-initiated from it. In terms of college structure, the department became the unit that represented the specialized discipline, and each department was responsible for developing and teaching the disciplinary courses.

With the decline of the old curriculum also came a new emphasis on developing programs that met students' differing interests, and this movement gave rise to the elective system championed by President William Charles Eliot of Harvard. Harvard's system was based on a new view of educational psychology. The old principles of mental discipline were jettisoned for a new emphasis on "individual differences and the importance of the student's pursuing his [or her] own natural talents" (Berlin *Writing* 60). Under Harvard's pure elective system, fully in place by the end of the century and a model for other institutions, students had virtually no required courses and took whatever interested them or prepared them for employment.[1] They graduated when they compiled enough credit hours, no matter what combinations of courses taken and passed. By 1900, the only required course at Harvard was English A, the first-year writing course. Because the elective system encouraged students to take a variety of courses, it helped establish the many new specialized courses and programs in science, technology, and other developing disciplines.

Throughout his career, Aydelotte questioned the value of intense specialization, and his curriculums attempted to mitigate some of the effects of this movement. At Oxford, he had experienced a system that combined in one integrated program several studies designed to prepare graduates for general careers. A specialist in English literature, for instance, would study not only literature but also English history and philosophy to learn how literature fits within these related intellectual contexts. Upon graduation, such students could teach in several fields. Aydelotte's Oxford mentor, Professor Walter Raleigh, for instance, took his degree in history but taught and wrote on English literature. Understanding relationships among disciplines became for Aydelotte the sign of an educated person. He considered the elective system a failure because it emphasized discrete courses that did not encourage students to understand these course's intellectual connections with other disciplines. In place of discrete courses, Aydelotte developed programs that combined studies. At MIT, for instance, he helped devise an English-History program that combined these two subjects in a series of courses to give engineering students a general understanding of literature within the contexts of broad historical movements such as the French and Industrial Revolutions. At Swarthmore, he used a similar model to develop his honors program that required juniors and seniors to read intensively in three related areas. During these two years, for instance, English majors took closely related seminars in English literature, history, and philosophy. Following the Oxford model, Aydelotte advocated the shift in American education from what he saw as the chaos of the elective system to the coherence of the Oxford approach.[2]

The Swarthmore approach, however, was not without its problems, two of which stand out. First, honors students were limited in the range of courses they could take and therefore could not develop secondary interests by taking courses unconnected to their major and its cognate seminars.[3] Swarthmore honors students, for instance, were allowed no electives during their last two years. The system did not encourage them to explore interests in unrelated disciplines, nor could they develop a minor outside their major and its cognates. The English major, for instance, who wished to take art history as a formal minor was out of luck. Second, the Aydelotte approach did not allow the depth of study that the elective system did. In the elective system, students could focus the majority of their course work on their major area and the rest of their work in other areas that interested them. At Swarthmore they were limited to a set program of seminars reminiscent in some ways of the limited curriculum of the $19^{th}$-century college.

But the advantage of Aydelotte's approach is obvious. Through the set seminars and the comprehensive examinations that followed them, students learned directly to see the connections among related disciplines in ways that the elective system did not encourage.

## Rhetoric and Composition

As the American college changed, so did its approach to rhetoric. In the old college, as Russell argues, speech was privileged over writing (38). Recitation itself was based on the spoken word, and students regularly prepared and gave public speeches, essays, debates, and forensics (40). Writing, however, was not completely ignored. Although spoken, many of these oral discourses were based on written versions, and these were often evaluated for written expression. With the rise of specialization, however, spoken discourse diminished in importance as the written discourse of the professions became the privileged means of academic communication. Every speciality developed its own professional organizations with journals to disseminate the written results of research, and part of a student's education, especially on advanced levels, was to master the discourse conventions of a chosen field. The emphasis on written discourse was intensified with the development of graduate programs at schools such as Johns Hopkins and Harvard that required students to write theses and dissertations. As writing became important to advancement in an academic culture dominated by the printed word, more writing courses were initially required. Harvard, for instance, in the 1880s recognized that students needed more writing instruction and instituted four years of courses (Adams *History* [11-12]), but this emphasis did not last long and few other colleges followed suit. Ironically, despite writing's growing importance to the academy and to the professions, by 1900, only the freshman English course was universally taught (Adams *History* 10-15), and it alone became the standard part of the college curriculum during much of the 20th century. Because of Harvard's national influence, this lone course was often modeled on Harvard formalist rhetoric, which later became known as current-traditional rhetoric.

By the end of the 19th century, when Aydelotte entered IU as a student, formalist rhetoric had established itself as the dominant teaching rhetoric in the nation (Goggin 3). It grew out of the Harvard reforms of Eliot, who assumed the presidency in 1867. Eliot initiated influential curricular innovations, which included the displacement of the classical curriculum that had dominated the old college, and the expansion of courses in science and technology. These new courses were designed to prepare the new middle class students for careers. One subject that replaced classical studies was English composition, for Eliot believed that students needed to be able to speak and write in the vernacular to succeed in the worlds of business, science, and technology. Eliot therefore hired Adams Sherman Hill, a former journalist, to develop a writing curriculum appropriate to the new pragmatic, vocational goals of the university. To assist Hill, Eliot gradually hired other composition instructors, including Barrett Wendell, LeBaron Briggs, and C.T. Copeland, and these early English professors designed courses, published research, and/or wrote textbooks that established formalist rhetoric as the standard approach to writing instruction in America up to about 1960.

By 1900 formalism had become almost universally established in textbooks and writing courses in America. Concern for discovering content had been replaced by a concern for conventional structure. As Adams Sherman Hill of Harvard put it in *The Principles of Rhetoric* (1878), rhetoric "does not undertake to furnish a person with something to say; but it does undertake to tell him how best to say that which he has provided himself" (65). This managerial stance pervaded the dominant approaches to rhetoric, reducing invention to outlining and applying conventional forms to essay writing (see Crowley *Methodical*). By excluding more sophisticated invention strategies from rhetoric, the Harvard formalists largely reduced composition to issues of form, style, and correctness. Students already had something to say, Hill and other late-century managerial rhetoricians assumed; these writers needed only advice on how to arrange that information and express it correctly and forcefully on paper.

Consequently, by the 1890s most composition textbooks offered students abstract rules for composing essays. Longer papers, for instance, were organized according to the modes of discourse—narration, description, exposition, and argumentation, although these terms varied slightly from text to text. Paragraphs, according to Scott and Denny's popular *Paragraph-Writing*, were organized by the methods of exposition—definition, division, illustration, classification, and so on. In *English Composition*, Harvard's Barrett Wendell offered the trinity of unity, coherence, and emphasis (he called the last *mass*) to guide student production of sentences, paragraphs, and essays. In *The Principles of Rhetoric*, Adams Sherman Hill reduced advice on diction and style to three principles: clearness, force, and ease (81-144). Finally, by century's end, teachers drilled students with the niceties of mechanical correctness, which included spelling, usage, grammar, and syntax. As Connors notes in *Composition-Rhetoric*, an examination of graded papers of the period indicates the intense commitment of composition teachers to form: they limited their comments to mechanical issues and largely ignored rhetorical effectiveness and quality of thought. This approach was somewhat understandable, Connors notes, since these turn-of-the-century composition instructors often taught classes with 100 students and lacked time and energy to make more thoughtful comments.

It was not, of course, that students, especially the weaker ones, did not need advice on formal elements. Many who lacked experience with the written word required some instruction in form and correctness. The problem was that students received little else by way of instruction, a fact that came to disturb Aydelotte. He recognized that students needed more emphasis on content and thought, and developed the thought approach to place more emphasis on the cognitive elements of writing.

One of Aydelotte's important contributions to composition theory and practice, then, was to serve as one of the few voices in the wilderness to question the wisdom of emphasizing only conventional form. First, he rejected the position that writing was a matter of following the modes of discourse. Few if any published essays, he argued in his book *College English*, follow a single mode. Instead, essays invariably reflect the habits of thought of the writer, Aydelotte argued. Some authors tend to think in narratives; others, in expositions. Furthermore, most essays mix the modes in complex ways. Consequently, teachers hamstring student thought by requiring them to follow slavishly modal patterns. Second, and more important, emphasis on conventional forms misleads beginning writers. All good writing begins with good thinking, Aydelotte assumed, and good thinking is always highly individualistic. The heart of the writing course, therefore, should be to help students think for themselves and then express that thought in prose that is both clear and personal. Aydelotte consistently rejected any approach that did not make thought and the expression of that thought the primary elements in the writing process.

Aydelotte's pedagogy, however, had two major weakness. While the Oxford approach that formed the basis of the thought approach worked with well-prepared students like those highly selective and educated undergraduates admitted to Oxford, it did not work as well with students lacking rich experience with the written word. This refusal to recognize that less well prepared students needed work on formal concerns placed Aydelotte at odds with much of the conventional thinking of his time and, as I will discuss later, contributed to the political problems at Indiana University that led to his resignation.

The second weakness resulted from Aydelotte's rejection of rhetoric. The thought approach assumed that good writing was good thinking written down. Consequently, rhetorical strategy–such as analyzing the audience, using formal invention strategies, studying stylistic devices and organizational strategies, and reviewing mechanics–received little direct attention in Aydelotte's work. A product of his time without training in the history of rhetoric, he conceived of rhetoric in formalist terms and rejected it, privileging thought over strategy. But, at a time when so much writing instruction emphasized form alone, Aydelotte's emphasis on thought was a much needed counter.

## Liberal Culturalism and Aydelotte

Recent histories of writing instruction in America sometimes mention Aydelotte but, since they do not examine the full body of his work, often mislead with half truths.[4] Aydelotte has been wrongly cast as a liberal culturalist, a kind of academic conservative at the time, a mistake that partly explains his thought being overlooked. I intend to rectify this mis-perception by showing that, while Aydelotte had some liberal cultural tendencies, many of his key assumptions about English studies are inconsistent with seminal liberal culture positions.

James A. Berlin presents the standard analysis of Aydelotte in *Rhetoric and Reality* by classifying him with the liberal culturalists, a group of English professors associated with Yale, Princeton, and Columbia who "held that all material reality has a spiritual foundation and that the business of education was to enable students to see beyond the material to ideal. The study of art was thought to be uniquely designed to do just this" (44). The liberal culturalists questioned the value of practical writing instruction for most students on the grounds that only the gifted few could learn to write well. The average student would be better served not by taking compulsory composition courses but by reading and discussing great literature. In addition to subscribing to this aesthetic position, the liberal culturalists also based their position on "a tacit social and moral code" that was aristocratic and suspicious of democracy (45)."Most proponents" Berlin continued, "were Anglophiles who favored class distinctions and aspired to the status of an educated aristocracy of leadership and privilege, a right that was claimed on their spiritual vision–partly a matter of birth and partly a product of having attended the right schools" (45). People achieved spiritual vision through years of reading important literature. Liberal culture rhetoric emphasized the centrality of "the individual voice, the unique expression that indicated a gifted and original personality at work" (45). While Berlin's claim that Aydelotte shared these assumptions is compelling at first glance, a closer look suggests that Aydelotte does not share many liberal culture values.

Most liberal culturalists criticized the growth of specialization and distrusted professional courses and programs in colleges and universities. Members of this group viewed professional training as limiting, culture as liberating. Brander Matthews, of Columbia, for instance, wanted his university undergraduates "to consider higher things than mere bread-and-butter studies" of the professional sort by encouraging them to breathe the heady "atmosphere of culture"(182). Other liberal culturalists rejected professional training because it limited the development of sound character, a key goal of most members of this movement. For instance, in "The Practical Value of a Liberal Education," William A. Merrill of Miami University argued that in college ". . . the course of study is not planned for the making of good lawyers, doctors, chemists, and merchants" (440-41). Instead, colleges should prepare men of sound character. Alexander Meiklejohn of Amherst College agreed. Unlike technical and professional schools, he argued, liberal colleges should not teach students to think like members of a profession; instead, such colleges should train students "to take human activity as a whole, to understand human endeavors not in their isolation but in their relations to one another . . ." (121). Writing particularly about the University of Nebraska, Herbert Bates put the proposition more strongly: "Some students graduate in educated illiteracy, mere thinkers of acids, contrivers of dynamos, computers of sentence-length, diggers after derivations" (606). Similarly, R. M. Wenley of the University of Michigan argued that education should "*educate* men, rather than *instruct* foresters, clerks, salesmen, agents, pedagogues, in their fecund kinds" ("Can We Stem" 245) (italics in original). Finally, in *The Spirit of America*, Henry Van Dyke of Princeton argued that the purpose of a liberal education "is not to fit men for any specific industry, but to give them those things which are everywhere essential to intelligent living" (227).

Unlike many liberal culturalists, Aydelotte valued professional training, in fact considered it necessary. Though he had been hired to broaden the background of

MIT's engineering students, Aydelotte was shrewd enough to recognize the importance of engineering education. Engineering students had to master the technical elements of their fields if they were to be effective professionals. But he also argued that engineers were more than technicians; they also had to interact with fellow workers, government officials, customers, and professionals in other fields. He believed that such interactions would be facilitated by a background in the humanities, especially in literature and writing. These studies would make them cultivated and articulate enough to be able to function in polite society. But they still needed their technical expertise to work as engineers.

Liberal culturalists also mistrusted specialization in English studies. As Graff puts it, the generalists (his term for the liberal culturalists) were "unfriendly toward practicality and minute investigation" (180). Most liberal culturalists looked with distaste upon the new German Ph.D. with its emphasis on philology, the linguistic analysis of literature. Dramatically, Bates, writing from a liberal culture perspective tested while teaching at the University of Nebraska (which had embraced German specialization), identified the problem he believed American education faced in the early 20th century:

> Education, we all know, is dividing into two parties: the party of those who seek fact, and the party of those who seek inspiration from fact; the party of mere science, and the party of those who demand not only science, but also beauty. Germany stands mainly on the side of mere fact; England and France mainly on the side of culture; America hangs in the balance. (605)

Fact-grubbing philologists, with their German Ph.D.s, were endangering the cultured generalist who sought Arnold's sweetness and light. Bliss Perry of Princeton and later Harvard cast the argument in a different form in *The Amateur Spirit*. This book distinguished between the professional and the amateur. The professional, whom he identified with German philology, "is apt to approach life from one side only." He continued: "from bending one's energies unremittingly upon a particular task, it often happens that creation narrows 'in man's view,' instead of widening. Your famous expert, as you suddenly discover, is but a segment of a man—over developed in one direction, atrophied in all others" (24-25). Taken too far, specialization damages the character. Professors and students, Perry argued, needed the broad training of a "liberal education" to counterbalance the "depth of technical research" (31-32). Four years later, in *Literature and the American College*, Irving Babbitt of Harvard, one of the most representative liberal culturalists, continued Perry's argument. Specialists trained in the German model with their philological Ph.D.s, Babbitt argued, became immersed in a minor subject that thwarted their growth as humans: "The work that leads to a doctor's degree is a constant temptation to sacrifice one's growth as a man to one's growth as a specialist" (107). Such specialization led to the "loss of mental balance" that the "old humanism" had maintained by demanding breadth rather than specialization (107). Wenley expressed the liberal culturalist rage at the new philologists' plans to shift American universities from general to specialist training when he wrote that

> the younger lions have roared at us that the university "exists to train specialists," and their din deafens, puzzles, or, where old women of both sexes abound, affrights.... But what kind of specialists? The humanistic sciolist who feels so keenly that he can assist at Elizabethan pot-house revels without turning a hair, but can find nothing except deliberate lechery in Whitman and George Bernard Shaw? ("Transition" 437)

Wenley thereby attacked the specialists on both intellectual and moral grounds.

Although Aydelotte questioned the value of philology with its emphasis on linguistic minutiae *(College English* vii), he did not question specialized research. In fact, he himself conducted such research throughout his career. His most significant research project was *Elizabethan Rogues and Vagabonds* (1913), the first book published in the Oxford Historical and Literary Studies series. While not philological, it is specialized research nonetheless. The book combined historical investigation and literary criticism to establish the nature of Renaissance rogues, sharpers, and crooks to shed light on these character types in Renaissance drama and pamphlet literature. The project, which applies historical evidence to literary problems, was in the Oxford, not the German, tradition. As Aydelotte became more deeply involved in teaching and administration, he did less research, but he did maintain an interest in the Renaissance and published in 1942 a scholarly essay based on Huntington Library research entitled "Elizabethan Seamen in Mexico and Ports of the Spanish Main" in the *American History Review*. In between, Aydelotte published pedagogical research on his thought approach, his MIT program, and his Swarthmore curriculum, as well as books and essays connected to his Rhodes Trust and Guggenheim work. (For a preliminary bibliography of Aydelotte's work, see Moran and Hardegree.) Furthermore, he designed his curriculum at Swarthmore to introduce honors students to the scholarship in their fields.[5] His goal was to create not generalists but scholars who could work in the nation's best graduate programs. Finally, in 1940, when he became Director of Princeton's Institute for Advanced Study, Aydelotte lamented that American Ph.D.s stopped doing research after completing their degrees and argued that all college teachers should be "functioning, creative scholars" ("Postgraduates" 60).

Perhaps Aydelotte differs most from the liberal culturalists in his attitude toward literature. According to Berlin in *Rhetorics, Poetics, and Culture*, the liberal culturalists tended to prefer a "passive receptivity to literature, rather than creative rigor" (32). By merely reading literature, these teachers believed, students absorbed as if by osmosis beliefs liberal culturalists valued. Susan Miller in *Textual Carnivals* identifies the accepted dynamic of the time. In the literature/composition binary, literature was commonly considered high while composition was the emblem for the low, the carnivalesque (1-4). As Berlin argued in *Rhetoric and Reality*, liberal culturalists viewed literature as the perfect vehicle to help students grasp the spiritual

(44). Princeton's Van Dyke in *The Spirit of America* (1910), for instance, connected literature with this realm: "literature," he argued, "...is more than half spiritual. For words are not like lines, or colours, or sounds. They are living creatures begotten in the soul of man .... They have a wider range, a more delicate precision, a more direct and penetrating power than any other medium of expression" (242). L.A. Sherman of the University of Nebraska made a similar point in *Educational Review*: "Polite literature appeals to taste, and must be spiritually discerned and appreciated" (52).

But the best representative of the liberal culturalist view of literature according to Veysey (183n) was Cornell's Hiram Corson. In *The Aims of Literary Study*, he argued that readers must respond spiritually to literature. "Literature," he argued, "more especially poetic and dramatic literature, is the expression in letters of the spiritual, cooperating with the intellectual, man, the former [the spiritual] being the primary, dominant coefficient" (24). He rejected scholarship because it presented "a great obstacle to the truest and highest literary culture" (43). He advocated reading aloud as the most effective way to express literature's higher, spiritual meaning. In *The Voice and Spiritual Education*, first published in 1896, Corson justified his classroom practice: "A poem is not truly a poem until it is voiced by an accomplished reader who has adequately assimilated it–in whom it has, to some extent, been born again, according to his individual spiritual constitution and experiences" (28). It follows, then, that Corson thought close reading of a poem for its meaning was less important than hearing it performed. Vocal interpretation, he claimed, is "spiritualized thought" (133). In other words, the listener did not have to think carefully about poetic meaning because meaning grew from the nebulous spiritual communion of poet, performer, and listener.

Unlike liberal culturalists such as Corson, Aydelotte did not substitute literature for religion, nor did he view literature as an expression of the spiritual realm. He did not believe merely reading literature made a student better. Instead, he thought that literature, when approached properly, stimulated thought. Writers, he argued, present unique interpretations of life, and reading these works helps readers wrestle with basic questions of human experience. But Aydelotte also argued that students bring thought to literature–they are not empty vessels to be filled with ideas. Aydelotte's thought approach asked students to compare the ideas in the literature with ideas they already possessed to test their own thought against the thought of other, more mature minds. Through this comparison, students developed their own beliefs and modes of conduct.

Finally, Aydelotte, unlike the liberal culturalists, valued writing instruction. The liberal culture position, as Berlin argues in *Rhetoric and Reality*, viewed writing "as the embodiment of spiritual vision"; this vision could occur only after "years of literary study" under the guidance of a teacher/seer (45-46). Liberal culturalists therefore rejected required college writing courses because they were unnecessary (Brereton, personal correspondence). These theorists assumed that students should learn to write in high school, and, since only competent writers should be admitted to college, writing courses there were unnecessary. In his 1911 *Harper's* essay

"Compulsory Composition in Colleges" (1911), Thomas R. Lounsbury, an Emeritus Professor of English at Yale's Sheffield School, stated the liberal culturalist position. He was

> thoroughly convinced that . . . the criticism of themes, even when it is fully competent, is in the majority of cases of little value to the recipient; that in a large number of instances the criticism is and must ever be more or less incompetent; and that when the corrections which are made are made inefficiently and unintelligently, as is too often the case, the results reached are distinctly more harmful than helpful. (869)[6]

If composition courses failed, how could students learn to write? Lounsbury provided two answers, both of which assume writing can be learned but not taught. First, students must develop their intellectual faculties through hard study, strengthening their mental just as they strengthen their physical muscles. In other words, "mental development . . . [lies] at the foundation of all good writing" (876). This mental development resulted not from writing but from reading. Second, since writing is an imitative art, students must read important authors, "one or some number of those whom the race regards as its great literary representative" (876). Such imitation developed style. Aydelotte, on the other hand, believed not only that writing could be taught but that it facilitated learning. He developed compulsory composition courses at Indiana and MIT; at Swarthmore, while he rejected compulsory composition, he made writing central to the learning process in honors seminars. Rather than using literature to achieve spiritual truth, he integrated reading and writing to make students effective thinkers in prose.

While Aydelotte believed that writing could be taught, he shared the liberal culture suspicion of Harvard formalism, and his thought approach, like the liberal culturalists' spiritual approach, reacted against the Harvard emphasis on the modes of discourse and mechanical correctness. Aydelotte, however, took a middle ground between Glenn E. Palmer's opposing ranks of liberal culture and efficiency. Centered at Yale and Princeton, according to Palmer (writing in 1912), liberal culture emphasized literary interpretation and development of "a few geniuses by the systematic treatment of enriching thoughts and broadening experiences" (488). This method's primary flaw, Palmer argued, was its isolation of practical training in the reading of literature from the students' lives (489). The Harvard method, on the other hand, emphasized efficiency in its attempt to "cultivate" in freshmen "good language habits" through "painstaking drill in the writing of short themes." This drill prepared "a class full of Philistines . . . for the everyday needs of democracy" (488). As did the liberal culturalists, Aydelotte rejected Harvard's composition theory. But he also rejected the liberal culture position, perhaps best expressed in 1915 by Charles G. Osgood of Princeton, that the students' lack of control of mechanics resulted not from educational deficiencies but from personality problems. Such deep problems, including the inability to organize or punctuate or spell, could only be solved by making students better people through reading literature. The teacher must "stir, enrich, and fertilize the soil" of the student's soul by teaching literature, not writing (232-33).

Aydelotte took a different position on formal elements. He minimized the importance of mechanics and assumed that all college students, with individual effort and with some help from instructors, could adequately master correctness to write acceptable prose. As Aydelotte wrote in *College English*, "Mechanical correctness is not a merit in writing; it is only a necessity.... Correctness is sort of like wearing a necktie, a condition of entrance into good society, but not an admission ticket" (119-20). For Aydelotte, then, correctness, like wearing a tie, is merely a convention, a convention that students can master, especially if teachers do not expect perfection. In fact, demanding error-free prose is foolish. Aydelotte believed it more important that students express their ideas forcefully. Once they have something important to say, he claimed, they would want to express thought correctly and learn enough about mechanics to do so.

Some conservative liberal culturalists went further than rejecting writing instruction of the Harvard stamp. Many of them yearned to restore the old Greek and Latin curriculum because that approach developed style. In *Literature and the American College*, Babbitt speculated on the value of translation:

> It is still an open question whether any direct method of teaching English [such as the Harvard daily theme] really takes the place of the drill in the niceties of style that can be derived from the translation of Latin; whether a student, for example, who rendered Cicero with due regard for the delicate shades of meaning would not gain more mastery of English . . . than the student who devoted the same amount of time to daily themes and original composition. (242-43)

While we might expect a foreign language teacher, in this case of French, to present translation as an alternative to vernacular instruction, English teachers sometimes also advocated translation. In *A History of Education in the United States* (1910), Charles Franklin Thwing, for instance, lamented the failure of composition instruction on the Harvard model. "The results obtaining, however, by such increase [of composition instruction]" he complained, "have not been adequate to the enlargement itself." Failure, Thwing argued, resulted from "the lack of attention paid to classical models. The style of great authors has been built up from a knowledge of Latin and of Greek. As the attention paid to these tongues has lessened, the sense of style in students who write at all has depreciated" (86). Finally, even an English professor such as Bliss Perry (who had moved from Princeton to Harvard) both questioned the Harvard method and offered translation as a solution. His evidence was that his Canadian students, who "had kept up their classics," wrote better than his American (*Gladly* 254).

Unlike liberal culturalists such as Babbitt, Thwing, and Perry, Aydelotte rejected translation. This rejection was due in part to his lack of training in Greek and Latin. His only exposure to Latin had been at Sullivan High in Indiana, and this training proved inadequate during every stage of his higher education. Because of his lack of background, he had problems with Harvard's philological work. He also had trouble passing the Oxford Responsions, the entrance examinations based partly on Greek and Latin. In *The Oxford Stamp* he expressed distaste for the dead languages when he argued that American students should not study a curriculum similar to the Oxford Greats, the traditional curriculum based on Greek and Latin language and culture. In place of the Greats, he advocated the study of English literature. This subject provided the modern American student the same breadth of treatment that the study of dead languages and literature provided earlier generations (77). In short, Aydelotte, unlike some of the liberal culturalists, had little interest in a dead language curriculum.

Aydelotte did share one liberal cultural position, a commitment to the British educational system, especially Oxford's version. In *Literature and the American College*, Babbitt argued for modeling American undergraduate education on the Oxford honors B.A. The Oxford degree, he claimed, was as demanding as the German Ph.D. but offered training "of an entirely different kind; it is at once a test of humane assimilation, and a discipline in thoroughness and accuracy" (139). Unlike the philologist who specialized in Germany, the Oxford graduate with an honors B.A. possessed, in Babbitt's mind, the breadth of reading that an instructor needed to teach liberal arts undergraduates to value humanistic scholarship. Aydelotte agreed with Babbitt. At a time when many American colleges lacked a demanding curriculum and encouraged sloth, Aydelotte proposed the British system, with individualized tutorials, reading lists, honors schools, and rigorous examinations, to remedy American mediocrity. All of his administrative and curricular innovations attempted to adapt the Oxford system to American conditions. Foremost among these were the Oxford Honors Schools, which Babbitt mentions favorably (79). In the United States, Babbitt wrote with some wit, exceptional undergraduates finished their programs of study early and departed while "the inferior or idle student who remains [was] labored over by a humanitarian faculty" (79). Oxford reversed the process. Average students received their pass degree in three years, while exceptional students remained longer to read independently for honors. Aydelotte agreed with this assessment and attempted throughout his career to raise academic standards, finally developing at Swarthmore an honors program partially modeled on the Oxford honors schools.

While Aydelotte distinguished much of his work from the liberal culturalists, some of his theory and pedagogy reflected liberal cultural influence. His MIT engineering writing program especially retained such assumptions. For instance, he realized that as the field of engineering became more complex and required more technical course work, liberal arts courses were forced out of the curriculum. He shrewdly recognized that his technical writing course could provide some of the lost humanistic background. Students read essays from *English and Engineering* designed in part to make them well-rounded so that they could communicate in polite society. But those essays had a more central purpose, too: to teach clear thinking, not only to inculcate culture and character. In his Indiana and Swarthmore curriculums, his goal was to develop not culture but thought, and even at MIT, the thought was more important than the culture.

## The Thought Approach

While Aydelotte had some liberal culturalist tendencies, he was not primarily a liberal culturalist. His work best fits into the separate category of the thought or idea course, which John C. Brereton in *Origins* identifies as one of the early 20th-century alternatives to Harvard formalism (16-17). The method emphasized the careful reading of essays and literature not for their style but for their thought. According to Aydelotte, two distinct forms of the course existed, the thought and the idea courses. The difference between the two is so slight, however, that commentators at the time such as Norman Foerster and Joseph M. Thomas used the terms interchangeably. Aydelotte, however, distinguished between his thought approach, which emphasized reading English literature, especially essays, drama, and poetry, and the idea approach, which drew on essays from different fields. The idea approach, Aydelotte argued in *The Oxford Stamp*, "took students too far afield in the search for ideas," while the thought approach "demands long application to one subject, turning it this way and that, tracing its implications in various directions" (136-37). Tracing out these implications and connecting them to different fields represents a true education. The idea course, he claims, provides students only with "[g]eneral information . . . not education" (137).[7]

The distinction he makes is not entirely convincing philosophically, however, since his thought approach draws on not just traditional literature, but also on essays by eminent Victorians that dealt with educational and cultural issues; consequently, the material for the thought course was diverse, too. The only difference was that English professors tended to read Victorian essayists such as Arnold, Newman, and Huxley; consequently, these essays had entered the literary canon in ways that essays by lesser-known writers had not. Aydelotte could in that sense be teaching only "literature."

Aydelotte's thought approach was based to a large extent on Matthew Arnold's analysis of critical thought, especially his views of on the difference between the literary critic's and the poet's roles in culture. The duty of poets, Arnold argued, was to interpret life and in so doing produce great literature. Each literary work therefore expressed that writer's thought or criticism of life. This activity, however, was not possible at the highest level in all time periods, especially those ages (like his own, Arnold concluded) with a dearth of great ideas. The Romantic poets wrote without a wealth of ideas and their poetry therefore suffered intellectually, Arnold argued. The critic's duty, on the other hand, was to provide poets with a stream of new and fresh ideas about life that writers could draw on to produce art. Aydelotte's thought approach therefore assumed that by reading major statements of criticism and literature, students were introduced to the important thought on life of significant authors that student writers, like any other writers, could use to sharpen their own thought.

Arnold, however, did not argue in his critical theory for the application of ideas to the world of politics and public affairs, and there exists a conservative strain, a support for the status quo, in works such as *Culture and Anarchy*, that influenced Aydelotte. As Chris Baldick argues in *The Social Mission of Literary Criticism 1848-1932*, Arnold consistently advocated for the postponement of social and political change (20). As Arnold stated in "The Function of Criticism at the Present Time," "Ideas cannot be too much prized in and for themselves, cannot be too much lived with; but to transport them abruptly into the world of politics and practice, violently to revolutionize the world to their bidding–that is quite another thing" (243). In other words, Arnold was not interested in using ideas to change the world or to work for social justice. Instead, his goal was to reform England's intellectual life. Implicit in this assumption is that radical social movements should be contained "within traditional frameworks in the interests of social and cultural harmony" (Baldick 22). Aydelotte shared this view. While he wanted his students to read literature for its thought, and to think critically themselves, he did not encourage that thought to lead to social action. As Aydelotte argues in *College English*'s chapter on Arnold, "practical reformers," who attempt to change social conditions through the machinery of political action, confuse means with ends:

> The end of life to them [Aydelotte continues] as shown by their propaganda, is physical comfort, wealth, increased trade, universal suffrage, the liberty to do as we please–not the culture and wisdom, not the spiritual improvement which these might serve, and the search for which alone makes wealth and comfort and liberty productive of good rather than evil. (19)

He wanted his students to think within the social and cultural boundaries of the world as it existed, to maintain the status quo, to strive for social harmony, not to imagine new worlds in which justice prevails for all. Aydelotte would agree with Arnold's assessment in "Function" that thinkers should examine life disinterestedly, with a calm removal from the "excesses and dangers" of real life around them. "Let us think," Arnold argues, "of quietly enlarging our stock of true and fresh ideas, and not, as soon as we get an idea, be running out with it into the street, and trying to make it rule there" (256). It is better, both Arnold and Aydelotte believed, to remove ourselves from the fray and let our thoughts mature within the confines of academia.

This position explains why Aydelotte could be a progressive educator with a conservative streak. While his pedagogy drew on many progressive ideas such as individualizing instruction and encouraging the development of individual thought to prepare the student for democratic life, it advocated for these principles without encouraging politically progressive thinking in the way that more liberal thinkers of the time such as his contemporary Alexander Meiklejohn of Amherst and later Wisconsin did.

## Aydelotte as Progressive Reformer

Where does the thought approach and Swarthmore reforms fit into the history of English studies and higher education in America? Although the Oxford method and Arnold's thought were two of the main influences on Aydelotte's educational philosophy, most of his educational reforms were consistent with the progressive movement in American education, and his contemporaries considered him a progressive educational reformer. The June 12, 1939, issue of *Time*, for instance, commented that "Progressive educators rate Quaker, co-educational Swarthmore as the No. 1 U.S. college, Frank Aydelotte as the ablest U.S. college president" ("Swarthmore's Aydelotte" 57). And R. L. Duffus, in *Democracy Enters College* (1936), a major Carnegie education study, labeled Swarthmore one of the progressive "New Deal" colleges because it created a flexible, responsive, non-traditional curriculum that educated all ability levels (149). Aydelotte with his search for excellence had more in common with a progressive educator such as John Dewey than with liberal culturalists such as Hiram Corson and Bliss Perry. However, while Aydelotte was progressive in educational theory he was socially conservative, a point to which I will return.

The term "progressive" is ambiguous because it was used loosely during the 19th and 20th centuries to describe various education reforms, especially in the lower grades. As Lawrence A. Cremin describes the movement,

> [p]rogressive education began as part of a vast humanitarian effort to apply the promise of American life–the ideal of government by, of, and for the people–to the puzzling new urban-industrial civilization that came into being during the latter half of the nineteenth century. The word progressive provides the clue to what it really was: the educational phase of American Progressivism writ large. In effect, progressive education began as Progressivism in education: a many-sided effort to use the schools to improve the lives of individuals. (viii)

Berlin notes in *Rhetoric and Reality* that progressive education shared with political progressivism "the optimistic faith in the possibility that all institutions could be reshaped to better serve society, making it healthier, more prosperous, and happier" (57), and Katherine H. Adams in *Progressive Politics and the Training of America's Persuaders* argues that progressives wanted "to make government more socially responsible [and place more emphasis] on active learning and problem-solving" (22). Aydelotte's reshaping of Swarthmore to meet the needs of honors students fits within these general aims to better society by producing better-prepared leaders. These leaders, he assumed, would work to improve society as a whole.

One idea Aydelotte shared with Dewey and other progressives was the role educational environment played in intellectual growth. In *Democracy and Education*, Dewey argued that the environment plays a crucial role in a student's mental development. The environment "leads [the student] to see and feel one thing rather than another; it leads him to have certain plans in order that he may act successfully with others; it strengthens some beliefs and weakens others as a condition of winning the approval of others" (13). Educators, therefore, must control the school's environment to produce the education they want students to experience. This educational environment is both the immediate social context of the school and the intellectual atmosphere created by the curricular methods, educational projects, and required readings.

Aydelotte developed curriculums to form healthy intellectual values. His thought approach, like Columbia's idea course, introduced students to the seminal ideas of modern society, such as the significance of literature, science, and business to modern thought. At Swarthmore Aydelotte constructed a complete environment that encouraged intellectual rigor lacking at most colleges. First, because they undermined academics, he cut back on the plethora of extracurricular "fun and games" for which Swarthmore had been famous (Clark 187). When he arrived at Swarthmore, he found that the school, because of its alumni's influence, placed undue emphasis on football. It admitted professional players so that the school could compete with much larger powerhouses, such as the University of Pennsylvania and Columbia University (Clark 182). To reign in this program, Aydelotte abolished athletic scholarships and required that the football team, now made up of students, play other small schools. He also questioned Swarthmore's extensive Greek system that encouraged "conformity and exclusiveness" inconsistent with democracy (Blanshard 266); he even convinced the women students to dismantle their sorority system. Second, he developed the Honors Program to create an environment that valued scholarship, hard work, and personal initiative. To attract brighter students capable of honors work, he established in 1922 a series of Open Scholarships, modeled on the Rhodes Scholarships, that paid full tuition and attracted exceptional students nationally.[8] He improved the faculty by hiring professors who knew their scholarship, could lecture to regular classes, and lead honors seminars. Within a few years, he changed Swarthmore from a typical small school that valued fraternities and sports to one of the most intellectually rigorous undergraduate institutions in the nation.

Aydelotte also shared with the progressives his commitment to the student-centered curriculum that considered individual differences among students. As Cremin notes, Dewey argued that the essence of progressive education "was to shift [the] center of gravity back to the [student]" (118), thereby making the student's "natural impulses to conversation, to inquiry, to construction, and to expression . . . the natural resources" of education (118-19). Aydelotte agreed with these goals, mainly because he had experienced himself the benefits of Oxford's conversations, tutorials, and small seminars, all methods that emphasized student interest and initiative. His American curriculums were inspired by Oxford and hence student centered. The thought approach, for instance, emphasized the students' individual responses to the readings through discussion and writing. Teachers functioned as midwives to help the student give birth to ideas while withholding their own beliefs. The Swarthmore Honors Seminar was also a model of the student-centered method. Teachers guided student discussion and research. When researching papers to be presented in seminars, students were not required to read only a set list of sources (although all participants read a small common body of central texts); instead, they followed their own interests by reading widely within the field of study. Since the student papers were in many cases the meat of the seminar, the seminar reflected student curiosities and interests. As Blanshard comments, however, Aydelotte did not take the student-centered approach to its most liberal end, as did schools like Sarah Lawrence and Bennington that developed "individualized programs often called 'functional' or 'life-enhancing'" (159). Such programs discarded traditional education and replaced it partly with individual projects, internships, and travel. Aydelotte remained committed to mastering the seminal texts in the fields, supplemented with individual reading.

A third principle that Aydelotte shared with the progressives was using education to prepare students to participate in a democracy. As Berlin comments in *Rhetoric and Reality*, progressive education ensured "the continuance of a democratic state that would make opportunities available to all without compromising excellence" (59). Blanshard, who studied with Dewey at the Columbia Graduate School, argues that Aydelotte's Honors Program was consistent with Dewey's educational philosophy in two senses. First, Dewey believed that in a democracy all students should have the opportunity "to bring [their] individual capacities to full growth" no matter what their social class (Blanshard 159), a position that Aydelotte generally supported. Second, Dewey and Aydelotte agreed that a democracy, since it did not have "hereditary rules or a self-perpetuating bureaucracy," needed to identify and educate its most able citizens (Blanshard 159). These most able students, Dewey and Aydelotte assumed, could contribute fully to American democracy only if their education helped them achieve their full potential. As Aydelotte wrote in "Lifting College Standards," "We have a truly democratic education if we give to each individual the opportunity to do his best, to develop his own powers to the fullest extent" (III 9).[9] The exceptional student who required the stimulation of the Honors Program should not take the same traditional courses that the pass student needed.

## Aydelotte's Social Conservatism

While Aydelotte was a progressive on curricular matters and was a life-long member of the Democratic party, he was not a progressive on all social issues. Although his pedagogy was liberal in that it encouraged open discussion and individualized freedom of thought and expression, his social policy was sometimes conservative, elitist, even racist. As Everett Hunt, Dean of Men during the Aydelotte years at Swarthmore, noted, Aydelotte's social conservatism grew from the assumption that a college social policy should never be in advance of the mores of the community in which it operates ("Frank Aydelotte" 31). In other words, Aydelotte did not believe that colleges should further social justice. He would not, for instance, address the issue of the salary discrepancies between professors and workers at Swarthmore because, as Hunt summarized Aydelotte's view, "the endowment funds of a college were to be spent for higher education, and not for experiments in social relations" (31). Aydelotte demonstrated other insensitivities to the plight of the downtrodden.

In particular, Aydelotte showed little sensitivity to African-Americans while he was president of Swarthmore. The case of George Arnold, a black student from Philadelphia who applied in 1932 for admission to Swarthmore, exposed Aydelotte's racism and deserves to be told in detail. Although Arnold wanted badly to attend Swarthmore and he and his father fought for his admission, his acceptance was never forthcoming. The college's Board of Managers, under Aydelotte's leadership, voted to reject Arnold by a wide margin. To avoid accepting him, Aydelotte and others took the extraordinary step of arranging a private scholarship so that Arnold could attend Dartmouth College.

To be fair to Aydelotte, Swarthmore had a history of discrimination well before he arrived. As Richard S. Walton notes in his history of the college, early in the 20th century, a light-skinned African American had been admitted on the mistaken assumption that he was white. When Swarthmore discovered his race upon his arrival, he was informed that Admissions had made a mistake and asked to leave (83-84). This anti-black bias is surprising, given that Quakers were among the early advocates of abolition and had long been devoted to the principles of racial equality.

The next major case that involved black admissions was Arnold's. If Aydelotte had been committed to racial equality, he would have fought to admit the young man because Arnold was a near perfect candidate. A graduate of a good school, West Philadelphia High, he had proved himself an outstanding student. As the Rev. Benjamin A. Arnold, the applicant's father, wrote to Aydelotte on July 5, 1933, his son had graduated with a 91 overall average and was sixth in a class of 393 students. As Dean Hunt summed up the case and expressed his own prejudices in his 1963 *Revolt of the Intellectual*, Arnold was an excellent all-around candidate, a perfect case to break Swarthmore's color barrier. He "was a prominent athlete; had a good background in classics...; was president of student government and popular with his fellows; and, *except for his color*, was a logical candidate for an Open Scholarship" (101-02) (italics added). He was such a fine all-around student that faculty members of West Philadelphia encouraged him to apply for one of Swarthmore's Open Scholarships that many of their white alumni of equivalent ability had recently won.

Swarthmore students as a whole favored Arnold's admission, and Aydelotte could have used such strong support to justify accepting the young man. According to Hunt in an unpublished March 8, 1933, letter to Aydelotte, both the men's and women's Student Governments had voted to express "positive approval for his [Arnold's] admission." While some students foresaw "minor embarrassments" from having a black on an all-white campus, most were "convinced that the admission of an able Negro is thoroughly consistent with our position as a liberal college." Furthermore, according to Hunt, the three white scholarship students on campus who had previously held Arnold's position as President of the student government at West Philadelphia all supported his admission.

Despite his excellent preparation and the student support, Arnold received lukewarm encouragement from Hunt and the Scholarship Committee when interviewed at Swarthmore. The case was sent to the Board of Managers for final decision. Arnold was ultimately rejected, Walton concludes, by a large majority of the Managers because his admission "would raise too many problems and create too many difficulties" (84). Aydelotte and the Managers were not willing to overcome those difficulties to fight for racial equality because they did not feel such equality was important.

While the Arnold affair did not generate much mainstream press, Aydelotte suffered hard questions from a few prominent black intellectuals understandably angry at Swarthmore's decision. Carl Murphy, owner and publisher of *The Afro-American*, wrote Aydelotte on September 14, 1933, asking him to confirm or deny Arnold's rejection because the paper "hesitate[d] to print a statement that a Quaker and Christian institute, such as yours reports to be, could have such an unchristian and un-American policy." He wanted to know if Swarthmore was "anti-Negro" because, if it were, the paper wanted to add Swarthmore to the list of discriminatory schools (mostly in the South) to avoid embarrassing future black applicants. The leader of the critics, however, was the gentlemanly Professor D. O. W. Holmes, Dean of the School of Education at Howard University, who engaged Aydelotte in a constructive dialogue on race. Holmes wrote on January 22, 1934, asking Aydelotte to clarify his stand on black admissions. After calling Aydelotte "one of the dynamic, spiritual leaders of this generation," he expressed his hope that Aydelotte and other white college presidents would help engender optimism in young blacks. This optimism would not develop, he maintained, "if events lead them to believe that places like Swarthmore College, with its Quaker heritage and its tradition of brotherhood, turns thumbs down upon his higher aspirations [by rejecting qualified black students]; for the deep South could do no more." In a March 6, 1934, letter to Aydelotte, Holmes continued his plea. Blacks take more offense, he argued, at "one act of injustice or discrimination [such as Arnold's rejection] in the Northern states" than at the "general set-up in the [overtly discriminatory] South." He reminded Aydelotte of his responsibility as a progressive leader to cure racial ills in America.

These and a few other elegant and pointed arguments did not move Aydelotte, who found himself in the uncomfortable position of defending Swarthmore's racist practices. His basic argument, heard so often during the Civil Rights Movement three decades later, was that black students would be uncomfortable at an all-white institution. The school, he wrote to Holmes on January 28, 1934, had "certain social difficulties" which made it impossible to admit black students. It was "co-educational" and "residential." In other words, white coeds lived on campus and would have to share that campus with Arnold. What of admitting black students to classes but having them live off campus? No, Aydelotte wrote, he would not admit blacks to classes if Swarthmore "were not prepared to make them at home socially." The assumption Aydelotte operated under was that blacks and whites could not socialize, that they had to remain segregated, supposedly for the good of both races. Aydelotte's cultural stereotype of black men was even more alarming: Arnold's presence would endanger white coeds. It would follow that white parents might stop matriculating daughters. And, if word got out that Swarthmore had integrated, donations might dry up from conservative alumni.

To reject a superbly qualified student because of his race was bad enough. But Aydelotte went further when he claimed that Swarthmore had no official, written policy that excluded blacks. While Swarthmore had no written policy, it had an unwritten one, a fact that Aydelotte denied privately to his black correspondents time and again. He refused, however, to make any public statement of his position. In the January 28 letter to Holmes, for instance, he claimed that Swarthmore had no "regulation" against admitting blacks, but he declined to state a clear policy because the college was gradually "becoming liberalized in, what is to me, a very satisfactory way." In a September 22, 1933, response to Murphy's letter, Aydelotte again claimed that his college's admission policy was not "fixed." But he refused to make a public statement for the *Afro-American* because such a statement "would only serve to defeat the efforts of those who are trying to work out a solution which shall be in harmony with the character and traditions of the College." Three years later, Aydelotte reiterated his position in a private letter of November 2, 1936, to Floyd L. Logan, the President of the Educational Equality League of Philadelphia, a black advocacy group: "We do not have a rule at Swarthmore against the admission of colored students, but since I have been President we have not thought it wise to admit a colored man or woman to the College."

Sadly, during Aydelotte's long tenure as President of Swarthmore from 1922 to 1939, no black student of either sex gained admission. Aydelotte was willing to exclude an entire race from the honors program that he saw as central to redeeming American education and creating a better trained political, social, and educational leadership. Let students like Arnold, he argued, attend other schools, preferably all male or larger, less intimate institutions. He, along with others, helped Arnold enter Dartmouth, but Aydelotte offered this assistance to avoid confronting his own racism. The first black students did not appear on campus until 1940[10] under the administration of President John Nason, Aydelotte's successor (Hunt *Revolt* 102), a fact suggesting that Aydelotte, not just the Board of Managers, fought black admission.

Many leaders have blind spots, but Aydelotte's prejudices are particularly troublesome. While we might argue that Aydelotte merely expressed the prejudice of his day, his position is still surprising, given the general liberality and progressiveness of his educational programs. It is also surprising given the Quaker tradition at Swarthmore. Furthermore, Aydelotte was in a position to do much good to help solve the racial problems of the nation and did worse than nothing–he actively worked to deny qualified black students opportunities that would have been of value to both them personally and the nation.

While it is tempting to reduce Aydelotte to a conservative racist, his racism is only part of the story. He worked in several ways to open Swarthmore to other groups often disenfranchised at the time. Upon arriving at Swarthmore, he established Open Scholarships for men. Modeled on the Rhodes Scholarships, Aydelotte designed them to attract excellent male students, no matter what their financial, religious, or cultural backgrounds. By attracting students from across the nation, these scholarships broadened the student body, introducing white minorities, such as Jews, to Swarthmore. Aydelotte also was an advocate for women. While the original Open Scholarships were limited to men, he later established a second set to attract excellent women students who might be tempted to go elsewhere. Furthermore, from the start of the Honors Program, Aydelotte encouraged women to participate, and they dominated the study of English during the first years of the program.

## Purpose of the Book

Despite his blindnesses, Aydelotte was one of the most significant curriculum developers in English studies during the first half of the 20th century. He was the foremost advocate of the Oxford approach to English studies, and all of his curriculums were innovative for their time and have left their marks on the current state of English studies. All, however, have their weaknesses, mostly due to Aydelotte's rejection of rhetoric. My study will examine the following innovations that Aydelotte made.

First, at Indiana University, Aydelotte developed the thought approach to freshman English, which was one of the few alternatives to Harvard formalism (Berlin *Writing Instruction* 75; Kitzhaber 73). While a handful of other teachers, most notably Lounsbury of the Sheffield School of Yale, had created literature-based writing courses, nobody before Aydelotte fully articulated a theory of teaching such courses. In *College English* (1913); *Materials* (1916), the anthology for the course; and *The Oxford Stamp* (1917), Aydelotte justified his approach and therefore created the fully-articulated model of the first of many freshman courses based on writing about literature.

The Aydelotte approach had weakness, however. By focusing entirely on thought, and assuming that good thinking led directly to good writing, Aydelotte de-emphasized technique and rhetoric, which led to two significant problems. The first was that weak students, those who did not have college-level writing skills, did not receive the instruction in technique that they needed. The second was that the courses contained little work in rhetoric, which meant that students did not master rhetorical principles, such as systematic strategies for invention, arrangement, and style.

Second, at MIT, Aydelotte contributed to the development of technical writing as an academic discipline. He was clever enough to recognize that engineering education, which at the time was becoming more technical, lacked emphasis on humane learning; consequently, Aydelotte modified the thought approach to broaden that education. *English and Engineering* (2nd ed 1923) was the first anthology of readings for an engineering writing course. This book modified the thought approach so that MIT students read and wrote on significant issues about engineering as a profession. It also contained some liberal cultural assumptions concerning the preparation of engineers to be cultured professionals ready to enter polite society. The weakness of the approach, however, was that, while it taught MIT students to think about issues important to their profession, it did not teach them the discourse conventions of their fields. After taking Aydelotte's engineering writing course, students did not know how to write like engineers.

Third, at Swarthmore, Aydelotte developed the thought course to its most advanced level. He created Swarthmore's influential Honors Program based on the honors seminar. Students worked in small groups to take a series of related honors seminars to prepare for written and then oral comprehensive examinations judged by outside academic specialists. At the heart of the honors seminar was the seminar paper. Students researched and wrote papers on topics seminal to the seminar and then presented them to their colleagues. The papers helped prepare participants for comprehensives and were critiqued for both form and content, thereby developing students' research, thinking, and writing skills. An early form of writing across the curriculum, the Swarthmore program became one of the models for honors education in the United States, and Aydelotte and the Swarthmore faculty produced four nationally important books analyzing honors education in general and their program in particular: Aydelotte's two books, *Honors Courses in American Colleges and Universities* (1924) and *Breaking the Academic Lockstep* (2nd ed 1944), Robert C. Brooks's *Reading for Honors at Swarthmore* (1927), and the Swarthmore College Faculty's *An Adventure in Education* (1941), written to honor Aydelotte upon retirement from Swarthmore.

Like Aydelotte's earlier curriculums, the Swarthmore program had a central weakness. Students neither directly studied rhetoric nor took a writing course, and, as I will show in Chapter Five, the writing suffered.

In fact, the weakness of all of Aydelotte's curriculums was their neglect of technique and rhetoric. This neglect was due, I suspect, to Aydelotte's identifying rhetoric with Harvard formalism, an approach he knew well and rejected. From Oxford he experienced the effectiveness of working with tutors who improved his writing by means of one-on-one critique, and he brought the spirit of that approach to the United States. While his curriculums ignored that fact that American students often needed work on technique because many did not have backgrounds as strong as the average Oxford student, his methods brought to this country a new emphasis on encouraging students to think for themselves as they worked out that thought in writing. As a profession, we would do well to examine the methods that he developed.

## NOTES

1. The elective system made possible the development of new disciplines that replaced the old set courses. Students demanded and took new courses that prepared them for careers. If it were not for student demand, the new programs might not have developed.

2. Aydelotte was one of several theorists who reacted against the elective system by developing more coherent programs. Another was John Meicklejohn, who established and administered the Experimental College at Wisconsin in the 1920s while Aydelotte was establishing his Swarthmore program.

3. Students could study other subjects on their own, of course, but the demanding work in the Honors Program did not give them much time to do so. They could, for instance, attend lectures or take additional courses, but honors work, if done properly, would take up most of their time.

4. Despite Aydelotte's importance to the development of English studies and higher education, few in-depth studies have appeared on him or his contributions to English studies and educational theory. Most of the best books explore his role in developing Swarthmore's Honors Program. The first of these is Robert C. Brooks's *Reading for Honors at Swarthmore* (1927), a description of the earliest form Swarthmore's program took. A second important study on the same topic is *An Adventure in Education: Swarthmore College Under Frank Aydelotte* (1941), which the Swarthmore faculty wrote as a tribute to his work at that college upon his resignation. This book discusses the development of the Honors Program under Aydelotte but contributes little to our understanding of his early career or to his work in English studies. The best single study remains Frances Blanshard's 1970 biography, *Frank Aydelotte of Swarthmore*. Since Blanshard worked for Aydelotte at Swarthmore as Dean of Women, and because she had his support in researching the book, the volume contains much useful information about Aydelotte and his work, especially while he was Swarthmore's president. The book provides essential background on the development of the Honors Program, but it is not as strong on Aydelotte's education and early career as an English professor and his thought approach. Nor is it critical of Aydelotte and his work. A good short introduction to Aydelotte's work is Michael G. Moran's essay "Frank Aydelotte" in *Twentieth-Century Rhetorics and Rhetoricians*, edited by Moran and Michelle Ballif.

While we have detailed analyses of Aydelotte's contributions to Swarthmore, few historians of education or of English studies have discussed Aydelotte's early work in depth. Laurence R. Veysey remains silent, as do Albert R. Kitzhaber, Arthur N. Applebee, John Michael Wozniak, Gerald Graff, Katherine H. Adams in *Progressive Politics*, Maureen Daly Goggin, and Susan Kates. Katherine H. Adams in *History* mentions in passing Aydelotte's MIT curriculum, and Frederick Rudolf in *The American College and University* discusses Aydelotte's work at Swarthmore but does not discuss his work at IU and MIT.

Some recent historians of composition, however, have discussed Aydelotte's work in first-year composition. In *Rhetoric and Reality*, James A. Berlin argues that Aydelotte should be read as a liberal culturalist (72), an argument that I critique above. John Brereton, in *The Origins of Compositions Studies in the American College, 1875-1925*, correctly identifies Aydelotte as one of the originators of the thought or idea approach to compositions studies but presents inaccurate details about Aydelotte's work and influence. He claims, for instance, that Aydelotte developed the thought course at IU in the 1890s. This would have been impossible since from 1896 to 1900 Aydelotte was an undergraduate there. He actually developed the course in 1908, after he had returned from Oxford with plans to reform freshman English instruction in America. Brereton also claims that the course "spread to Columba" by 1915 (17). All evidence suggests, though, that Columbia developed a similar course, the idea course, independently. Finally, Michael G. Moran has published "Frank Aydelotte, Social Criticism, and Freshman English," a short discussion of Aydelotte's contributions to English study that this book expands.

Aydelotte's work in technical communication has also received some attention. Robert J. Connors in his short history of technical communication claims that Aydelotte developed the "broad" approach to engineering writing that emphasized reading in various related fields to expand students' intellectual backgrounds. John Hagge in "Early Engineering Writing Textbooks" argues briefly that Aydelotte's anthology, *English and Engineering*, "indicates a strong interest in the idea that engineering students should acquire general humanities-based culture" (464), and David R. Russell, in *Writing in the Academic Disciplines, 1870-1990*, asserts that when MIT hired Aydelotte, utilitarian writing concerns gave way to "claims of culture" (464), position that I examine in Chapter 4. Teresa Kynell in *Writing in the Milieu of Utility* mentions Aydelotte as a liberal culturalist, but misidentifies *English and Engineering*, his MIT textbook, as a "prose model reader" (40). Aydelotte used the essays not as prose models but primarily as vehicles for stimulating thought about the nature of engineering as a profession. Michael G. Moran has published two essays on Aydelotte's contribution to technical communication. The first, "The Road Not Taken: Frank Aydelotte and the Thought Approach to Engineering Writing," examines the strategies that Aydelotte used to modify for MIT the thought approach that he had developed at IU. The second essay, "Frank Aydelotte: AT&T's First Outside Writing Consultant, 1917-1918," evaluates the writing and thinking course that Aydelotte designed for AT&T employees in 1917. Both of these essays are expanded in Chapter Four.

5. While students in honors seminars would read the classic texts in their fields, they were required to update that research by reading more current work.

6. Oddly, despite this negative view of the efficiency of writing instruction, Lounsbury was a life-long teacher of writing.

7. See Sharon Crowley's *Composition in the University* for a criticism of Aydelotte's position (98-100).

8. These scholarships were only for men, but Aydelotte eventually established a similar set for women.

9. This elitism permeates Aydelotte's thought. He never considered the benefits of having brighter students helping less talented students in some classes. He was interested in creating a cadre of elite scholars who were prepared to take leadership roles in their various professions, and he thought the best way to accomplish this was to isolate them so that they worked together to reach high standards.

10. These students appeared under the auspices of government training programs during World War II.

## 2: Education in America and Britain

To understand the significance of Aydelotte's theoretical contributions to teaching literature and writing, it is useful to understand his own education in these subjects during the late 19th and early 20th centuries in the United States and Great Britain. It is important to understand his American training because he rejected many of its assumptions. In his own approach to writing instruction, he repudiated pedagogies emphasizing form and mechanics, two central elements of the dominant, Harvard approach that had become fully established in American colleges by the early years of the 20th century. He rejected the segregation of composition and literature, another tenet of the Harvard method, which largely isolated composition instruction from literature. But he also rejected the liberal cultural position with its assumption that students should be taught to read literature but not to write essays.

While our understanding of his American education is important because he rejected its assumptions and methods, our understanding of his Oxford education is important for the opposite reason–it provided him with the tenets of the thought approach, which he implemented differently at Indiana University (IU), Massachusetts Institute of Technology (MIT), and Swarthmore College, where it reached its apex in the Honors Program.

Aydelotte earned degrees at three schools. He began his college education at IU, taking his A.B. in English in 1900. After teaching at several schools as an instructor and working as a journalist, he matriculated at Harvard in 1903, where he received his A.M. in 1904. Finally, after being selected a Rhodes Scholar from Indiana, he matriculated at Oxford's Brasenose College in 1905. Although the scholarship was awarded for three years, he first studied there for two, through 1907. Upon marrying, he could not continue in residence so he returned to IU. However, to prepare *Elizabethan Rogues and Vagabonds* for the Clarendon Press, he received special permission to return for his third year of Oxford residency in 1912-13. From Oxford, he received in 1908 the B.Litt. degree, which was, as opposed to the B.A., a research degree that Aydelotte claimed at the time he earned it equaled in rigor the German and American Ph.D.[1]

At both American schools, Aydelotte studied composition as a distinct subject. While attending IU he took the required Harvard-influenced freshman English course, which emphasized mechanics, the paragraph, writing short personal essays, and the modes of discourse. At Harvard, he took the famous English A, and later helped teach the course himself as Professor C. T. Copeland's assistant. While he occasionally wrote favorably of English A and integrated a few of its methods into his own writing courses, the thought approach he later developed opposed the assumptions of the Harvard course. The thought approach, with its integration of composition and literature, developed out of his experiences at Oxford, where composition was not taught as a separate course but through individual tutorials in which papers were critiqued.

## Undergraduate at Indiana University

In a 1918 letter congratulating Aydelotte on the publication of *The Oxford Stamp* (1917), Margaret Clapp, one of his fellow undergraduates at IU, confided that "[a] good many years ago, when I first went to Indiana University and sat behind you, a foot-ball 'hero' with your head in bandages, in Mr. Harding's class in English History, it didn't take me long to perceive that the clearest, most intelligent and most interesting thinking that was being done on the student benches was going on in your bandaged head." Aydelotte must have taken pleasure in learning that his classmate thought highly of his intellect, for he himself remembered in notes for a chapter of his unfinished autobiography, "Bloomington Indiana, 1896-1900," that he entered college with "slender preparation" from high school in Sullivan, Indiana. His memories of college life included "the hard work which I had to do in preparation of every assignment" (1) because of his weak academic background.

Despite his thin preparation, Aydelotte enjoyed a successful college career, both academically and socially. He became a star football player–who was selected an all-state right end in 1900–and also developed intellectual interests. In 1900 he edited *Arbutus*, IU's student literary magazine and yearbook. According to this source, Aydelotte was active on campus. He was a member of Sigma Nu fraternity, he was a director of the Publishing Association (82), he played Orlando in *As You Like It* (121), he sat on the yearbook's Board of Editors (236), and he published a short story entitled "A College Case" (132-36) in the yearbook. He was drawn to English studies and decided on a career in either journalism or teaching.

The English courses that he took at IU were typical of those then taught at anAmerican university. If Aydelotte had entered IU earlier, his studies would have been limited to one of three old-fashioned curriculums–science, ancient languages, or modern languages (Gray 56)–but by the mid-1890s, IU had reorganized itself. Instead of following a set curriculum, students enjoyed flexibility in course selection and could major in many subjects, including English. In 1893, the English Department had created three divisions from which students could select courses. According to the *Annual Catalogue of the Indiana University* for that year, the three groups were 1) Rhetoric, 2) Language, and 3) Literature. Interestingly, these areas corresponded to three approaches to English studies then in vogue nationally. The first, rhetoric, reflected the new sense, growing largely from Harvard's influential writing program, that students needed to write good English to be successful in business and industry. The language group, mostly courses in historical linguistics, reflected the influence of philology, the scientific study of language. The third grouping, literature, reflected the growing importance of literature as an intellectually challenging discipline.

IU's literature offerings were designed, according to Professor Martin W. Sampson, the chair of the department, to teach students to read, understand, and appreciate good literature ("English" 6-7). Significantly, the IU approach to literature rejected the four approaches to the subject current at the time—the philological, the liberal cultural, the historical/biographical, and the aesthetic—and emphasized teaching students to read literature carefully. In an 1894 essay in The Dial, Sampson explained what the study of literature did not mean at IU:

> —to one teacher it meant to fill the student full of biography and literary history; to another it meant to put the student in possession of what the best critics, or the worst ones, had said about the artist and his work; to another it meant making a pother over numberless details of the text (a species of literary parsing) [philology]; to another it meant harping on the moral purposes of the poet or novelist; anything, in short, except placing the student face to face with the work itself and acting as his spectacles when his eyesight is blurred. (6)

IU's English Department, in other words, taught students to engage literature directly.[2] The IU approach undoubtedly influenced Aydelotte's later thought approach for he, too, argued that instructors should encourage such engagement. His sense of engagement was a little different, though. He viewed literature, following Matthew Arnold, as a repository of the best thought about life, and advocated studying literature to provide thoughtful material for compositions.

Students specialized in one area of English but also took courses in the other two, with a pair of courses required of all majors. These set requirements were English 7 (English Composition) and either English 5 (Old English) or English 14 (History of the English Language). The purpose of the first was to teach students to write clearly; the second, to teach historical linguistics, which many teachers then, especially philologists, felt prepared students for all other work in composition and literature.

At IU, Aydelotte had opportunities to take writing courses, starting with the required English 7, freshman composition. After completing that course, he could take English 15, described in the 1894-95 *Indiana University Catalog* as an "Advanced course designed to stimulate original production" and open to students "who have distinguished themselves in Course 7" (43). The department also offered Professor Sampson's English 10, Rhetorical Seminary. This course, designed particularly for future teachers, taught rhetorical principles and included a "detailed investigation of text-books in rhetoric and composition" (43). While in the course, students taught composition classes and corrected themes under Sampson's supervision. Although there is no way to determine Sampson's approach to writing instruction, his 1907 textbook for high school students, *Written and Oral Composition*, coauthored with Ernest O. Holland, offers some insight. Unlike many contemporary texts, the book combined instruction in oral as well as written discourse. But much of the rest of the book was familiar material. Sampson organized the book according to the modes of discourse–narration, description, exposition, and argumentation, with an additional section on "Letter-Writing," a nod to business communication. The text also emphasized drills in mechanical correctness and provided writing assignments removed from meaningful thought and reading. Given Aydelotte's later rejection of form-driven rhetoric, he certainly did not embrace Sampson's formalist assumptions in his own writing courses. The primary lasting value of the course was that it gave him an intellectual grounding in current methods of composition instruction, most of which he later rejected.

Since Aydelotte, like all students, took English 7, Composition, I will examine this course carefully. It was based on formalist principles, as the 1895-96 *Indiana University Catalog*, which lists the textbooks for the course, proves. The first book listed is *Paragraph-Writing*, by Fred Newton Scott of Michigan and Joseph Villiers Denney of Ohio State. Scott was one of the important rhetoricians of the period whose rhetorical theory, Berlin argues in *Rhetoric and Reality*, had epistemic underpinnings and democratic tendencies (47-48). *Paragraph-Writing*, however, expresses little of this philosophy. Instead, it emphasizes formalist principles. As the title suggests, the book teaches the paragraph as the primary discourse unit. Scott and Denney spelled out clearly their reasons for this emphasis. Following Barrett Wendell of Harvard, Scott and Denney argued that the paragraph, unlike the sentence, requires "prevision," the ability to plan (iii-iv). Learning to write, Scott and Denney argued, meant learning to manipulate these larger "units of discourse," as the preface makes clear:

> Learning to write . . . means learning to construct units of discourse which have order and symmetry and coherence of parts. It means learning theoretically how such units are made, and practically how to put them together; and further, if they turn out badly the first time, how to take them apart and put them together again in another and better order. The making and remaking of such units is in general terms the task of all who produce written discourse. (iii)

Instead, Aydelotte argued that students should write longer, more demanding papers on significant issues raised in the essays and literature they read.

The formal emphasis continued in English 7's other texts, three short books in a 1895 series based on the modes of discourse: *Specimens of Prose Description*, edited by Charles Sears Baldwin of Yale; *Specimens of Narration*, edited by William T. Brewster of Columbia; and *Specimens of Exposition*, edited by Hammond Lamont of Harvard. Each volume begins with a theoretical discussion followed by the meat of the book, selections of fiction and non-fiction that illustrate the mode. The books assume that students would read the models and then write essays that imitated them. These assumptions suggest that English 7 continued the formal emphasis by moving beyond the paragraph to the whole essay. Students such as Aydelotte read the models, listened to lectures about them, and wrote essays imitating the forms.

While at IU, Aydelotte established close ties to many of the administrators and faculty. In "Bloomington, Indiana, 1896-1900," he remembered some of the people who influenced him. He took an ethics class from Dr. William Lowe Bryan, who would later become IU's President and, as a member of the three-person Indiana selections committee, help Aydelotte win his Rhodes Scholarship and later hired him as an Associate Professor of English at IU. Aydelotte also became friendly with Dr. Joseph Swain, IU's current President, who soon assumed that same office at Swarthmore and many years later recommended Aydelotte as his successor (Perkins 24).

As an English major, Aydelotte studied with much of the faculty in that small department, but the English teacher who most influenced him was Professor Sampson, the chair. While not well known when he taught Aydelotte (he was only 34 when Aydelotte graduated in 1900), Sampson later developed a modest academic reputation by editing minor editions of novels by Henry James and Mrs. Gaskell, plays by Shakespeare and Webster, and selections from Washington Irving and Milton. He also demonstrated interest in composition with the Harvard-inspired *Written and Oral Composition*, discussed earlier. But Sampson most impressed Aydelotte not as a scholar but as a teacher. Many years later he remembered Sampson favorably in a vague way as a man who possessed "a rare genius in the teaching of [English]" ("Bloomington" 1). Sampson also had an important influence on Aydelotte's intellectual development. One term when Aydelotte finished a science laboratory in one month designed to take three, he spent the rest of the term reading independently. When he asked Sampson what to read, the professor gave him what was standard advice at the time: "Begin with Matthew Arnold and go where he leads you" ("Bloomington" 3). Arnold, along with other Victorian essayists such as Ruskin and Newman, provided Aydelotte with the heart of his educational approach that he later developed (see Chapter Three). Sampson thought highly of his student, and wrote of him:

> In scholarship Aydelotte has ability of unusually high order. He has a keen quick mind, which seems at first at odds with his athletic boyish appearance. His keen quality of mind I have tested again and again in the classroom, for it seemed too good to be true that I should have in the same person a young fellow of searching mind, of indefatigable diligence, of hearty sanity, of attractive manners—and he never failed at any point. I could always count on him when all the rest of the class had come to their limit. (qtd. in Perkins 29-30)

By the time he graduated in 1900, Aydelotte was recognized as a young man with a future. He had been introduced to the dominant methods of teaching writing and literature in America and probably had accepted them uncritically. After spending the next few years working at temporary jobs–teaching at a high school in Louisville and working as a newspaper reporter–he decided to continue his English studies at one of America's best graduate programs in English, Harvard's.

## Graduate School at Harvard

In 1902 Aydelotte matriculated at Harvard. As Bliss Perry, who began his popular teaching career there a few years after Aydelotte arrived, remembered in his autobiography, *And Gladly Teach*, graduate students from lesser Southern and Midwestern schools who matriculated for the M.A. often had trouble with Harvard's graduate requirements because these students lacked advanced knowledge of languages, including French and German, to keep up in the demanding core philological courses (250). Aydelotte was disappointed to learn that he was accepted not for the M.A. but for the B.A., the same degree he had completed at IU, to make up deficiencies in his background. Aydelotte remembered in his autobiographical notes "Harvard University, 1902-1903" that Harvard was especially concerned that he lacked preparation in Latin, his only training being three years at Sullivan High (2). Harvard had accepted him because he had been a star student at IU but still expected him to make up deficiencies before entering the graduate program.[3] As he had at IU, according to his notes, he found Harvard demanding, especially since its graduate work emphasized the language-based philological approach which played to a major weakness (1), and he did not do as well as he had hoped.

The Harvard English Department contained some of the most famous English teachers in the nation. Barrett Wendell, who had just published his *Literary History of America* and was well-known for his rhetoric, *English Composition*, taught there but was on leave that year. But Aydelotte got to know three of Harvard's celebrated teachers: George Lyman Kittredge, who taught Shakespeare philologically; Charles Townsend Copeland, under whom Aydelotte served as assistant in freshman English; and Le Baron Russell Briggs, Dean of Harvard College, who became one of Aydelotte's best friends and appointed him Copeland's assistant (Blanshard 41).

While studying literature, Aydelotte had to wade through the philology courses. Liberal culturalists like William Lyon Phelps and Bliss Perry criticized this emphasis. Phelps, who attended Harvard as a graduate student a few years before Aydelotte, remembered the iron grip that philology had on the English Department:

> At that time it was considered both by the faculty and students in the Harvard Graduate School, that everyone who took advanced studies in English must spend nearly all his time on philology. Thus I found the students were all studying Anglo-Saxon, the history of the English

language, Historical English Grammar, Old Norse, Gothic, and what not; furthermore, the Doctor's theses were on linguistic subjects. (246)

This is strong criticism since Phelps as a professor at Yale rejected philology and advocated a less scientific approach to literature. Bliss Perry also criticized the philological emphasis. "The steel core of the English work at Harvard, then [1907 and before] as now," he lamented, "was in the old linguistic and historical courses covering the period from the earliest Anglo-Saxon writers to the decline of the Elizabethan drama. These courses were essential for candidates for honors in English and for the higher degrees" (*Gladly* 244). Aydelotte therefore took philology courses, including Kittredge's Shakespeare, for which he earned a disappointing B plus (Blanshard 44).

Perry complained that at Harvard the "'fact' men triumphed" (253). Graduate students were expected to master many facts but study no ideas; there was little emphasis on philosophy even though American universities granted the German-style doctor of philosophy. Perry lamented that at Harvard he sat through many Ph.D. oral examinations that addressed facts about literature but "scarcely a question dealing with the contributions to thought which were made by major thinkers in the Western tradition" (253). Aydelotte eventually rejected the Harvard philological approach with its emphasis on linguistic form and factual minutiae and developed the thought approach, which empathized reading literature for its ideas.

While Aydelotte rejected philology, he appreciated Kittredge's Shakespeare course. He also felt that he "gained the most intellectually" from Kittredge at Harvard (Blanshard 45). Through Kittredge's instruction, Aydelotte came to appreciate, as Blanshard notes, "the rigors and satisfaction of pure scholarship" (41). Aydelotte recognized that Kittredge, one of Harvard's great scholars, transcended the narrowness of mediocre philology. He accomplished this through "both [classroom] histrionics and a vast store of humanistic knowledge" (Earnest 143). And Aydelotte in turn favorably impressed Kittredge, who, as the student tells it, advised him to apply for the A.M. rather than the A.B.:

> One day I was working in the stacks of the Harvard Library when Kittredge came along and asked to see what book I was taking our of the stacks. I showed it to him. He apparently was impressed. He talked to me a little about it and then asked me what degree I was applying for. I said I had been required to put in an application for the A.B. He said: "Go to the office and change that to the A.M." I accordingly did this, but I never knew until Commencement whether I was going to get the A.B. or the A.M. (qtd. in Blanshard 45)

He received the A.M., much to his relief.

According to Perry, Harvard was not then best known for its literature instruction; it was far better known in the popular mind for its composition program: "the courses offered by the English Department in Linguistics and Literature," he remembered, "were then much less known to the general public than the course in composition" (*Gladly* 223). English A influenced the teaching of composition across the nation, and, in fact, it had influenced the writing course Aydelotte had taken at IU. English A had been originally created by Adams Sherman Hill and was gradually developed over the years with the help of others, including Briggs and Wendell. By the time Aydelotte arrived, the course was under the direction of Copeland. Oddly, upon matriculating at Harvard, Aydelotte discovered that he himself was required to take English A, even though he had taken a similar course at IU.

By the time Aydelotte arrived at Harvard, writing had been taught there using formalism for a quarter century. The English A that he took had recently been redesigned and described by C. T. Copeland and H. M. Rideout in *Freshman English and Theme Correcting in Harvard College* (1901). Hill continued to influence the course through the required textbook, his *Principles of Rhetoric*, first published in 1878. The book placed most of its emphasis on mechanics and form. The first two parts updated much of the material on grammar and usage found in George Campbell's *Philosophy of Rhetoric* (1776), emphasizing, first, good usage and violations of good usage, including barbarisms, improprieties, and solecisms. The book then covered word choice, use of the proper number of words (neither too many nor too few), and arrangement, covering sentences, paragraphs, and compositions. The book ended with a discussion of the four modes of discourse, following Alexander Bain's types with a few modifications: description, narration, exposition, and argument. The book attended little to invention, limiting itself to teaching students the formal elements of diction, usage, style, and organization.

Perhaps the most famous element of English A was the daily theme. Although he no longer taught English A by the time Aydelotte arrived, Wendell, along with Briggs, had introduced this technique (Brown 56). Wendell had gotten the idea from a journalist friend who told him that young reporters learned to write by writing every day (Kitzhaber 210-11). Briggs had profited from keeping a diary and thought that students, too, would benefit from daily writing (Brown 57). English A therefore required students to produce a theme of one page four days a week (the other two days–one of which was Saturday–they translated a short passage from another language and wrote a summary or response to Briggs's weekly reading or lecture) (Copeland and Rideout 7). Consequently, students wrote one page–either an essay, a translation, or a lecture summary–six days a week. Students put finished themes in a box outside the instructor's office, and each one was corrected, often by a course assistant like Aydelotte. The subject matter for most of the early themes was the students' immediate experience and surroundings. Students commonly wrote descriptions of their environment and brief narrations of events.

As Copeland and Rideout made clear, the purpose of these themes was not to make students into "interesting" writers; it was to make them into "correct" writers (9). Most of the writing at first was trite,[4] according to Copeland and Rideout: "the general run of themes will be stock accounts, in stock phrases, of the melancholy falling leaves, of the gloom that attends waking on a rainy day, or the gray squirrels that frisk in the Yard, or runaway horses that 'dash madly,' of Saturday football games, marvelously dull, and of trips to Bunker Hill" (8-9). Although bad, the themes allowed teachers to attack the formal problems of trite language, poor spelling, bad punctuation, poor organization, and other weaknesses of student prose. English A teachers worked hardest on word choice and essay structure and assumed that once students could write correctly, they could then make their writing interesting (9). While most of the daily themes were on open topics, some teachers in the program assigned particular subjects. Some required students to translate passages from foreign languages; others to imitate passages of "great English writers" (20); others to provide a summary of a longer paper before writing it; and others to write conventional correspondence such as invitations, letters of introduction, and application letters.

The translations, an approach that had deep roots in the old classical curriculum, appear to be Adams Sherman Hill's idea, and he described the method in his 1885 essay, "English in the Schools," which outlined his principles for using translation to teach good English. He argued, for instance, that each sentence translated must "be a good English sentence at all points" (126), not merely a word-by-word rendering of the original. A word-for-word translation such as "No one will be about to be a thief, we being the aid" is inadequate because it is not idiomatic (126). The effective use of translation, Hill argued, could provide "a means of enriching the vocabulary and stimulating the powers of expression" (126). Given Aydelotte's weakness in languages, especially the dead ones, one can only speculate on his view of translation.

While students found the daily theme a grind, one anonymous Harvard graduate explained its importance in the *Atlantic Monthly* ("The Daily Theme Eye"). The requirement forced students to develop a "daily theme eye" (427), the habit of noticing subjects appropriate for short, personal essays. Students could write on anything, "a fleeting impression of life" (428) or an incisive response to a book or a play. Successful students developed the ability "to watch for and treasure incidents that were sharply dramatic or poignant, moods that were clear and definite, pictures that created a single clear impression" (428). In short, students had to develop a writer's eye that saw things vividly. Given the goal of the dailies to teach correctness before interest, however, the experience of this student, a professional writer, might not have been representative, and he admitted that few of his classmates appreciated these essays.

The daily theme in fact put a burden on both teacher and assistants. Phelps remembered seeing Wendell in his office, surrounded by student themes, using a stack of them as a pillow while he napped. Phelps remembered, too, his own days as Wendell's assistant when he read 800 freshman themes a week. He "read all day and a good part of the night. Once [he] was sick for two days, and a substitute read for [him], because even one day's lapse made it impossible to keep up" (274). And not all the English faculty valued the method. The liberal culturalist Perry was critical of the time that men like Child, Hill, Wendell, Briggs, and Copeland spent reading themes. He claimed that Wendell and Child became skeptical at the end.

As editor of the *Atlantic Monthly* for a decade, Perry reviewed essays from across the country, and he "kept to [him]self the dreadful secret that in ten years reading manuscript . . . [he] had never observed that Harvard men wrote any better than" other college graduates (*Gladly* 253-54). Having taught at both Harvard and Yale, Phelps claimed that he could tell no difference between the writing of the two student bodies, even though Yale students at the time took no required writing course (273-74).

In addition to the dailies, English A students wrote three to six page "fortnightly themes" on an assigned topic. Copeland and Rideout's book provided some of the topics, which suggest that many of these themes taught the modes. The first semester emphasized exposition. Students wrote various explanatory essays and an autobiography. The second semester's themes were organized around the remaining modes: two descriptions followed by two narratives, followed by a brief and an argument (4-5). As with the dailies, the instructor made no attempt to help students generate ideas. Students came up with their own topics and generated their own materials as best they could. Most teachers evaluated the themes for form and correctness—usage, punctuation, arrangement, etc.–not for thought.

While students met in two classes a week, they also had two other kinds of contact with instructors. These two elements influenced Aydelotte because, when he developed his freshman course at IU, he used both. The first was the conference. Each English A student met once a month with the instructor "to review his work and learn his individual needs" (Copeland and Rideout 3). Some instructors, including Copeland, held conferences more often. The second element was the "third hour" (3). As Brown relates, the third hour developed when Hill and Briggs asked the faculty that the course be changed from two- to three-hours a week. The faculty reluctantly agreed if students had to do no out-of-class work for the third hour (54). After students met their own class for two hours a week, all sections congregated for another hour with Briggs, who either read aloud or lectured on a topic to orient students to college (Brown 56).

Aydelotte's disappointments with Harvard continued. He wrote home that his mid-year grades were unexceptional, all B's, including English A. He lamented that, even though he had taken a similar course at IU, a "B in English Composition, is as good as I can expect" (qtd. in Blanshard 45).

He did, however, have the good fortune to become Charles Townsend Copeland's assistant. Copeland was one of Harvard's most idiosyncratic teachers. He had been hired as an instructor in 1893, and he remained in this lowly position for seventeen years (Adams 100). Like all new instructors, he began in English A, reading themes; by the time Aydelotte arrived, Copey (as he was affectionately known) directed the program, coauthoring *Freshman English*, which described it. His methods of teaching writing were unusual. He had once been the drama critic for a Boston paper, and he retained a dramatic flair. He often gave public readings of sample passages that exemplified the plain style (Defoe was a favorite). He held regular student conferences similar to Oxford tutorials in which he required students to read their papers aloud. As he listened, Copeland acted out elaborate responses, groaning extravagantly and pretending to snore loudly at dullness. As students read, he would stop them to write down his verbal comments. According to Dean Briggs, these comments were brusk: "Write, 'What a swag-bellied sentence!' Write, 'March of the elephants!'" (qtd. in Adams *Copey* 176-77).

For all his posturing, Copeland stressed the importance of thought in essays and influenced Aydelotte. In the T. S. Eliot paper that Adams includes in *Copey of Harvard*, with Copeland's dictated comments, Copeland clearly attended to more than form. At least one of Copeland's former students, the writer Walter D. Edmonds, recognized Copeland's emphasis on thought:

> The purpose of writing [Copeland maintained] is to set down truthfully one's meaning; and style, therefore, is not a manufactured process, the manipulation of words for their own sake, but the organization of ideas. A writer cannot 'create a style' any more than he can create himself, but he can train himself to think, and if he hopes to succeed, he must. (qtd. in Adams *Copey* 175)

This is as good a statement as one can find on part of the position that Aydelotte eventually adopted. Many years later in his autobiographical notes, Aydelotte admitted that he owed Copey "no little debt for the values which I received at Harvard" ("Harvard" 1). He also mentioned the work Copeland required of him. Like Phelps a few years earlier, Aydelotte corrected student papers. He also advised Copeland on "what might be said to" student writers in conference (2).

Copeland in turn appreciated Aydelotte as a teacher, as evidenced by the recommendation letter that the Harvard instructor wrote to the University of Colorado. He praised his assistant as an excellent teacher and "as one of the few best out of the many young men that have helped me teach English Composition during the past ten years." He continued:

> Besides doing his work faithfully and well, he was a friend to his pupils, and made it pleasant for them to go to see him at his lodgings. In this human, highly important, generally neglected department of a teacher's duty Aydelotte did far more than any other assistant of mine has even tried to do. I wish he might live in Harvard "Yard," teach Harvard undergraduates, and be their genial yet highly respected associate. (qtd. in Blanshard 46)

This letter suggests that Aydelotte adopted Copeland's conference method by meeting students at his rooms. It also suggests that Aydelotte, like Copeland, established personal relationships with his charges. Aydelotte continued using conferences in his own teaching in part due to Copeland's influence.

What did Aydelotte learn about teaching writing from Harvard? For the most part, he learned what he did not want to do with a writing program. He rejected the daily theme approach, which he thought led to superficial prose. In an attack on the dailies in *College English*, Aydelotte argued that students should write one careful essay a week rather than "a larger number written more rapidly," as Harvard required (133). In "The History of English as a College Subject," Aydelotte again attacked. As he put it, the daily essay required students in a year-long course to "produce . . . an amount of writing which, if it were really to say anything, would tax the strength and fertility of most professional men of letters, even though they gave all their time to the work" (189). "Such work," he continued, "encourages glibness and facility and wordiness rather than sincerity and brevity and care" (189). While he agreed with Hill's stress on the plain style, he rejected the Harvard emphasis on form and correctness, emphasizing critical thinking instead. He came to believe that correctness cannot be taught until the student writer had something important to communicate and the desire to write it well. Finally, he rejected the assumption that writing and literature should be studied separately.

But he also found methods that he continued to use in his later teaching. Two of these were the individual writing conference and Dean Briggs's third-hour talk. In short, while he borrowed techniques from America's most famous writing program, he rejected its soul and pointed his programs in new directions. The inspiration for these changes he found in England when he attended Oxford University.

## Rhodes Scholar at Oxford

Aydelotte matriculated at Oxford as a Rhodes Scholar from Indiana in 1905, a member of the second class of Americans to hold the scholarship. He remained at Oxford for two years, receiving his B.Litt. in 1908 after leaving England. He returned for his third year in 1913 to prepare his *Elizabethan Rogues and Vagabonds* for publication at the Clarendon Press. During his first two years, he worked closely with Sir Walter Raleigh, the university's first modern English professor, and came to the conclusion that an Oxford undergraduate education, especially the honors degree, was superior to its American equivalent. The Oxford experience in fact became the defining episode in his education and deeply influenced his future curriculums. He became the foremost American advocate of the Oxford approach. He also remained active in the American Rhodes Scholarship program, serving as the founding editor of the *New Oxonian*, the official magazine of American Rhodes scholars, and eventually becoming the first American Secretary to the Rhodes Trust, a post that he held for years. In this position, he oversaw the evolution of the American Rhodes Scholarships into one of this country's most prestigious academic awards. He was knighted by Queen Elizabeth II for his life-long contributions to the Rhodes Trust.

The Rhodes Scholarships were established by the will of Cecil John Rhodes, an English colonialist and racist who made his fortune in South Africa and the African nation formally named after him, Rhodesia (now Zimbabwe). In Africa he speculated in diamonds and gold, excluded black Africans from mine ownership, and stole large tracks of land from the native peoples, all the while wrapping his greed in the British flag.[5] While amassing his fortune, he found time to meet the residence requirements for a pass degree at Oxford and considered the experience valuable, especially since it threw him in with the future British political elite who would help him achieve his colonialist ambitions. An ardent supporter of the British Commonwealth and the superiority of Anglo-Saxon values, he established his scholarships to bring together young men throughout the English-speaking world, and Germany, to study at Oxford. By including men from the colonies, he hoped to teach them the importance of "the retention of the unity of the empire" (Rhodes 22). He also hoped that they would spread what he considered healthy Anglo-Saxon values throughout the world. He believed such a system would secure world peace through shared understanding.

He was particularly interested in bringing young Americans to Oxford. While he did not expect them to reject the United States, he developed the bizarre hope that they would help unify the English-speaking world, perhaps under the American flag. To facilitate their educations, the Rhodes will allocated each student 300 pounds per year to matriculate at any Oxford college for "three consecutive academical years" (Rhodes 29). Under the plan as initially conceived, each state was allotted two scholarships (34). According to the Rhodes Will, the criteria for choosing scholars were the following:

1. "literary and scholastic attainments";
2. "fondness" for sports such as "cricket[,] football[,] and the like";
3. civic qualities "of manhood[,] truth[,] courage[,] devotion to duty[;] sympathy for the protection of the weak[,] kindliness[,] unselfishness[,] and fellowship" [sic]; and
4. leadership qualities such as "moral force of character," "instincts to lead," "interest in his schoolmates"–in short, qualities that "will be likely in after life to guide him to esteem the performance of public duty as his highest aim" (36).

Aydelotte was an excellent candidate for the scholarship. He was interested in things literary and scholarly, having majored in English, edited IU's literary magazine, and worked as a journalist and English teacher for a few years after graduation. He had also been trained at Harvard in philology, which was the primary scholarly approach to literature at Oxford then (although that was to change under Raleigh). Though interested in the intellectual world, Aydelotte was no bookworm. He was an athlete of some prowess, having lettered in football for IU. While his leadership skills had not yet manifested themselves, his friends among the IU administrators recognized his potential. In fact, on the day when the establishment of the scholarships was announced in 1901, IU's President Joseph Swain immediately thought of Aydelotte. Swain said to him in his Quaker diction, "Frank, has thee heard of these Rhodes Scholarships? Thee ought to get one of them." As Aydelotte remembered in his unpublished autobiography, "Bloomington,

Indiana," he replied, "Dr. Swain, I had already thought of it" (4). Aydelotte was to fulfill his potential for leadership later in life by becoming the American Secretary of the Rhodes Trust, Swarthmore's president, and, in his final post, Director of Princeton's Institute for Advanced Study.

In part because he had the support of his former teacher, Bryan, a member of the Indiana selections committee, Aydelotte won the nomination. His major problem was finding a way to pass the Oxford Responsions, an entrance examination which required knowledge of "algebra, geometry, Latin translation at sight, and Latin prose composition" as well as some Greek (Beirne 666). While Frank F. Beirne, a 1910 Rhodes Scholar from the University of Virginia, remembered the examination as "far from severe" (666), Aydelotte possessed so weak a background in classical languages that he had to bone up. He crammed while he taught English at the Louisville Male High School, his first job after Harvard.

While he had studied Latin in high school, he had never studied Greek and had to learn the basics quickly. He knew Abraham Flexner, the head of a preparatory school in Louisville and an expert on teaching languages, and approached him about the Greek. Flexner gave him a system for learning the language on his own which Aydelotte supplemented with full-time study during Christmas break with tutors (Flexner *I Remember* 322). The cramming paid off when Aydelotte passed (Blanshard 46-49). In the notes for his memoirs, Aydelotte commented wryly that he had "often said that no one was ever exempted from Responsions with a more slender balance of Greek than [he]" ("Harvard University" 4).

At Oxford, Aydelotte fully participated in university life. As an athlete, he enjoyed sports such as rugby and rowing. As a young man interested in scholarship, he appreciated the emphasis on the academic life, especially the university's library, one of the best in the world. He valued the internationalism of Oxford that threw Americans like himself among students from around the world. Like many Americans, he found the emphasis on pomp and circumstance intriguing, and for the rest of his life, he traveled to Oxford to participate in academic ceremonies as often as he could.

The English educational system was different from the American. The Oxford degree, especially the pass degree, did not primarily train scholars but created gentlemen. Writing in 1903, two years before Aydelotte matriculated, William T. Harris outlined the benefits of an Oxford education. Rather than training academic specialists, as did the German universities, Oxford attempted to train well-rounded scholars who possessed "good breeding," a love of "fair play" gained on the playing fields, and an appreciation of scholarship (2-9). Students were required to reside for three years in Oxford within a 1.5 mile radius of Carfax, the location of the old St. Martin's Church, to receive a degree (Blauvelt 368). This requirement was sometimes called sleeping for one's degree. The purpose of the residence requirement was to ensure that all undergraduates participated in Oxford life, which included, along with study, outdoor sports such as rowing, cricket, and rugby. As Blauvelt noted in 1902, "For the majority of Oxonians the life counts more than the work. Oxford trains few scholars, a great many gentlemen" (371). Consequently, in addition to athletics, Oxford valued social life. The honors degree, on the other hand, emphasized scholarship of the highest degree and required more work than the pass degree.

The Oxford experience revolutionized Aydelotte's concept of university teaching. After his two years there, Aydelotte believed that the English had worked out many problems that dogged the American system. These problems revolved around a series of related issues, including the lack of high standards, the fragmentation of the curriculum under the elective system, the emphasis on memorization at the expense of deeper understanding, and the separation of writing instruction from meaningful content. All of these problems he saw as stemming from a central cause: American students were neither required to read widely nor to think deeply about significant issues. At Oxford Aydelotte found a system that encouraged students to think at full capacity.

Aydelotte was most impressed with Oxford's honor schools, which in 1903 consisted of English Language and Literature, *Literae Humaniores* (The Greats), Mathematics, Law, History, Theology, Oriental Studies, and Sciences (Harris 16). While Oxford students could take a pass degree, a degree less demanding than an American B.A., most ambitious students chose to take an honors degree, which required considerably more work than the American degree. The distinction between the two, Aydelotte argued, was as "sharp" as the distinction between the American B.A. and Ph.D. While pass students worked little more than the average American undergraduate, honors students entered for their last two years a "final honors school" in which they read under a tutor to prepare for comprehensive examinations ("Honors Courses" 2). English honors was therefore more demanding than American honors. In America, honors could be gained in two ways, Aydelotte argued in "What the American Rhodes Scholar Gets Out of Oxford." In the first, excellent students could win honors with little effort. In the second, lesser students could win them by grinding out the course work and studying every waking hour. In Aydelotte's view, the Oxford system ensured that the first group did "the hardest and best work of which [they were] capable" (678). As Aydelotte argued in "Honors Courses," "The pass degree is for the man who is not primarily interested in the intellectual life; the honors degree is for the man who is" (2). Students who entered an Oxford honors school had to meet "a higher standard" and complete a more specialized curriculum than the pass student did (Crosby "Courses" 56-57).

Each school taught a series of related subjects, and each had its own examinations, board of examiners, lectures, and faculty (Crosby "Courses" 57). Based on the results of the examination, students were ranked, with the highest, most valued distinction being a "first class" (57). Crosby comments that American Rhodes scholars entering Oxford, "even those who have done some post-graduate work, find the Honours B.A. a task worthy of their mettle; while those who have not finished or have just finished undergraduate work in America will have their hands full if they attempt to win a first or second class" honors degree (57).

One of the main advantages of the honors program, according to Aydelotte, was its emphasis on mastering two or more related subjects. Discovering connections between disciplines, he argued, was one way to create knowledge. In the United States, students were not encouraged to make such connections. Under the elective system then popular, students took discrete, loosely-related courses. The educational philosophy behind this approach was that, since all students are different, they should not take a set program of study. This system, Aydelotte was convinced, blinded students to relationships among bodies of thought. Instead of experiencing connections, students accumulated credits, and administrators assumed that such accumulation resulted in knowledge.

At Oxford, on the other hand, the honors student developed knowledge in an honors school, which was broader than an American academic department. In these schools, students studied several related subjects. As an example of Oxford's success, Aydelotte pointed to the School of Modern History in which students studied–in addition to history–languages, literature, economic theory, and international law. The purpose of this program was to bring together related disciplines that would give students the disparate knowledge needed to solve modern political and economic problems ("Honors Courses" 2).

Another advantage that Aydelotte saw in the Oxford method was the "thoroughness" with which students studied their subjects ("Rhodes Scholarships" 581). Once again, he found that American education was limited by the superficiality of discrete courses. The American method, Aydelotte argued, resulted in "killing rather than in stimulating the mild interest which prompted the student to understand" the course content (581). After earning the B.A., American students then needed an MA to specialize. At Oxford, Aydelotte claimed, undergraduates specialized immediately. They read to gain depth of understanding that American undergraduates rarely achieved. As Aydelotte argued, the American "method of taking scattered courses in order to widen the range of our interests is only a clumsy and extravagant way of getting the benefit which could be obtained far more naturally and easily from a certain amount of general reading" (581). American education, to Aydelotte's mind, achieved breadth by requiring many loosely related courses; the Oxford system, by contrast, required students to read thoroughly a few related subjects. "What the English academic discipline lacks in extent as compared with ours," Aydelotte argued, "is made up in thoroughness" ("American Rhodes Scholar" 678).

Aydelotte was also impressed with Oxford's tutorials. From his perspective, the tutor was the heart of the Oxford system. By his time at Oxford, the tutorial system had been formalized. No longer hired privately, tutors were part of the colleges' teaching staff. When students arrived, they were assigned a tutor in their intended subject. In the first interview, the tutor determined current knowledge of students and informed them of examinations and other degree requirements. The tutor then planned an individualized course of study by providing a list of readings and identifying appropriate lectures. Once the term started, students met with their tutor once a week to discuss issues and read papers tutors had assigned (Bailey 127-

28). Since the "only hard-and-fast academic engagement," Aydelotte writes, "is to call on [one's] tutor once a week at a specific hour" ("What" 678), the Oxford system avoided many of the problems of the American with its emphasis on unrelated courses and collecting credits. By organizing a body of reading at the beginning of one's studies, the tutor told students not what to take "but what [they were] supposed to know" ("What" 679). "Whereas the American undergraduate takes courses," Aydelotte continued, "the Oxford man studies a subject" (679).

The tutor oversaw the student's individual development by assigning weekly topics. While the tutor assigned the topic, the student enjoyed freedom of approach. As Aydelotte explained, ". . . the choice of books to be read, of how much or how little shall be done, or the point of view from which to topic shall be treated–all of these are left to the student" (*Oxford Stamp* 16). Oxford valued individual initiative in "the [person] who is able to plan . . . , and who has the energy and initiative to work without constant supervision." Such a person "can go as far and as fast as he [or she] likes. Perhaps capacity for independent work is the most important academic result of the Oxford system of education" ("What" 680). Unlike the German-inspired American instructor, who "pour[ed] out a stream of facts and ideas over the heads of the class," the Oxford tutor placed "the emphasis upon the individual reaction to the work, and . . . [on] personal teaching which has illumination and driving power many times as great as anything which the instructor can do in the classroom or lecture alone" (*Oxford Stamp* 63-64).

In terms of writing instruction, Aydelotte developed his central concepts at Oxford. In the tutorials, students presented weekly papers on the reading completed, and the tutor critiqued papers for both content and expression. The critique was meaningful because students wrote on a known topic to a known audience for a known purpose. Aydelotte concluded that the Harvard emphasis on form at the expense of content and rhetorical situation was an inferior approach. This emphasis on integrating writing instruction with course content became one of the marks of Aydelotte's approach to composition instruction.

To balance freedom and discipline, Oxford developed comprehensive examinations to make students work hard. Undergraduates took these only after the conclusion of one or two years of study. Aydelotte often compared the Oxford comprehensives to American course examinations. American examinations emphasized the mastery, often by memorization, of small amounts of material. Such tests encouraged cramming and forgetting. Students therefore neither synthesized material nor built systems of knowledge. Oxford examinations, by contrast, were in essay form and demanded that students answer questions to demonstrate "one's power of dealing with a subject," not a small body of information ("What" 681). Since the tests required the synthesis of a year or two of reading, students could not cram; they had to know the reading well enough to write intelligently when questioned. Students were rewarded when their papers presented "answers which not merely contain[ed] information but [were] also well thought out and well written" ("What" 681).

An element of the Oxford experience that Aydelotte valued was student conversation. As he argued in *The Oxford Stamp*, Oxford was designed to encourage a rich social life by giving students leisure. Andrew Lang, an Oxford graduate, recognized this fact in his book entitled *Oxford*:

> For three years men are in possession of what the world does not enjoy-leisure; and they are supposed to be using that leisure for the purposes of perfection.... The boy who has just left school ... finds himself in the midst of books, of thought, and discussion. He has time to look at all the common problems of the hour, and yet he need not make up his mind hurriedly, nor pledge himself to anything. (263-64)

The colleges were set up to encourage such discussion. As Aydelotte remembered in *The Oxford Stamp*, each student had quarters (a large study and a smaller bedroom) in one of the colleges. Students entertained each other in their studies, often hosting breakfasts, "the great social meal in Oxford" (7). After the meal, students talked well into the morning. Aydelotte considered this social interaction, with its emphasis on intellectual conversation, an essential part of an Oxford education missing from American colleges:

> It offers Oxford men an opportunity of acquiring, in the numberless discussions which this social life makes possible, an openness and alertness of mind, a certain independence in thinking, and a readiness, which it is almost impossible to acquire any other way. Perhaps there is no teaching which American undergraduates need so much and of which they get so little, largely because of the external arrangements of our college life. (9)

Oxford conversation broadened students by introducing them to differing opinions. Aydelotte argued that American students studying there found the talk useful because they mixed with "men from every nation and every class [who were] living together and surveying the nations of the earth in human and humorous companionship." Americans returned home "a citizen of the world" ("What" 682-83). "Most Rhodes Scholars would say," Aydelotte argued, "that Oxford talk is the best talk in the world" (682), in part because it lacked the provincialism of undergraduate talk in the United States. Oxford conversation, Aydelotte thought, helped students "translate thought into action"(*Oxford Stamp* 4). In other words, the Oxford undergraduate "learns, or has the chance to learn, how to present his ideas in action rather than merely how to hold them suspended in his mind" ("What" 682).

Aydelotte, however, dismissed the purely social element of Oxford conversation. He noted that discussion cannot provide ideas where none exist and that too much of Oxford's "social life offers only social training," which in England was the mark of "a university man." "But at its best," he went on, "this intellectual discussion, freed from pedantry and self-consciousness by the leaven of healthy, enthusiastic, undergraduate life, is one characteristic of Oxford that we of the American universities ought most to envy" (*Oxford Stamp* 12). In other words, Aydelotte did not highly value the gentlemanly graces for which Oxford was famous, and he did not want American colleges to foster them. Instead, he advocated that American undergraduates partake of challenging discussions seminal to their intellectual development. While it was not until he created Swarthmore's honors program in the early 1920s that Aydelotte fully integrated Oxford-like conversation into his teaching methods, he based his thought approach to writing instruction on the notion that students work out intellectual positions in discussion.

He arrived at Oxford at an exciting time for English studies because he arrived the year after Walter Raleigh, the university's first modern Professor of English (earlier ones had been philologists). Raleigh was by all accounts an unusual but brilliant lecturer who, unlike his philological predecessors, taught literature, not language. He was a critic who wrote books on major literary figures such as Wordsworth and Shakespeare. He also wrote a book on style and one on the history of the English novel. These books were not scholarship of the highest order but reworked lecture notes, and all have the weaknesses of such productions. It was not as a scholar but as a teacher and educational theorist that Raleigh influenced Aydelotte.

Raleigh was born in London in 1861, the son of a Congregationalist minister. He took his B.A. at London in 1881 and then entered King's College, Cambridge, where he studied history. After teaching in India and England for several years, he took a Chair of English Literature at Liverpool, replacing the famous critic A. C. Bradley. In 1900, he replaced Bradley again at Glasgow (Smith *Letters* I v-xi). He took a professorship of English literature at Oxford in 1904, where he revived the moribund honors school in English literature established in 1894 (Smith I xiii). When he arrived, only five men and fifteen women took the final honors examination in English literature; by 1922, when he died unexpectedly, 70 men and 46 women took it (Smith I xiv).

Raleigh was, according to H. W. Garrod, "one of the great figures of the Oxford of his time" (266). He was an eccentric but effective lecturer who began each talk by throwing out dates, facts, and stories and then reading passages of literature from books that he had marked with slips of paper (Smith I xii). He read with expression, all the while annotating passages with "a running commentary of inspired or ingenious notation" (Garrod 269). As Raleigh himself said of his lecturing, "I lecture in a very picaroon, jolly beggar kind of way, think it wakes them up" (*Letters* 125). His teaching method was not systematic because too much system, he believed, destroyed literature. Likewise he believed "dogma" was unhealthy in literary interpretation and demanded that his students "read and think for themselves" (D. Nichol Smith, "Raleigh" 703).

Raleigh, as Chris Baldick argues, was suspicious of literary criticism. He viewed literature as the expression of individual genius and was most interested in the individual thought of the writer, as he made clear in the following lines of verse:

> One book among the rest is dear to me.
> 'Tis when a man has tried himself in deed
> Against the world, and falling back to write
> Sated with love, or crazed with vanity,
> Bemused with drink, or maimed by fortune's spite,
> Sets down his Paternoster and his Creed. (*Letters* 329)

Raleigh therefore viewed literature as the expression of the author's thought, or creed, and rejected critical method that de-emphasized literature as personal expression. It followed for Raleigh, then, that literature consisted of an individual comment on life (Palmer 144).[6] Aydelotte drew on this notion of literature being an expression of the writer's thought when he developed his thought approach at IU starting in 1908.

Upon becoming director of the English program, Raleigh rejected philology and developed an approach of his own. In his letter in support of the School of English Language and Literature, he criticized philology on the grounds that it used "the minuter methods of Science without achieving any notable results" ("Professor Raleigh's Letter" 50). He considered his method, which combined criticism with history, as "another, more ancient way" that he convinced Oxford to adopt (50), and this combination of history and criticism became identified as the Oxford approach to literature.

Raleigh expressed a clear but traditional sense of purpose in undergraduate education. He made an Arnoldian distinction between two kinds of education, scientific/professional and liberal education. The purpose of the first was to train students in a subject; of the second, to help them develop as individuals. As Aydelotte summarized Raleigh's views in an address before the 1926 American Philosophical Society, echoing Pope's *Essay on Man*, "It is assumed that the proper study of mankind is man. It has taken as its aim the preparation of men to live together in society" ("Universities" 2). While many of Raleigh's views on liberal education were traditional, he expressed an innovative sense of its purpose: such education should value individual intellectual growth. To encourage this growth, the liberal arts professor had to "look at the way [the student is] looking," not just at the subject ("Universities" 1). In other words, the professor should center instruction not on subject matter, but on the students' responses to it. This emphasis was consistent with the Oxbridge tutorial method, which had traditionally emphasized individualized instruction.

When Aydelotte arrived at Oxford to study English, he enrolled in Brasenose College but found this college had no English tutor so he had to look elsewhere. He was assigned to Ernest de Selicourt of University College ("Oxford 1905-07" 1), then the only tutor of English literature in all Oxford. Aydelotte soon recognized that the Oxford honors B.A. would repeat much of what he had covered at Harvard, so he decided to work towards both the B.A. and the new research degree, the

B.Litt.(Blanshard 60-61). But he soon discovered Raleigh and wrote to his mother in October 1905:

> My English work is looking up, since yesterday. Professor Walter Raleigh from the University of Edinburgh [sic]–a new man here--is organizing the work in a way that is going to be fine, better than the German University methods and better than Harvard for original work anyway because the classes are smaller and you get more individual attention and because of the libraries here. He is a kindly sympathetic fellow and I like him much. (qtd. in Blanshard 61)

He took Raleigh's seminar on Renaissance literature. In this, Raleigh introduced Aydelotte to pamphlet literature of the period by Robert Greene and others that exposed "tricks and habits of the sharpers and criminals of London" (Raleigh *English Novel* 65). Raleigh had a particular interest in these pamphlets, having discussed them in two books, *The English Novel* (1894) and *Shakespeare*, published in 1907 while Aydelotte was in residence. Aydelotte wrote a paper on these pamphlets that received such praise that he decided to switch from the B.A. to the B.Litt. degree and do original research ("Oxford 1905-07" 2).

Aydelotte spent the remainder of his two years expanding his paper into a thesis under Raleigh and Professor C.H. Firth, the Oxford historian. Because of his advanced thought and preparation, they gave Aydelotte special permission to work independently without reading weekly papers, and he sought the professors out when he needed advice. He remembered that he once consulted Firth on a historical problem related to the project. Rather than giving him superficial advice, Firth went to his shelf and handed Aydelotte books until he "had around [him] on the floor a little mound of historical work" that Firth recommended he digest ("Oxford 1905-07" 2-3). While writing the thesis, Aydelotte experienced the combination of intellectual freedom and rigor that Oxford offered.

The experience of writing the thesis deeply influenced Aydelotte's views on education. He realized the importance of making connections between disciplines. Typical of Oxford literary research, the thesis combined work in literature and history, using each to illuminate the other. The project began by examining Robert Greene's "Coney-Catching pamphlets" and expanded to determine their historical accuracy ("Oxford 1905-07" 2). As Aydelotte remembered, the two professors "gave [him] . . . a conception of scholarship which [he] had never had before" ("Oxford 1905-07" 2). Later in his career, when Aydelotte developed Swarthmore's Honors Program, he attempted to give American students a similar sense of scholarship that helped them connect disciplines. Swarthmore students read in at least three related fields, not just one.

This type of scholarship was different from much being done in America. It was not philological research, which emphasized linguistic analysis; it was not literary history, which emphasized names and dates; it was not *belle lettres* or liberal cultural research, which emphasized random observations on the spiritual nature of the literary experience. Instead, as the finished book demonstrates, Aydelotte's approach was sophisticated cultural analysis that used historical research to elucidate the 15th- and 16th-century English coney-catching pamphlets of Greene and other prose writers. By examining various historical documents, including laws, discussions by contemporary commentators, state papers, and other such manuscript materials, Aydelotte proved that many of the discussions of the Renaissance rogues and vagabonds in the pamphlets and on the stage were accurate. He also demonstrated that these groups of misfits resulted from the economic disasters of the early 16th century growing from the enclosure movement that displaced peasants from their hereditary places in the feudal system. While much of the argument verified historical truth of Renaissance con-men, Aydelotte also established the literary value of the pamphlets, differentiating, for instance, between the early, innovative ones and the later, plagiarized ones produced to profit from the genre's popularity.

*Elizabethan Rogues and Vagabonds* received excellent reviews. Most reviewers commented on its sophisticated research strategies, and some noted Oxford's influence on its methodology. The unnamed reviewer for the *English Historical Review* called the book "an admirable opening volume" of Firth and Raleigh's Oxford Historical and Literary Studies and praised Aydelotte's use of manuscript material (792). The reviewer for the *Scottish Historical Review* commented on Aydelotte's "wide knowledge of the rogue history and literature" (220). Several reviewers remarked on Aydelotte's combining the study of English literature and history, the reviewer for the *Saturday Review* noting the success with which Aydelotte created a "complete . . . picture" of disreputable Elizabethans by drawing on the two fields (624). In the *American Historical Review*, Wallace Notestein commented appreciatively on the Oxford flavor of the book. It "shows," he wrote, "an intimate understanding of the Oxford way of thinking. . .which associates history with literature and interprets each by the aid of the other" (886). "Mr. Aydelotte," he continued, "has written an excellent monograph. He has made brilliant use of his materials. He has done more: he has caught the deeper significance of his subject. Moreover he handles with ease and lightness what might be called the English of Oxford" (887). Notestein essentially argued that Aydelotte was doing research different from most being done in the United States. The monograph not only used historical and literary analysis, but it was also written with a light touch, with a style that lacked the ponderousness of much German-inspired academic prose.

Aydelotte had Raleigh to thank for the development of his prose style, and his experiences working with Raleigh convinced him that the Harvard method of teaching writing was ineffective. Raleigh valued good writing, demanded it from his students, and sometimes bemoaned American Rhodes scholars' lack of ability. In a letter written to Oxford historian George W. Prothero on May 23, 1906, he mentioned a Rhodes scholar in a research class who read a paper "that was empty, magniloquent, abstract, flatulent, pretentious, confused, and sub-human. I could have wept salt tears" (*Letters* II 298). We get some sense of the kind of advice Raleigh gave on writing from a December 22, 1907, letter to Aydelotte critiquing *Elizabethan Rogues and Vagabonds*. Raleigh criticized the introductory material of the manuscript because it repeated what would come in the body of the work. He also critiqued the style and advised Aydelotte to "polish its nails, so to speak.... Read it through once solely with the view of expression. E.g. 'raged with great vigour'– how else would you rage? Or 'father(in law?)'. Try reading this aloud–it won't go. It is shorthand for what you ought to express fully." In this short passage, he asked Aydelotte to cut redundancies, clarify unclear expressions, and read the material through for rhythm and flow.

Attending Oxford as a Rhodes Scholar was Aydelotte's formative educational experience. He had attended two major American universities, IU and Harvard, but, after Oxford, found them lacking. He came to view the Oxford system as superior to the American and devoted his professional life to adapting the Oxford methods to American conditions. The Rhodes Scholarships were important, he believed, because they created a cadre of American educational reformers who could introduce parts of the Oxford system in the U.S. As he wrote in 1922, in the "History of the Operation of the Rhodes Scholarships in the United States,"

> Rhodes Scholars are leaders in the serious and wide-spread attempt to introduce into the American educational system the best features of the English Universities, including the tutorial system, final comprehensive examinations, and the differentiation between the Honours and the Pass degrees which allows the ablest students to progress at their natural pace instead of being held back to the rate which is not too fast for the average. (211-12)

He also came to believe two other related principles. First, writing instruction succeeded best when it takes place within content instruction, especially in small tutorials or seminars where students could receive individual attention of the kind he received from Raleigh and Firth. Second, the Oxford method of having students study a few related subjects offered a better education than the American method that required a variety of elective courses to achieve breadth. While he would not develop a curriculum that incorporated most elements of Oxford until he became president of Swarthmore, he began implementing some Oxford principles, greatly modified, at Indiana University, where he met his first and only major failure as an educational reformer.

## NOTES

1. The B.Litt. was a research degree in that it required a thesis of original work. The thesis subject often developed out of a seminar, as it did in Aydelotte's case. His thesis, after revision, was published by Oxford University Press.

2. This method assumed that literature had one interpretation and that the teacher's job was to provide that interpretation when the student reader foundered. Aydelotte's method differed from this in that he assumed that students would read differently according to their backgrounds, intellects, and interests. He valued independent thought.

3. This requiring students from other schools to retake work was not uncommon at Harvard. Dr. Will B. Howe, IU's chair of English while Aydelotte taught there several years later, had taken a B.A. at Butler College in Kansas. Upon matriculating at Harvard late in the 19th century, he took a second B.A. there before he began graduate work.

4. It apparently did not occur to the Harvard instructors that the triteness and other writing problems were due in part to the number of papers the students were required to write. Aydelotte recognized this as a problem: students could not write a thoughtful paper every day.

5. While Rhodes was clearly a racist, Oxford University did not enforce a racist policy. It accepted students from all races and did not administer the Rhodes Scholarships along racist lines.

6. The Arnoldian element is clear in Raleigh's theory–literature represents the individual writer's criticism of life.

# 3: Developing the Thought Approach at Indiana, 1908-1915

When Aydelotte married and left Oxford after his second year, he needed a job. He applied to the English Department at Indiana University (IU), his alma mater. It made sense to return home: his family lived in Sullivan, Indiana; he had many supporters at IU, especially William L. Bryan, now IU's President; and he saw an opportunity to influence his undergraduate English department. That he had been an all-state football star made Aydelotte an attractive candidate to many; that he had starred on IU's first state championship team made him even more so (Blanshard 102).[1] Aydelotte's old mentor, President Bryan, wrote letters inviting the young Rhodes Scholar back to IU, and Aydelotte joined the English faculty as a Visiting Associate Professor in January 1908 (Blanshard 102). While Aydelotte took the job with high hopes, he soon found himself in a conflict over teaching methods that led to his resignation.

From the first, Aydelotte did not intend to fit into the English department as it was structured. In a letter designed to lure him back to IU, Bryan informed him that the department needed "building up" (Blanshard 102) and that IU would do what was necessary to support curricular changes. Aydelotte was interested in the offer in part because he saw an opportunity to change the freshman writing program. In his May 1, 1907, letter to Bryan, Aydelotte outlined his plans for freshman English:

> While . . . I should model [the new course] roughly on English A at Harvard, I should make a number of modifications suggested by [Oxford]. . . . The daily themes and personal conferences of the Harvard course I should keep . . . . At Harvard English A seemed to me to be the most important single factor in giving the men some conception of what the University stood for in scholarship, in culture and in content. I believe such a freshman course would fill a need at Indiana. I should plan to start with one section of perhaps 30, and study the results.

Interestingly, Aydelotte did not develop a course similar to Harvard's English A; perhaps he mentioned English A only because he knew that the freshman course then on the books was based on Harvard's famous model, and he would not be hired if he threatened the status quo. At any rate, when he arrived at IU and began designing his freshman English course, English 2A, he angered many members of the department who supported the Harvard method. English 2A, which became known as the thought approach, was his first attempt to introduce an Oxford-inspired pedagogy in America. As he wrote in a September 17, 1954, letter to Frances Blanshard, "the Stamp of Oxford was certainly on all this educational program of mine at Indiana."

The thought course represents an important development in the history of English studies because it contrasted so sharply with the methods of Harvard's writing program. While the Harvard approach emphasized form and correctness, the thought course emphasized reading essays and literature for content and writing about it. The course therefore broke down the Harvard separation between literature and composition and cast writing and literature into a new relationship that taught students to think and write critically about literary texts. Unlike Harvard's English A, Aydelotte's course emphasized high level critical thinking and problem solving skills by requiring students to reflect on significant problems raised in the reading. Most importantly, Aydelotte saw himself as training a different kind of person than did Harvard. While Harvard trained the middle-class professional for a position in business and industry (Berlin *Writing Instruction* 60), Aydelotte's thought approach prepared future leaders who could reflect on the world and change it, not serve established masters. Oxford, he believed, had prepared generations of students to solve the infinite problems of building the British Empire; Aydelotte wanted to prepare future Americans who could achieve similar results.

The weakness of the course is apparent, however. It did not meet the needs of many IU students. While such an approach might work well at elite colleges such as Oxford, which accepted only the best students from selective preparatory schools,[2] it did not work as well for IU students, who often entered college from diverse educational backgrounds and with questionable writing skills. Before they could think in prose, many of these students needed more work on the formal elements of discourse that Aydelotte largely neglected. For the very best students, those well-prepared for college work, however, the thought approach was successful, but Aydelotte had no way to limit his approach to this group at IU.

## Theory of the Thought Approach

Before turning to Aydelotte's pedagogy, I will first discuss the theoretical grounding of the thought approach. While developing English 2A, Aydelotte articulated his theory in essays that appeared in the *Nation*, the *Atlantic Monthly*, *Educational Review*, and *English Journal*. He collected many of the essays in The

*Oxford Stamp, and Other Essays* (1917). As this title suggests, the essays express positions on education that grew out of his Oxford experiences. He also published *College English: A Manual for the Study of English Literature and Composition* (1913), a book articulating the thought approach designed for students and teachers under the assumption that even the instructors needed guidance in the novel method.

In general, this book and the earlier essays attacked then current American composition and literature instruction and argued for Aydelotte's approach, which made critical thinking the primary concern of American education in English studies.

Aydelotte established the historical basis for his attack on American English studies in "The History of English as a College Subject in the United States," a piece originally written for C. R. Mann's Carnegie report on Engineering Education. In this essay, he identifies the twin traditions of composition and literature instruction that emphasized form rather than thought. In his discussion of composition studies, he traces the development of rhetorical theory and practice in the United States from its dependence on the British rhetoricians Hugh Blair, George Campbell, and Richard Whately to the emergence of American theorists in the British tradition. He criticizes Blair and Campbell for their emphasis on correctness, and their condemnation of the writing of the best 18th century stylists as mechanically imperfect. He attributed the contemporary obsession with correctness to their influence.[3] To Aydelotte, correctness is "a sterile ideal . . . which never existed on sea or land" (179). Since the most carefully-edited professional prose contains errors, it is unreasonable to demand perfection from freshmen. Such an emphasis, Aydelotte concluded, attempts to "cultivate taste by a negative process" (179), by which he meant that this emphasis neglected the real value of literature, its criticism of life.

Aydelotte objected to any approach that taught writing as a rule-governed activity because such an artificial approach privileged form over content. He points to G. P. Quakenbos's 1854 *Advanced Course of Composition and Rhetoric* as one of the seminal texts that made instruction artificial. The book emphasizes rules of rhetoric, style, and discourse forms on the assumption that students learn to write by following rules. As Aydelotte notes, "the fact was ignored that men do not write to illustrate principles of style, and that whatever is written for that purpose, even if successful, is useless for any other" (183). The assumption that form and style should be studied as a set of rules separated from content held firm throughout the 19th century, Aydelotte argued, as indicated by textbook writers such as "Bascum, Day, Haven, J. S. Hart, Bain, Hunt, Hill, Genung, and Wendell" (183), all of whom shared an interest in formal approaches. These texts had the same weakness: "they are constantly concerned with the form of thought rather than the substance, and hence the tendency toward artificiality in their results with the average beginner" (183).

In another *Oxford Stamp* essay, "Robert Louis Stevenson[:] Darkening Counsel" (first published in 1912), Aydelotte attacks one of the oldest and most pervasive formal approaches to composition instruction, the imitation of passages.

The method had its beginnings in classical rhetoric, and it was widely used in the 19th-century classics classroom. It was also used extensively in the century's composition classes. To Aydelotte, the method justified not only the imitation of short passages, but also the modes of discourse, models for entire essays. Stevenson claimed that he learned to write like a "sedulous ape" by aping notable passages from other writers. Because of Stevenson's popularity, many English professors included imitation in their composition classes. The method was used at Harvard, and Aydelotte claims to "have heard of a big sophomore composition class at Harvard which finally came to the point where they would stamp whenever Stevenson's name was mentioned, as at the mention of the ladies or of Yale" (152).

Aydelotte took an interesting approach to undermine Stevenson's claims. He argued that imitation does not explain the writer's development. Instead, Stevenson acquired his style from the forces that shaped his intellect. When he read, Stevenson did not read "models of style" (156); instead, he read a mix of writers who interested him intellectually. In short, he read to think "things out for himself, . . . the one motive to make a young man with blood in his veins and the world stirring about him to become a reader of books" (159). His style is his own, and the reader would be hard pressed to discover obvious influences. When writing, Stevenson did not focus on formal techniques; instead, he discovered form as he worked out his argument. The problem with Aydelotte's position is that it is probably wrong. As an aspiring writer, Stevenson would have read with at least one eye on technique. He would have read to master various formal, rhetorical, and stylistic strategies that he applied to his own writing. By denying freshman writers knowledge of technique, Aydelotte could not help the weaker progress. While critical thinking is important and was too often ignored in the dominant pedagogies of the time, critical thinking in prose could not occur without control of formal conventions.

Aydelotte also criticized the 19th-century tradition of literary study for its emphasis on form. He rejected the *belles-lettres* tradition because Hugh Blair and his followers viewed literature instrumentally as a source of illustrations for rhetorical principles. These rhetoricians approached literature not as a body of thought but as a collection of illustrations of effective prose techniques–stylistic turns, discourse structures, and so on. As Aydelotte explained his position in an untitled biographical manuscript, "I took the line from the beginning that the study of English literature should be a study of what the author said and not merely his style in saying it" (1).

Aydelotte, however, was wrong in his assessment of Blair. While Blair did emphasize style, he did not reject the importance of thought. As he makes clear in Lecture I of *Lectures on Rhetoric and Belles Lettres*, his object of attack was artificial scholastic rhetoric with its "false ornament" (31). In its place, he called for a rhetoric that emphasized substance over "show" and simplicity over "ornament" (31). As did Aydelotte, Blair, following Bacon, rejected "the study of words alone" (31) and placed his primary emphasis on the thought itself. In fact,

Blair's introduction expresses many of Aydelotte's positions on the form/thought opposition.

Aydelotte also attacks a second tradition, the philological. Philologists applied rigorous linguistic analysis to English literature. Like the *belle-lettres* approach as Aydelotte conceived it, this method emphasized form over content. To find literature that lent itself to detailed linguistic analysis, philologists turned largely to Old and Middle English as well as Renaissance texts. This approach led to heavily annotated school texts, and these annotations, Aydelotte comments wryly, caused "[a] great deal of literary study [to become] a study of notes rather than texts, and the story is universal of the undergraduate who, not having time in preparation for an examination to read both text and notes, chose the latter to his profit" (*Oxford Stamp* 195). Since he was interested in teaching students to read literature for its thought, Aydelotte emphasized reading literature itself rather than philological notes.

In another *Oxford Stamp* essay, "An Experiment with the Freshman Course," Aydelotte attacked a third approach to contemporary literature instruction, the historical survey. At the time, the course usually took the form of a superficial, "rapid" survey "from Alfred or Chaucer to Tennyson" (89). Aydelotte feared that the purpose of the course was not to help students understand literature; instead, its

> purpose is to give the members of the class a bird's-eye view in order that they may understand, so to speak, the possibilities of the subject, may have their curiosity excited by different periods and authors, and be thus stimulated to further reading and study, and that they may learn at the beginning the place of each author in what is often called the evolution of English literature. (89)

Aydelotte thought that the rapidity made the approach superficial because students were not encouraged to read literature carefully to understand the author's thinking. Instead of encouraging thoughtful understanding, the method demanded only that students strengthen their memory by memorizing names, dates, and titles (Aydelotte "Correlation" 140). "The value of literature as a stimulus to thought," Aydelotte comments, "is its educative value," and this value "lies in its meaning rather than its history" (140).

While the term "rapid" would bother many contemporary teachers because it implies superficial treatment, Aydelotte did not seem to recognize the usefulness of broad surveys. Their purpose was to introduce students to a wide range of literature within historical and cultural contexts and thereby prepare them for more specialized courses. The thought approach, on the other hand, because it limited itself to a few major works, did not provide the same breadth of coverage that the survey did. The method did, however, encourage depth of treatment and therefore better prepared students to write on literary topics.

While these three essays attack common approaches to composition and literature, Aydelotte articulates his thought approach in "An Experiment" and in

*College English* (1913), both of which discuss his English 2A goals. These pieces argue that literature and composition should be taught together, that the freshman English course should teach students to think about significant ideas in the readings, and that concerns of form and correctness should be secondary. Aydelotte grounds his approach primarily in the work of two Victorian thinkers with close ties to Oxford, John Henry, Cardinal Newman, and Matthew Arnold.

*College English* discusses the work of Newman, who in *The Idea of the University* outlined his views on university education. Like Newman, Aydelotte placed problem solving at the center of his educational theory. He assumed that humans have an innate desire to understand themselves and their environments. As Aydelotte put it, "All the desires of man become in the end desire for understanding the mysteries of his environment and of his own nature, the conditions of his existence" (1). Following Newman, Aydelotte argued that the university exists to make it possible to identify, explore, and solve these problems. Each discipline (or *science* in Newman's language) offers a partial solution to a central human problem by offering a distinct "method of attack" (2). Each discipline therefore offers a limited view of the "truth." Since each disciplinary view is limited, students learn the scope of knowledge by studying disciplinary methods and findings. It is only by studying many disciplines, not just one, that students avoid narrowing and thus warping their perspective. Students therefore gain from the university a "broader outlook," what Newman terms "philosophy." What should result from a university education is a "philosophical habit of mind, or liberal knowledge" (6), which includes the ability to think critically about the world.

Liberal knowledge is a key term for Aydelotte. Such knowledge results not from memorizing information but, as Aydelotte defined it, develops when "information [is] transformed by thought" (7), a position central to Aydelotte's educational theory. While students need to gather information as material for thought, merely collecting and memorizing information is not enough. As Aydelotte states, "Education is something more than storing the memory with facts. The essential part of it is assimilating these facts, reasoning about them, fitting them together, perceiving their relations and their significance" (48). One way that students learn to transform information into knowledge is through conversation of the kind that Aydelotte experienced at Oxford. Transformation can also be achieved through writing, as students work out their thought in prose.

For Aydelotte liberal thought is independent thought, and independent thought can be learned through practice. As did Newman, Aydelotte assumed that a major purpose of education is to help individual students develop independent thinking *(College English* 9). Education itself, therefore, must focus on the individual, a principle that Aydelotte had learned first-hand at Oxford. As Aydelotte argues, "Each man's education, in reality, must be his own, something which he has thought out for himself.... Real knowledge cannot be learned; it can only be acquired by individual thought" (2). While a teacher or a book can assist intellectual development, neither can create better thinkers; only students can learn to think for themselves as they create world views. As Aydelotte put it, "in the end nothing is true for him [the student] except what he himself can think . . . ; he cannot borrow another's [thoughts] and use them as his own unless he can think them, that is understand them and believe them, for himself" (52).

A related educational assumption borrowed from Newman was the rejection of "smatterings" of information (9). Instead of studying a lot superficially, Aydelotte argued that students should learn "a few things well" (9). The purpose of education is not to learn everything about all disciplines but to learn the most important elements of each. Such centrally important knowledge offers several benefits. Not only do students learn the "truths" of each discipline; students also learn the "limitations" of each (9). The end of education, Aydelotte argues, following Newman, "is [the development of the] power of mind, the development of a man's own nature, his capacity for independent thought . . . . In other words, its end is the making of an intelligent man" (9). This end can be achieved, Aydelotte believed, by studying a few subjects thoroughly.

In addition to Newman's thought, Aydelotte also drew on Arnold's views on culture in his theory. For Arnold, culture referred to the best that had been thought and said by any age in any nation. Aydelotte borrowed Arnold's idea to argue that one purpose of education is to introduce students to the best thought available from which to develop the kind of individual world views that Newman valued. As Aydelotte argued, culture in Arnold's sense offers a "criticism of life, that is as something more than mere information or learning, as implying a theory of life thought out by the individual on the basis of the soundest knowledge and best thought which the world had produced" (24).

An important difference exists between Arnold and Aydelotte, however. Arnold argued that the best that has been thought and said should be drawn from all Western cultures and all periods, especially from the classical tradition. Aydelotte, on the other hand, limited that knowledge to the English tradition, which he viewed as a source of seminal thought for American intellectuals. Aydelotte therefore limited his students' reading almost exclusively to British essays and literature. One of the reasons he did this was to further Cecil Rhodes's ends of encouraging the spread of British intellectual ideals in America. Aydelotte would have been on firmer ground if he broadened the literature he taught to include the literature of other nations and cultures.

It is largely from Arnold that Aydelotte took his views on literature. Arnold viewed literature broadly, including any written text of significance in any field, including the sciences. In *College English*, Aydelotte echoes Arnold's famous dictum that literature is "the record of the best that has been thought and said in the world" (20). "Literature," Aydelotte continues, "is a record, one of the fullest and most adequate that we possess, of man's thought about life" (52). As Arnold argues in "The Function of Criticism at the Present Time," "the elements with which the creative power [of the writer] works are ideas" (238), and writers draw on the ideas about life available in their time when producing literature. Literature therefore offers a criticism of life and all serious poets present their individual analyses of life and its problems. Again echoing Arnold (and Shelley), Aydelotte argues that "The poet is the prophet of his age, the thinker, the revealer of truth, the commentator upon the life which he portrays" (20). All literature is the expression "of personal, subjective thought" (23), "the expression of man's thought about life and the world we live in" (28). The more valuable the literature, the more significant the thought it expresses. Because each major poet presents a body of thought on the human condition, students can read each in order to come to a deeper understanding of their own views on life. In other words, students should read literature not merely to appreciate or understand it but to clarify their own thoughts about their conditions as humans.

This process, however, is individual for each student, for each brings a different set of beliefs and a distinctive body of experience to the reading. As Aydelotte notes in *College English* on reading *Hamlet*, "[t]he thoughts we think about it, our interpretations of it, are many and different and they belong to us. The value of the play is the value of all great literature, that it stimulates and inspires these thoughts" (53). For students, therefore, reading is an active process of analyzing the thought contained in literature and comparing that thought to the thoughts that they bring to the literature. As they gain knowledge from their reading, students modify their world views and sharpen their thinking.

For Aydelotte, thought unifies the study of literature and writing. He bases his view of the student writer on his view of the poet. Just as poets express their thoughts about life in literature, students must recognize that their writing is valuable to the extent that it too expresses careful, honest thought. As Aydelotte argues, "Good writing is a matter of good thinking. The writer's task is to use his intellect, to see into the truth of things, and to express his ideas as exactly as he can" (47). Aydelotte believed that understanding the thought of a writer like Shakespeare will help the student write thoughtfully: "writing in the one case as in the other is a matter of seeing truth and honestly expressing it in words. The difference between the ordinary man and the genius lies first in what each sees in the world, and second in the degree to which each is faithful to his ideas" (46). While few if any students can become a Shakespeare, they all, with work, can learn to express their own thoughts accurately, and reading Shakespeare can help them achieve this goal.

Aydelotte assumed that no writers can write "until [they have] ideas to express" (47), and he therefore rejected any approach to instruction that begins with technique. "Too much cannot be said against the idea of writing, so common in the teaching of English composition, which makes it merely a matter of juggling words, a trick to be acquired without reference to the idea beneath the word" (46). Technique will not help a vacant student; "no one," Aydelotte asserts, "can give [a student] a style better than his ideas deserve" (46).[4]

Aydelotte, however, does not recognize that the opposite is often true. Some students with interesting ideas lack the experience with the conventions of written discourse to fashion effective prose that expresses their thought. As Mina Shaughnessy argues in *Errors and Expectations* (1977), students who write error-filled prose are not necessarily lazy or stupid; many have not yet mastered "the dominant code of literacy" (13). Learning this code is not a matter of willing oneself to write correctly, as Aydelotte assumes; it is a matter of learning a complex set of linguistic and formal conventions that appear transparent only to those who have "already mastered that code" (13). Aydelotte's approach, therefore, would not work for the Indiana farm boy who arrived at IU with little experience with reading and written discourse. It would work better with the fully prepared student.

## IU as Aydelotte Found It

The continued Harvard influence on IU's English Department was probably due partly to Professor Will D. Howe, who had become Head in 1906, six years after Aydelotte had graduated. After a B.A. at Butler College, he took a second B.A. at Harvard in 1895, an M.A. in 1897, and a Ph.D. in 1899. He attended Harvard during some of the years when Adams Sherman Hill, Dean Le Baron Russell Briggs, Barrett Wendell, and others developed English A. As Rollo Brown noted in his biography of Briggs, men trained at Harvard "went all over the country to teach in colleges and universities, and they carried with them the gospel" of Harvard composition (59). Howe was undoubtedly one of the disciples.

In many ways Howe's training and assumptions were different from Aydelotte's, and these differences created tension between the two men. Howe held the Ph.D., a specialist degree based on the German model of graduate education. He brought to Indiana the assumptions that English courses should be separated into specialized courses and that professors should be specialists in literary areas. As the IU catalog shows, he clearly assumed that courses in writing should be distinct from courses in literature. He also assumed that literature courses should be organized historically, and that introductory literature courses should be surveys. The literature sequence should begin with a broad historical survey of English literature and continue with more specialized period courses to trace the historical development of English literature.

Aydelotte, on the other hand, coming from Oxford, brought a different set of assumptions about English studies. Rather than separating courses of study, he preferred the Oxford model that made connections among them. He assumed, for instance, that writing instruction should not be separated from literature instruction. Like Arnold, he viewed literature as including not only poetry, fiction, and drama, but also non-fiction prose, including scientific discourse. He rejected the notion of broad coverage on the lower levels, preferring instead that students read deeply a few important writers to understand their thought and its application to life. He emphasized critical reading and critical thinking. Finally, he did not hold the Ph.D., but the B.Litt. His was a generalist degree in the sense that he, under the guidance of his Oxford tutors, had read widely in English literature and history, drawing on both to write papers for his tutors and for his seminars. He had initially enrolled in the English Literature honors school and had witnessed the workings of the Oxford honors B.A., which emphasized individualized reading under a tutor. One of Aydelotte's purposes in returning to Indiana was to adapt some principles of the Oxford educational system to the American university, a project that led to conflict.

To understand the work Aydelotte did at IU, we must examine the writing curriculum before he arrived. The *Indiana University Bulletin* for 1908 outlines the composition courses then offered and suggests that the writing program had changed little philosophically since Aydelotte's undergraduate days. Only the course numbers had changed. English 1, "Entrance Composition," was for students who could not yet write on the college level. This course prepared students for English 7, "Elementary Composition," the required freshman course. English 11, "Composition," was a more advanced composition course, and English 15, "Advanced Composition," was for juniors and seniors. Finally, English 35, "Composition Seminary," was described as "[a] course in writing, restricted to those who have passed with distinction in Course 15" (118). These courses suggest two things about IU's writing program. First, students could take writing courses throughout their undergraduate years. Second, the Department viewed writing as distinct from literature, a position that Aydelotte attacked by combining the freshman writing and literature survey courses.

The main course that Aydelotte targeted for revision was English 7, freshman composition. As the description makes clear, the course emphasized form: "A course planned for practical work in writing English. Special drill in sentences, paragraphs, and all the principles of composition" (117). The texts listed support this view. Students used Edwin C. Woolley's *Handbook of Composition*, which Connors calls the first "modern handbook of mechanical correctness" ("Handbooks" [91]). The subtitle suggests its coverage: "A Compendium of Rules Regarding Good English, Grammar, Sentence Structure, Paragraphing, Manuscript Arrangement, Punctuation, Spelling, Essay Writing, and Letter Writing." As this list suggests, the text discusses mechanics and form prescriptively. The "Preface" illustrates the degree to which Woolley concerned himself with correctness: the book "may be used, first, by students of composition for reference, at the direction of the instructor, in case of errors in themes" (iv). From the first page, he argued that English is of two types, good or bad:

> English discourse employing words generally approved by good usage, and employing them in the senses and in the grammatical functions and combinations generally approved by good usage, is called good English. English discourse employing words not generally approved by good usage, or employing words in senses and in grammatical functions and combinations not generally approved by good usage, is called bad English. (1)

Bad English appeared in newspapers, "recent fiction," and in conversations with low people; all such language should be expunged from theme writing, which required, to Woolley's mind, a highly formal language. To encourage mechanical perfection, he discussed errors in diction, syntax, grammar, and style. The book suggests, therefore, that one of the main aims of English 7 was to teach students to avoid common writing errors.

In addition to Woolley, the course used two other texts in the Harvard tradition. One was Arlo Bates's *Talks on Writing English*, which continued the formal approach from a different angle. As Bates asserts in the preface, his method owed much to the work of two Harvard rhetorics, Adams Sherman Hill's *Principles of Rhetoric* and Barrett Wendell's *English Composition*. Bates, a professional writer and chair of MIT's English department, focused some attention on drafting and revising, but his main emphasis was on technique, which included the modes of discourse. The course also used Natter, Heresy, and Greenough's *Specimens of Prose Composition*, an anthology of prose models for imitation. Clearly influenced by Alexander Bain's theory of discourse as well as by later theorists such as Adams Sherman Hill, the editors divided the book into four modes: exposition, description, narration, and argument, the EDNA approach. They identified each mode with a mental faculty (as did Bain), so that exposition and argument are "in mood *analytic*" because they appeal to the intellect, and description and narration are "in mood *pictorial*" because they appeal to the senses and imagination (xiii). For each mode, the editors provided model essays to imitate, including some student themes. The Harvard influence is strong in that the book includes sample "daily themes," which look more like journal entries than finished essays, and "fortnightly themes," which are longer, more finished pieces. The model essays are unrelated thematically, making it clear that teachers used them to teach form, not to explore a topic or to trace a theme across a series of essays. Consequently, English 7 placed primary emphasis on teaching students to write essays in the four modes and to write those essays correctly.

English 7, therefore, had all the elements of a Harvard-influenced writing course: students wrote regularly, perhaps daily, probably about their personal experiences; they learned principles of correctness using Woolley; and they mastered essay form from the modes of discourse. While the textbooks were different, the course was similar to the one Aydelotte had taken a decade earlier.

The second freshman course that Aydelotte targeted was English 2, "Survey of the History and Development of English Literature," a freshman introduction to the history of English literature. The description in the 1910 *Indiana University Bulletin* gives a good idea of the course: "Rapid and extensive reading in the English classics, prose and poetry, from Chaucer to Tennyson" (154). The word "rapid" in the description explains why Aydelotte disliked the approach. Students were introduced to a range of material superficially, an approach that did not encourage the critical thinking Aydelotte valued. On the other hand, the course, which covered two semesters, had the advantage of introducing students to many of the texts in the English canon, and this broad coverage, if done well, would have prepared them for their advanced literature courses. Aydelotte, however, rejected the survey approach. As he argues in *The Oxford Stamp*, teachers can best teach introductory literature by identifying key literary topics– "Wordsworth's theory of the imagination or Arnold's conception of the critic" (137-38), for instance,–that the teachers can relate to each other "so that they [the topics] lead to the mastery of a connected body of thought" within the field of English studies (138). By selecting a few writers to read in depth, English teachers, Aydelotte assumed, could help students understand issues of literature and life.

One last important piece of information: English 2 was Howe's course in that he personally coordinated its staffing and syllabus. Any attack that Aydelotte made on this course Howe probably viewed unsympathetically.

Evidence suggests that Howe was indeed committed to the current English 2 and English 7 courses. In the *Indiana University President's Report 1908*, he wrote to President Bryan about his efforts to improve the courses. "I believe," he wrote, "that the division of the elementary classes English 2 and 7 into small groups of twenty to twenty-five is working most satisfactorily. Besides the regular class meetings we try to give to each student of these classes from two to three or more personal conferences during each term" (1). He wrote this while Aydelotte was developing English 2A but does not mention specifics about the new course.

In the same report, Howe makes clear that the purpose of English 7 was to help students master the basics, a purpose that Aydelotte consistently questioned as a primary goal. Howe in particular complained to Bryan about the students' poor control of mechanics:

> Our great despair is the poor and uneven preparation of these students who come from the various high schools. The students in so many instances show the result of flabby and superficial training, a curious disregard for the principles of . . . correct writing and a dearth of a liking for good books. (2)

Howe went on to mention that the program tried its best to "reach every student" and help him or her advance only "when he [or she] can write with a degree of correctness" (2). Howe, in short, was aware that many IU students lacked the high school preparation to write well, a fact that Aydelotte tended to ignore, and this was one area of disagreement between the two. Aydelotte objected to making correctness the center of writing courses. He viewed correctness as a holdover from the 18th-century rhetoricians and their followers. He particularly objected when courses taught correctness at the expense of thought. As he argued in "An Experiment," the essay that justified his Indiana approach, students in 2A "were never allowed to believe that mechanical correctness alone constitutes good writing. Correctness, they were told, is an absolutely necessary but yet subordinate matter: good writing depends upon having something to say and upon getting it said" (126). When students had something important to say, he argued, they would learn enough about mechanics to express their thoughts correctly because "most mechanical difficulties are not really mechanical but logical" (131). Selecting the right word, Aydelotte believed, was not a matter of knowing correct diction but a matter of working out one's meaning in prose. Aydelotte therefore took a modern view of teaching mechanics, a view that was influenced by the more advanced linguists of the period such as Lounsbury and Krapp, both of whom viewed usage descriptively rather than prescriptively. While students needed to learn "[a] few grammatical forms and usages" (131), Aydelotte argued, they needed to learn this information within the contexts of their own writing. And they would learn it when they needed it to communicate an idea important to them. To teach mechanics separately, as Howe advocated, distorted the writing process. But to ignore the students' needs for instruction in form and mechanics as Aydelotte did led to its own difficulties, especially for the weakest students of the kind Howe described.

## Aydelotte's English 2A

Bryan hired Aydelotte to improve freshman instruction. Whether or not Howe approved of this arrangement is unclear. What is clear, however, is that Aydelotte took his charge seriously. In a letter of May 3, 1908, Aydelotte asked Bryan for an appointment to speak "of some things in the Department which seem to me to prevent it from being efficient . . . ." In other words, he saw problems in the department and went over Howe's head to notify the President of them. One of the problems, he went on to say, "is to improve the freshman work." He received encouragement from Bryan, for in four months, in a letter of September 12, 1908, Aydelotte announced that his freshman course was almost ready:

> I have nearly completed the plans for my Freshman course. They embody all the features we spoke of: conferences, small classes and large lectures, composition work based on reading and a sliding scale of reading according to the preferences and ambitions of the student. I begin with three very thoughtful books: Newman's *Idea of a University*, Arnold's *Culture and Anarchy*, and Carlyle's *Heroes and Hero Worship*, which I expect to study very slowly and carefully in order to teach the students how to work and in order to give them a conception of civilization as a product of thought and our world as a triumph of technique. (Italics added)

Here Aydelotte briefly outlined what would be listed as English 2A in the 1909 catalog. Four elements deserve attention. First, the course combined reading and writing. Students were to read literature, in this case Victorian essayists and four major English poets, and write about the ideas in their work. The course would be student-centered in that it allowed students some leeway to decide, as they did at Oxford, how much reading to do and what topics to discuss. Second, the course was not a survey but limited the literature to a few important pieces that Aydelotte intended to work through carefully to teach methods of analysis. Third, Aydelotte did not mention any attention to mechanics and form. Instead, he emphasized teaching students to reflect on the thought of the reading and then write thoughtful essays in response. Fourth, the course combined several methods of presentation including large lectures (which Aydelotte would deliver), small class discussions guided by other teachers, and one-on-one conferences with those teachers. Aydelotte considered the course in the Oxford tradition.

Most importantly, Aydelotte designed English 2A to combine in a single freshman course instruction in writing and literature. Because of his articles and books justifying the approach, it was one of the first fully articulated theories of the writing-about-literature approach and is therefore the prototype of all such freshmen courses. The course, however, never advanced beyond the experimental stage and never fit comfortably into the curriculum, as the suffix "A" suggests. The reasons are clear: it was philosophically incompatible with the dominant ideology of the department, which assumed two things. First, on the freshman level, literature and writing should be taught separately, and, second, freshman literature should be a broad, introductory survey from Chaucer through Tennyson. Hence the department taught writing in English 7, literature in English 2.

As the 1910 *Indiana University Catalog* makes clear, 2A was competing with both English 2 and 7. Like English 7, it taught students to write, and like English 2, it served as an introductory literature course that was a prerequisite for more advanced courses in the discipline. The catalog describes the differences between English 2 and English 2A for students, who were undoubtedly perplexed. The reading in the courses, the catalogue explains, was

> practically the same, but in English 2 emphasis is laid on the historical development of literature as well as on subject matter, while in 2A the stress is laid upon the subject matter and the meaning of the works studied. No student beginning either English 2 or 2A is allowed to change to the other course. (153-54)

While the two courses satisfied the same prerequisites, they were distinct in their conceptions of English studies. English 2 assumed that students needed grounding in literary history, with little attention to close reading. The course was primarily concerned with biographical information about the writers, with the titles and dates of the works, and with the social movements that influenced literary history. Students spent little time reading closely or discussing individual works. The description of the course in the 1910 *Indiana University Bulletin* implies that little careful reading took place:

> Rapid and extensive reading in the English classics, prose and poetry, from Chaucer to Tennyson. In general it is planned to familiarize the student with the character of the chief literary productions of each century, to show him how these productions express the life of the people, and how there is thus a continuity in literary history through the continuity of social history. (154)

English 2A, on the other hand, emphasized close reading of fewer works in order to understand their "meaning." As the description shows, English 2A moved away from the historical model by focusing on a few authors:

> A study of the elementary principles of literary interpretation and criticism, illustrated by one book each of Newman, Arnold, and Carlyle, and the works of five English poets from Tennyson to Shakespeare. Readings from the minor poets and prose writers of each period sufficient to give the student an outline of the history of English literature. (154)

The five English poets included, in addition to the two above, Milton, Pope, and Wordsworth. Introduction of the terms "interpretation and criticism" is important because it suggests that Aydelotte emphasized close reading and critical writing skills. Finally, he subordinated literary history to the careful reading of a few important works.

English 2A also paralleled English 7, "Elementary Composition." Students read literary works and wrote about them. This dual focus created an administrative problem because some students would have taken English 7 before enrolling in English 2A. Others might begin 2A or 2 and want to switch. So the department developed guidelines. First, students who had previously taken English 7 could take 2A as a three-hour course and be "excused from the themes and from part of the conferences" (154). Such students would learn the close reading strategies without writing essays. Second, students were not allowed to move from 2 to 2A. This rule suggests that the courses had become so different as to constitute distinct courses rather than variations of one. It also suggests that the department wanted to prevent such transfers.

One of Aydelotte's goals in developing 2A was to combat what he considered the superficiality of American education, a quality he undoubtedly saw in English 2, with its emphasis on rapid reading. English 2A, then, was to be a more demanding, more thorough course, a fact that Aydelotte made clear in a set of notes dated December 22, year unknown, to the teachers of 2A he supervised:

> This term's work in Wordsworth and Pope is much harder than any we have before attempted. If it proves too much we can perhaps cut down on the schedule but I am eager to carry it out if possible. At the rate we are going it will be impossible to lay stress on any but important passages in the Prelude. These should be pointed out for special study when lessons are assigned. It will also be impossible, on account of the length of the lessons, to require the class to look up historical material illustrating the poem: supply the most necessary information in class. ("Notes" 1)

This note suggests much about Aydelotte's teaching method. He expected students to read with understanding, but he was willing to select passages from longer works and have teachers supply contexts and historical information. He wanted the course to be demanding, a fact that Professor Frank Davidson noted many years later in an undated *English Department Newsletter*: "Some students thought him [Aydelotte] severe in the demands he made upon them, but they respected him as did the rest of us [instructors]. . . . He was firm in his conviction that a student, instead of being spoon-fed, should be a major factor in educating himself" (80-81). The value that Aydelotte placed on educating oneself later became one of the cornerstones of his honors program at Swarthmore.

To encourage students to educate themselves, Aydelotte made "freedom of discussion" central to English 2A. While he presented a common weekly lecture to all 2A students, he did not encourage teachers to lecture. Instead, they were to lead discussions on the course readings. These discussions made the course student-centered because they allowed the students freedom to gear the course to their interests. Aydelotte viewed this discussion as central to the Oxford method. As he wrote on September 17, 1954, to Frances Blanshard, at IU he "welcomed this [questioning and discussion by students], and indeed the whole atmosphere of the course and of our conferences was a little like an Oxford tutorial session."[5] This claim is not entirely convincing, however, for the Oxford tutorial usually took place between the tutor and a single or a few students while IU's class discussions took place between a teacher and 25 to 30 students. But Aydelotte's discussion method represents an important pedagogical advancement over the recitation and the lecture methods which both gave the teacher almost absolute power over class content.

Each year Aydelotte offered English 2A over three quarters. While he coordinated the program, training the teachers and lecturing weekly to all sections, instructors under his direction did most of the actual teaching. These young instructors were dedicated to Aydelotte and his approach and put themselves at some risk. As Alfred Brooks, a member of the English Department at the time, commented to Frances Blanshard in an unpublished letter in 1954, by teaching English 2A these powerless young instructors risked the ire of the older professors who disagreed with the thought approach. These professors favored Harvard formalism.

Aydelotte's model syllabi show that in each part, the course integrated three kinds of instruction. For most classes, Aydelotte assigned a fairly short literary selection for students to read and discuss with their individual teachers. During one class per week, usually Monday, he, as Dean Briggs had done at Harvard, gave a background lecture on an issue raised in the readings to all classes, which met together in a large common room.[6] According to Frank Davidson, this lecture "supplied the theme subject for the week" (80), and the topic was often demanding. Davidson remembered that "Once [Aydelotte] talked on the divergent points of view of Wordsworth and Darwin on nature, and left the class to ponder and to write a paper on which was the more profound view" (80-81). Aydelotte thereby encouraged students to compare literary and scientific thought and then decide which view appealed to them. After the lecture, during other class times, students met with their teachers to discuss issues and prepare to write papers.

Brief analyses of three of Aydelotte's 2A syllabi will give a better idea of the content and approaches. These syllabi were designed as common course schedules for the instructors he supervised. The fall course covered the Victorian essayists: Newman, Huxley, Arnold, Ruskin, and Carlyle ("Eng. 2A–Fall Term, 1911"). As the syllabus for the fall term of 1911 shows, Aydelotte spent three weeks on Newman, discussing some of his ideas on education, the nature of a university, the nature of liberal knowledge, and the distinction between knowledge and information. During those three weeks, Aydelotte lectured on the following topics: "Newman's Life and Times," "Newman's Idea of Liberal Knowledge," and "Knowledge and Religion." While the first lecture attempted to provide some background on both Newman and the Victorian period, the other lectures addressed key positions in Newman's *Idea of the University*. During the three weeks, students wrote three essays. The first assignment asked them to write about what they expected from the course. The second was vague–to write on "some point" connected with Aydelotte's lecture and Newman's "Discourse V." The third is more representative of Aydelotte's assignments: students were to write either on "Knowledge vs. Information, or Liberal vs. Professional Knowledge," both important issues in Newman's book.[7] During the fourth week, Aydelotte covered Huxley, addressing in his lecture the relationship between science and literature. He covered Arnold's *Culture and Anarchy* during weeks 5 through 7. Week 8 took up Ruskin; weeks 9, 10, and 11, Carlyle.

Throughout the course Aydelotte attempted to accomplish two major goals. First, he tried to focus the reading on those sections of longer works that he considered essential to understanding contemporary life. Aydelotte made certain, through his lectures and through the writing assignments, that students connected the ideas in the text with contemporary American culture. Examples of this connection appear in one of the Arnold assignments, in which students applied the ideas of *Culture and Anarchy* to some contemporary social problem. Another example is the application of Ruskin's economic reflections, *Unto This Last*, to "present day business." Second, he limited his lectures to one per week and gave the rest of the time to discussing the reading. Aydelotte required students to participate; they were not to expect him or instructors to feed them information. Instead, they were to work out their own positions in relation to the readings.

During the winter quarter, Aydelotte designed the course around two major poets, Wordsworth and Pope, again selecting a few important works for close study ("English 2A. Winter 1912"). He spent the first five weeks on the *Prelude*, finishing it in the sixth and then turning to "Tintern Abbey." During weeks seven and eight, he covered some minor Wordsworth poems and a few poems by other Romantics. He then spent the rest of the quarter on Pope, teaching *Essay on Man*, *Essay on Criticism*, and *The Dunciad*. It is interesting to note that by teaching Pope after Wordsworth Aydelotte disrupted the expected historical arrangement of works.

During the spring term, Aydelotte covered Milton, Shakespeare, and Sidney, with some attention to contemporary drama, such as Ibsen's *Hedda Gabler* and Sir Authur Wing Pinero's *Iris* ("English 2A, Program of work, Spring term, 1912").

As earlier, Aydelotte was careful to integrate reading, lectures, and writing. When covering *Sampson Agonistes* during week three, for instance, Aydelotte lectured on "The nature of tragedy, with special reference to SAMPSON AGONISTES." For the essay, students wrote a character analysis of Sampson as a tragic character. During week six, when the class was reading *Macbeth* and a few modern tragedies, the lecture was on the character of Macbeth, and students, drawing on the earlier tragedy lecture, wrote an essay analyzing modern tragedy.

While English 2A was to teach students to think about issues in literature important to them, Aydelotte recognized the need for minimum writing instruction. It is clear that the thought approach alone did not teach all students to write adequately. In an undated, handwritten set of notes about the course, someone working in the program outlined how 2A handled such instruction (Anon.). All students were required to own a dictionary, and 2A teachers required a "*minimum but continuous amount of class work on common errors and principles of composition*" (italics added). This concession was due to the need for such instruction by under prepared students. Aydelotte did not, however, emphasize the writing process or multiple drafts to help students improve their writing, but he did tie writing to the learning process. The writing topics, which Aydelotte introduced in his large lecture, were "to be over [the] week's work and constitute a review," and the papers were written in class on Thursdays from 3:00 to 4:30. Even though students wrote in-class essays, the essays resulted from considerable earlier preparation: the reading, Aydelotte's lecture, class discussion, reviews of the week's work. Students therefor had many opportunities to reflect on the essay topic and determine their own stances before writing. They did not write cold as Harvard students often did.

The goals of Aydelotte's approach, the notes make clear, were two-fold. The first was to develop a "facility in writing"; the second, to test the students' knowledge of the material. As Aydelotte more formally stated in *College English*, the essays served "the double purpose of (1) developing his [the student's] ability to think and to write, and (2) testing and confirming his understanding of the books studied" (132).

This approach is problematic. By using writing to test student knowledge, the writing itself becomes subordinated to the reading. The approach could therefore degenerate into an academic exercise not an experience growing out of a real rhetorical purpose–for students writers to express their opinions on the content of the reading. It also encouraged superficial test writing that, because it was produced under time restraints, did not allow for careful drafting and revision. Aydelotte's approach would have been stronger if he had allowed out-of-class essays with adequate time for students to work out thoughts in prose.

Aydelotte is on firmer ground concerning writing assignments. According to the notes, topics should be specific. In *College English* Aydelotte explained that he rejected those that required students to "comment on the literary merits" of the texts (132). This approach he calls "infant criticism," a term that echoed a *Nation* controversy in 1908 about writing instruction. In an editorial titled "Our Infant

Critics," an unnamed commentator argued that student literary criticism "must be stilted and stupid little compositions" because such critical writing was beyond the ability of college students. J.H. Gardiner of Harvard, in an essay of the same title, answered, arguing that writing about literature caused in students a "repugnance . . . [for] the idea of learning to write" (258). Both commentators called for more concrete, practical writing topics that were less demanding. Because of this controversy, Aydelotte felt obligated to demonstrate that his approach differed from standard literature-based approaches at the time.

Instead of asking students to write "infant criticism" about a literary work as a whole, Aydelotte and his teachers gave students one significant point from the reading on which to write. As Aydelotte argues in *College English*, giving students "*one point* to explain and illustrate rather than a whole book or chapter or section to summarize and condense" stimulates thought (italics in original). Asking students merely to summarize ensures "dull and deadening" writing. Assignments should be carefully focused on a particular issue in a reading to encourage "the thoughtful student . . . [to] enlarge to the limits . . . his intellectual resources" (133). When students wrote on novels and plays, for instance, Aydelotte discouraged the traditional character sketch because it was too unfocused. The 2A notes offer examples of bad and good assignments. A poor one would be "Write a character sketch of Malvolio" while a better one would be "Why is M. not a tragic character?" or "Why can Manoa not persuade Sampson to go home with him?" As another approach, he suggested that students write on the single speech of a character, explaining its meaning while at the same time analyzing what the speech illustrates about the speaker. Good students, he commented, could write papers that offer different interpretations of the same speech "and outline the different conceptions of the character as a whole implied in each interpretation" (133). As these topics suggest, Aydelotte gave students writing assignments that not only addressed a particular issue but also required writers to draw on larger concepts, such as the nature of tragedy.

The notes also briefly address grading. Since students were expected to do more than summarize literature, to receive a C or better students had to write analytically. Mere summaries would receive a D. The best way to respond to the essays was not through written comments but through individual conferences (*College English* 133). Aydelotte probably modeled the method on Copeland's Harvard conferences and on Oxford tutorials. As another strategy, he advised against commenting verbally on student papers in front of the class but strongly recommended reading aloud the best papers to inspire others (133-34).

The course had other important elements. Teachers were to assign outside reading, but this reading should not be traditional literature. Instead, it should be histories or biographies for background information. As the notes make clear, students kept a notebook of their responses to this reading. Before class they were to write the "*point*" of the reading in 10 to 50 words (an early form of free writing), and be prepared to read aloud this response at the beginning of class (italics in original). The teachers were also to give frequent, five-minute quizzes. Their purpose was to require students to define "*one* important idea in the current lesson in . . . 25-100 words" (italics in original). The notes give examples of possible test topics: "What does Arnold mean by Literature?" or "What does Huxley mean by artificial education?" These topics were designed to highlight central ideas in the readings and to determine if students understood them, and the reading of notebook responses in class encouraged discussion on the issue at hand.

While Aydelotte refused to dedicate class time to form and mechanics beyond the minimum, he did recognize that some students needed extra help. Weak students could get this help, the notes make clear, by attending a "Laboratory class." Like a contemporary writing center, the laboratory provided students a place to work on writing problems and difficult class material, and offered a partial solution to the problem of poor preparation of freshmen. The solution distinguishes Aydelotte's approach from Howe's in an important way. Howe assumed that all students needed work on the basics, and the study of mechanics should be the center of instruction. Aydelotte, on the other hand, individualized instruction so that only students needing special help could get additional help.

English 2A was successful, at least for well-prepared students, perhaps because it satisfied both the freshman writing and the introductory literature requirements. Students could kill two birds with one course. Aydelotte's handwritten notes give the student enrollments of the three courses–English 2, 7, and 2A–for 1909. During the winter, English 2 enrolled 135 students, while English 7 and 2A enrolled 250 and 114 respectively. During the fall of that year, the figures were 138, 278, and 124, which meant that the department ran 7 sections of English 2, 10 of English 7, and 4 of English 2A. These numbers suggest that English 2A was at least holding its own but that the other two, more established courses remained more popular. By the next year, 1910, however, the numbers changed. The *Indiana University President's Report* for that year mentions that 387 freshmen took either English 2A or English 7 (18). The majority, 237 of them, however, elected Aydelotte's course, which was being taught by Aydelotte and his assistants, Hawkins, McDonald, Stonex, Wylie, and Miss Hannel. These numbers suggest that 2A was growing in popularity while English 7, the original freshman composition course, was declining.

## Problems at IU

It is not entirely surprising, therefore, that Aydelotte began to experience problems with colleagues and the head of his department, Howe. As IU colleague Alfred Brooks remembered in 1954, "higher-ups" including Howe and two other established English professors, Sembower and Stephenson, "were against it [2A]" and even President Bryan seemed enthusiastic only in comparison. The reasons for this hostility are complex, but they resulted from at least two factors. First, Aydelotte was President Bryan's hand-picked representative to shape up the English department, and he apparently went over Howe's head to Bryan in order to get English 2A approved, a decision that Bryan came to regret. Second, 2A was a successful course that drew students away from the established courses. Since Howe was committed to these, he was hostile to Aydelotte's new ideas. Traces of the resentment began to surface. Howe, for instance, wrote Bryan on August 15, 1909, to mention that "Aydelotte with [two assistants] are trying to work out the problem in Eng 2A (a combined literature and composition course)." Howe himself, he continued, would work closely with Rice, another faculty member, to "give very close supervision of Eng. 7," the course that was losing enrollment. Frances Blanshard notes that Aydelotte confided to her that "a strong member of the department" who had been on leave when Aydelotte developed English 2A returned and did not approve of the new approach to freshman English (110). She also notes that the entire department might have rejected Aydelotte's approach once he went on leave to Oxford in 1912-13 for his third year of Rhodes scholarship.

As long as Aydelotte had President Bryan's support his course could survive, but he eventually lost that, too. At first Bryan encouraged his work. In a letter dated April 27, 1908, Bryan wrote that he "very strongly desire[s] to have [Aydelotte] at Indiana University" and goes on to promise him "that we shall be able to offer you from time to time such promotions as will make you willing to remain one of us." In a letter of recommendation to the Principal and Fellows at Braesnose College, Oxford, dated April 28, 1913, Bryan praised Aydelotte's work, noting that Aydelotte

> has been very successful in his work at Indiana University, both in his own advanced teaching and in the supervision of elementary teaching. He has given particular attention to the methods of teaching English to Freshmen. I regard his studies in this field as an important contribution to a difficult problem.

But all was not well between the two men, and when Aydelotte returned to Oxford, a series of letters about 2A passed over the Atlantic. These letters suggest that the course was in trouble. On March 11, 1913, Aydelotte wrote Bryan enthusiastically about the appearance of *College English*, published by Oxford University Press. He wrote that he hoped that he would be "allowed to resume English [2]A" because the book would make the course "more effective than ever with the Freshmen." When he wrote Bryan again on April 30, he expressed "surprise" that Bryan thought that in his previous letter he was "appealing" to Bryan to be allowed to offer 2A the following year. So the decision not to offer the course had been made.

Meanwhile, Bryan wrote a letter critical of Aydelotte's management of the course. Since Aydelotte lectured each week to all sections but was not the teacher of record for any, Bryan accused him of not teaching enough students. In a letter from Oxford dated May 25, 1913, Aydelotte defended himself against the accusation that he taught only four students the previous year: "The fact is, however, that in theory one-half, and in reality more than half, my work was done in English 2A–in lecturing, in conferences with students and instructors, and in administering the course. This half of my work does not show in the reports." He went on to explain that initially he put his name with the instructor's on each roll but that he stopped doing so because the two names confused "the office staff," a lame explanation. Bryan wrote back on June 9, 1913, to apologize and to claim that Aydelotte misunderstood him. Bryan only wanted to assert the principle that it is "quite wrong to turn over overflowing classes to illy prepared teachers while the teachers who are prepared are teaching very few. This is in my opinion one of the worst evils in our American institutions." In short, Bryan was attacking an early form of the teaching assistant system that used beginning, under-prepared instructors to teach classes that more mature instructors preferred not to. But circumstances forced Aydelotte to use instructors; nobody else in the department was willing or able to teach 2A. Aydelotte justified the approach by arguing that he carefully trained and supervised the instructors. As he explained to Frances Blanshard in a letter of September 17, 1957, when new teachers had trouble with the unfamiliar, demanding approach, Aydelotte would teach their sections himself to "try to straighten [the teacher] and [the students] out."

Although Bryan seemed satisfied with Aydelotte's explanations, the damage was already done. English 2A would not be offered again. Despite its growing popularity with the students and despite Aydelotte's continued commitment to the approach, the course did not have the support of some of his more powerful colleagues. Even Aydelotte admitted, in his April 21 letter from Oxford, that the course had caused problems:

> I am rather relieved on the whole [that the course would not be offered again] for while 2A is one of the most intensely interesting courses I have ever had anything to do with, it has always been by far the most difficult and taxing part of my work, and it seems to have given rise to a perfectly endless amount of opposition and misunderstanding.

Because of this opposition and misunderstanding, 2A vanished from the curriculum and English 2 and 7 remained.

## Aydelotte's National Influence

Although Aydelotte did not have faculty support (and eventually left IU because he could not get promoted), he developed a small national following among English teachers. While the thought approach received attention and support from all over the country, it mostly influenced teachers in Midwestern universities. Some embraced it enthusiastically. His books describing the approach received eager responses. Not only did teachers adopt Aydelotte's ideas, but several published readers and textbooks based on Aydelotte's principles. The method was important enough to generate some debate in the scholarly journals that most English professors read.

One of Aydelotte's earliest supporters was Norman Foerster, then a young instructor at the University of Wisconsin.[8] He had taken his B.A. at Harvard in 1908, where he was a disciple of Irving Babbitt. In 1912, he finished his M.A. at Wisconsin, where he taught freshman English. He was a member, with Babbitt and Paul Elmer Moore, editor of the *Nation*, of the conservative new humanist group that advocated a literary criticism based on ethical content and that attacked philology as a critical method on the grounds that it valued fact grubbing. Foerster initially learned of the thought approach through Aydelotte's 1912 *Education Review* essay, "English as Training in Thought," the first full justification of the method. In a letter dated October 28 of that year, he wrote that the approach "seemed entirely sound as well as extremely refreshing . . . . Your view of the matter, at once free from pedantry and dilettantism, is so natural that . . . I am amazed it is not the conventional view." Foerster, along with his colleague Karl Young, began applying Aydelotte's thought approach at Wisconsin. In a February 5, 1913, letter, Foerster described Wisconsin's reaction to Aydelotte's work:

> Your name and your convictions are by this time familiar to our entire teaching staff in freshman English, and our plans for next year have been made in such wise that we shall devote the whole second semester to exposition, using one of two complete books–Carlyle and Hazlitt, or Newman and Thoreau–as a basis for class discussion and theme writing.

He commented that Harrison R. Steeves of Columbia had co-edited an anthology of readings entitled *Representative Essays in Modern Thought* which "lays great emphasis on 'Cultivation of Ideas'" and this publication, along with Aydelotte's work, suggested to him "that throughout the country substance is to be stressed, rather than 'artistic' fluency and accuracy of detail [mechanical correctness]." In other words, the English profession had an alternative approach to the dominant Harvard method of writing instruction. When *Materials*, Aydelotte's anthology of readings for English 2A, appeared in 1916, Foerster wrote on March 5, 1917, that the book was "admirably suited to the purpose, and entirely consonant with the trend of the times. Indeed, except for the title, it seems to me one of the very best collections of essays for use in Freshman English anywhere."

Foerster not only appreciated Aydelotte's work but also participated actively in arguing for the method and developing a textbook based on it. His first book was an anthology entitled *Essays for College Men*, which he edited with Frederick A. Manchester and Karl Young of Wisconsin. As Young wrote to Aydelotte on November 20, 1913, the book was designed for a course based on Aydelotte's "*method*" (italics in original). Unlike Aydelotte's *Materials*, this book devoted itself almost entirely to questions of education, and the teachers at Wisconsin required students to write themes that applied "the thought of the essays to conditions more or less local," thereby connecting the ideas read to the themes written. Young gave an example. The anthology contains the 1912 "Inaugural Address" of Alexander Meiklejohn, president of Amherst College. The address argues that liberal education should be rigorously intellectual and demand the best thought of both faculty and students. Wisconsin students were to write on "The Wisconsin A.B. Curriculum as Judged by President Meiklejohn."

Foerster's most important contribution to the thought movement was his 1916 essay in *English Journal*, "The 'Idea Course' for Freshmen." This essay argued the practical benefits of the new approach, which he called "the latest widely popular type of Freshman course in English–the 'idea course,' or 'thought course,' or 'content course'" (458). Although he did not mention Aydelotte, he did justify his methods in language that echoes Aydelotte's. Foerster claims, for instance, that the new approach "awakens" freshmen to the intellectual life through complex reading. The course also "fosters the faculty of judgment" (462) by requiring students to write arguments that address significant issues. Because the assigned reading is difficult, Foerster argues, freshmen learn to read and critique complex discourse. The essay also echoes Aydelotte through its attack on the formalism of the dominant approaches to composition. The thought course, Foerster argues, protects against "hollow" discussions and "precise but dull" themes that result from methods emphasizing form over matter. The thought approach introduces "substance" to the course to remind students of "the relation of form and substance" (464). He also took the argument about correctness to the enemy's camp by arguing that the thought course teaches students to write correctly: "experience has proved abundantly that the Freshman does learn to express himself with a degree of clearness, vigor, and interest, not to mention elementary correctness, that he did not attain under the old [Harvard] system" (464).

Aydelotte found another important ally in the philologist and descriptive linguist George Philip Krapp of Columbia, who helped Aydelotte get *College English* into print. Because Krapp had connections with Oxford University Press, he was an invaluable mentor. Krapp first became interested in Aydelotte's work in 1910 when reading "The Freshman English Course," a note Aydelotte published in *The Nation* that first described the thought approach to a national audience. When Krapp read Aydelotte's longer, more thorough "English as Training in Thought" (1912), he wrote Aydelotte in a May 27 letter that he gave the piece his "heartiest approval" and commented that the approach was similar to one E. R. Carpenter had begun developing at Columbia before his death. Krapp also suggests that Aydelotte explain his approach in a book, a book that Krapp would "be glad to assist in any way to bring ... [ to] publication." Krapp recognized that the book was needed not only for students but also for teachers "who themselves are not much given to thinking. I mean you will have to teach the teachers to think as well as the students." This insight gives *College English* its peculiar double vision of addressing both groups. Krapp was probably interested in Aydelotte in part because of his flexible view of usage and mechanical correctness. As Connors argues in *Composition-Rhetoric*, Krapp, along with Loundsbury of Yale's Sheffield School, questioned the "correctness-only standards" being promulgated in composition handbooks (156). As a descriptive linguist, Krapp recognized that usage and related issues of language use were more complicated than the prescriptive hand-book writers allowed. In *A Comprehensive Guide to Good English,* for instance, Krapp argues for a contextual and flexible view of usage, recognizing that usage varies situationally (3). In *Modern English,* published in 1909, a few years before he worked with Aydelotte, he rejected absolutist positions. "[S]peech arises," he argues, "out of the immediate social relations of man to man," and this communicative and social position provides "the final test of [usage's] value" (9-10). He also recognized the various levels of acceptable usage, ranging from the literary to the colloquial. While he argued that some usage was indeed simply wrong, his main interest was to describe English as various groups used it.

Krapp saw *College English* through to publication and gave Aydelotte advice as needed. It was Krapp, for instance, who, in a letter of August 6, 1912, recommended that Aydelotte change the title from the vague *Literature and Education,* a title in the Oxford tradition of yoking together two subjects, to the more informative *College English: A Manual for the Study of English Literature and Composition.* In a follow-up letter of August 23, he criticized the manuscript for its lack of unity and sent it back for revisions. On February 27 of the next year, however, he wrote that he liked the completed manuscript and would recommend Oxford begin production. He predicted that it would have a "good and strong influence on the teaching of literature and composition in the colleges." Without the enthusiastic support and sound advice of an established scholar such as Krapp, it is doubtful that Aydelotte would have gotten the full discussion of his approach in print as soon as he did.

Aydelotte had a direct influence on one of his colleagues at IU, Richard Ashley Rice, who produced a thought anthology after he moved to Smith College entitled *College and the Future* (1915). Rice, the same man whom Howe chose to help him improve English 7, was a specialist in Romantic poetry and published a series of forgettable books and monographs on Byron, Wordsworth, and Rousseau. In many ways his best work, *College and the Future* anthologized essays about education and the college experience, and was similar in aim to Foerster, Manchester, and Young's *Essays for College Men* in that both books focus on education. Aydelotte's influence appears throughout. The selection of essays follows Aydelotte's principles in that the essays identify significant problems about education for discussion and writing. The first two anthologized essays address one of Aydelotte's particular interests, the value of an Oxford education. While Rice chose many American essays (which Aydelotte did not do in *Materials*), he also chose selections from two Victorian essayists, Newman and Stevenson, commonly anthologized at the time.

Aydelotte's approach to English instruction influenced most forcefully the introductory essay that Rice wrote for the book entitled "Learning to Write" (1-44), which was popular enough for Scribner's to publish as a separate pamphlet under the same title in 1917. Here Rice not only quoted two substantial passages from Aydelotte's *College English* (5-6) but also echoed and expanded Aydelotte's views on the relationship among thought, writing, and technique. Rice's main contribution was to place these discussions within a generalized developmental scheme by claiming that "boys" (he mentions no girls) must learn to think like men. As Rice comments, "Learning to write is difficult for the same reason that it is difficult for a boy to think like a man. It can be done. Little by little it is done. But to do it outright is rare. All this means that learning to write is but part of learning to grow up. For writing is thinking" (1). Rice took a position similar to Aydelotte's on the relationship between thought and technique. Both rejected the position that what Rice called technique and Aydelotte rhetoric should be taught separately, apart from reading, discussing, and thinking. Rice, however, unlike Aydelotte, viewed technique and thinking as interactive, even dialectical, as he made clear in this passage:

> In the practice of any art, thinking and acquired technical skill must constantly support each other, ideas at once fashioning their technique, and technique helping in the formation of ideas. In their final effects these two elements may scarcely be separated. It is hence unwise to separate them to begin with the process of learning to write.... Thus what you say (or write) is simply the shape of what you think, and the study of technique is the study of representative, convenient, and effective shapes for thought from which the principles of correctness and of structure are to be deduced. (3-4)

Here Rice articulated Aydelotte's position more clearly than Aydelotte himself did. Writers produce discourse by putting their thoughts in language. This process requires the application of certain techniques, which are actually forms of thought themselves. However, composition teachers should not attempt to teach these principles separately from reading, writing, discussing, and thinking, a position that Aydelotte embraced. While Rice was somewhat more willing to grant technique a significant role in the composition course than was Aydelotte, both men agreed that thought should receive the primary emphasis.

Rice expanded one of Aydelotte's key concepts, the idea of thoroughness (see Moran "Concept"). Aydelotte used this term somewhat informally when arguing that students should think about topics in depth and examine issues from multiple points of view. Thoroughness was an ambiguous but powerful term in Rice's rhetoric. In one use he meant that the student must fully explore and understand the topic before writing on it. In this sense thoroughness is related to invention. Through reading and thinking about a subject, the student should fully understand the connections, especially the causal connections, among all parts of the topic.

Originality is another term closely related to thoroughness, and the former results from the latter. The student can cultivate originality by comparing his mind and acts to those of a great artist. Great writers, whom Rice defined as geniuses, possess an expanded intellect that causes them to be thorough in their thinking and writing, and the student writer, even one who lacks great abilities, benefits from studying the works of the great. Only by doing this "can he best cultivate his own originality—through seeing the further possibilities, the wide importance of what he is doing. And only thus is he apt to realize the necessity for thoroughness" (11). Thoroughness is therefore a central term in Rice's conception of education, for it is the process of "expanding intellect" and "cultivating originality" (9). He presented as synonymous terms "trained observation, craftsmanship, imagination," (21) but he preferred "thoroughness" because it suggests an ability and a habit of character, both of which the student writer can cultivate. The great writer is "persistent and serious-minded" enough to be original in thought and writing. This genius possesses "a superior type of energy" to reach "comprehensive thoroughness" needed to produce great writing (15). The student must therefore read great writing not only to develop writing abilities but also to develop as far as possible the character of greatness. Rice therefore developed thoroughness into a God term in a way that Aydelotte did not. Aydelotte did not discuss important writers as those possessing great characters; instead, he viewed such writers as those who identified central human problems and solutions to them. But he agreed with Rice that the student benefits from reading great writers because the student can model problem-solving strategies on theirs.

Other anthologies based on the thought approach appeared (see Hardegree 82-99). University of California professors Benjamin P. Kurtz, Herbert E. Cory, Frederick T. Blanshard, and George R. MacMinn edited a freshman anthology entitled *Essays in Exposition* (1914) which combines elements of the thought approach with current-traditional methods (Hardegree 94). As did Aydelotte, the editors encouraged student thought by presenting essays that raised questions about modern life, especially the role of education, the relationship between science and literature, and the place of art in daily life (iv). The next year, Maurice Garland Fulton edited *College Life: Its Conditions and Problems* (1915), which, as the title suggests, collects essays for freshman English courses designed to stimulate thought about the college experience. Aydelotte's influence appears in Fulton's introductory discussion of thought in writing: "Thought without expression is, as every one knows, very indefinite and it is only when we think our thoughts out into words that we seem really to have thoughts.... Thus every time we try to express ourselves faithfully, we make the outlines of our own lives more distinct and create further opportunities for new activities" (xiii). While Fulton departed from Aydelotte by including American essayists, he also, as did many anthologists, selected some of the same Victorians that Aydelotte did: Cardinal Newman on the nature of knowledge, Matthew Arnold on literature and science, and Thomas Henry Huxley in response to Arnold. Another anthology that shows Aydelotte's influence is *Essays for College English* (1915), edited by James Cloyd Bowman, Louis I. Bredvold, Leroy Bethuel Greenfield, and Bruce Weirick, all from Iowa State University. Slanted to the agricultural student, the book introduces these students "to the more fundamental and far-reaching movements of thought of our times," which, thanks in part to Aydelotte's influence, "are being more and more widely used in freshman work in English" (I). As did Fulton, the editors included essays by Huxley and Arnold on the relationship between science and the arts.

These anthologies, like Foerster, Manchester, and Young's of Wisconsin, suggest that the thought approach had become by the middle of the 1910s an established approach to teaching freshman English, especially in the Midwest and West. They also suggest that Aydelotte's approach tended to establish itself in particular departments where a group of instructors became fond of it and edited anthologies for their own programs. Finally, they suggest that the approach had become important enough to encourage many of the publishing houses producing freshman English textbooks to develop their own thought anthology to keep their offerings current and competitive (Brereton 1997). Oxford published Aydelotte's *Materials*; American Book, Steeves and Ristine's *Representative Essays*; Houghton Mifflin, Foerster et al.'s *Essays*; D.C. Heath, Bowman et al.'s *Essays*; and Scribner's, Rice's *College and the Future*.

Before many of these books even appeared, Aydelotte warned against some of the directions that the thought approach was to take. He questioned the wisdom of using essays from fields other than English as many of the anthologies did. In "The Correlation of Literature and Composition," originally published in *English Journal* in 1914, Aydelotte argued against "going too far afield in the search for ideas" in fields other than English such as philosophy, history, political science (136). Topics such as the Panama Canal might be interesting, but, in the hands of an English professor, they would not contribute to sustained, analytical thought that only the study of a coherent and related body of reading could provide. "Thinking power is not to be got," Aydelotte argues, echoing Newman, "through smatterings but demands long application to one subject, turning it this way and that, tracing its implication in various directions" (137). The only subject that an English instructor could effectively use to build up this body of thought is English literature, broadly construed, Aydelotte concluded. The English instructor lacked the necessary training in other fields to teach their thought effectively.

This position is not entirely convincing, however. In his own pedagogy, Aydelotte includes in the category of English literature a great number of Victorian essays on a variety of subjects–the nature of criticism, of education, of science, of literature. Since these essays address a wide range of subjects, many of them loosely related, it is unclear how they are different from the kind of contemporary topics that Aydelotte criticizes. After all, Newman wrote *The Idea of the University* as a discussion of the Catholic university, not as a piece of literature. If one accepts Aydelotte's position that students should read thoughtful essays as well as literature, a teacher could achieve that goal by collecting essays on many subjects, as Harrsion Steeves and Frank Ristine did in their anthology, *Representative Essays in Modern Thought* (1913), which addressed contemporary political and social issues.

One explanation for Aydelotte's hesitancy to open the thought approach to a variety of subjects was his advocacy of conservative social and political views. Since one of his goals was to advance British thought and values, he wanted to limit the approach to the handful of approved British intellectuals whom he valued.

More importantly, however, was his desire to maintain the status quo socially and culturally. Aydelotte did not want the thought approach to become a vehicle for radical thought that questioned the somewhat conservative social views that he held.

Not all responses to the thought course were positive. In 1916 Joseph M. Thomas published in *English Journal* an essay entitled "Do Thought-Courses Produce Thinking?", a paper originally presented in Chicago at the November 1916 college section of the National Council of Teachers of English meeting. The fact that the essay was read, and then published as the lead article in its issue, suggests that Aydelotte's method had become a threat to traditionalists. Thomas seems a bit overwhelmed by the force of the movement. He claims to have had on his desk six thought anthologies. While Thomas was not a major figure of the period, his essay powerfully debunks the thought approach in one of the most widely-read journals of the English profession and therefore demanded attention.

Thomas's attack is multi-pronged. He argues that the old, form-based methods, the ones that Aydelotte attacked, had merit because teaching students "to spell, to punctuate, to paragraph properly, to use words with propriety and accuracy, is no slight accomplishment" (80). He objects to the essays being chosen not to illustrate rhetorical principles but to illustrate problems and stimulate discussion. He complains that the method requires students not to write about their own experiences, which should be the starting place of all writing; instead, they write about issues they do not fully understand. He accuses teachers of fashioning courses on topics in which they, not the students, are interested. Finally, a point with which Aydelotte would agree, Thomas notes that English instructors themselves are inadequately trained to teach essays from a variety of non-literary disciplines. Thomas concludes with two suggestions. First, the thought course, due to its demanding nature, should be a junior or senior capstone course because at that point students would likely possess enough intellectual sophistication to benefit from the work. Second, the course should be staffed with mature instructors. Only "[t]he man of the broadest interests, the most diversified experience, and the most liberal culture in the entire college faculty should be chosen . . . . Certainly it ought not to be taught by the callow youths, themselves just out of college, so many of whom cut their professional teeth in courses in Freshman composition" (88).

If criticism is more desirable than silence, Aydelotte must have appreciated some of Thomas's critique. He himself would have agreed that the thought course should not draw on material from fields unrelated to English, and he might have taken note of Thomas's point of not using raw instructors in the course, especially since his own such use contributed to problems at IU. But Aydelotte probably would have questioned two of the points. He would have rejected Thomas's call for a return to formalism. Aydelotte viewed formalist methods as a return to the 19th-century tradition that, he believed, encouraged inane writing. And he would have rejected the claim that students should write only about personal experiences. Such an approach, he believed, did not encourage critical thinking about human problems.

## Aydelotte's Views on Rhetoric

Throughout his work in composition, Aydelotte expressed a Platonic suspicion of rhetoric. This suspicion is best expressed in the epigraph for *College English*, Bacon's statement from *The Advancement of Learning* on the first distemper of learning: "when men study words and not matter." He makes the Platonic implication of his position clearest when he echoes Socrates's position from the *Gorgias* in *College English*: writing "is a thought process which strikes down to the roots of their [writers' and speakers'] being, not an acquired *knack* of juggling with words" (117) (italics mine). Socrates used the term "knack" to attack Gorgias on the grounds that he treated rhetoric as a superficial skill, a knack, and ignored the search for truth that should be the foundation of all discourse. These statements express Aydelotte's conviction that composition students must begin the writing process by thinking through their positions on an issue, but they also suggest his view of language as a distorting medium. Although this is a traditional position with a long history, the immediate influence on Aydelotte's language/thought opposition was probably Sir Walter Raleigh, his Oxford mentor. In *Style*, Raleigh argues that writers who express "real meaning," who communicate profound, timeless thought, do not succumb to flagrant abuses of style such as unnecessary variety (50). "Language," Raleigh continues, must be "fitted to thought" (61). Later in the book he argues that "The idea pursues form not only that it may be known to others, but that it may know itself, and the body in which it becomes incarnate is not to be distinguished from the informing soul [the thought]" (62-63). Aydelotte, then, followed Raleigh in assuming that thought, the soul of prose, exists before its incarnation in language. The writer's work, therefore, is to discover language that fits the thought, that gives the thought form. To reverse the process, to begin with language or form before thought, would lead to sophistry, the manipulation of language ungrounded in meaning, which is one of Socrates's criticism of Gorgias. This fear of language caused Aydelotte to write critically of the 18th- and 19th-century English and American rhetorical tradition in his attacks on formalism, and evidence suggests that he largely limited his idea of rhetoric to Harvard formalism and its immediate influences in the 18th and 19th centuries.

Aydelotte's theory of rhetoric, then, is Platonic in its suspicion of rhetoric. It is also Platonic in a second sense: it places its primary emphasis on the individual writer's search for and expression of personal truth. This emphasis on personal truth makes Aydelotte an expressivist. In an 1982 essay entitled "Contemporary Composition," James A. Berlin connects expressive rhetorics and Platonic theory by arguing that expressivism finds its "ultimate source" in Plato (239). Plato was suspicious of concrete reality, locating abiding, unchangeable truth in immutable forms that exist beyond the flux of everyday reality. To discover truth, humans must escape their prejudices and blindnesses, and strive to see beyond the worldly.

Thinkers discover the immutable through a form of dialectic, the Platonic dialogue, in which a philosopher leads a less advanced thinker to deeper insight. This knowledge takes the form of a private vision, a personal understanding to which each participant must remain true.

Expressive rhetoric, according to Berlin, assumes that writing expresses private vision, and writing can only be effective when it remains true to that vision. Aydelotte's view of rhetoric rests on this assumption, and many of his methods are consistent with expressive strategies. First, Aydelotte assumed (with later expressivists such as Peter Elbow) that the purpose of writing is to express individual thought. From Raleigh at Oxford, Aydelotte had learned that humanistic education should not teach facts or a body of information; it should develop in the student a personal understanding of the subject matter. All education is self education, Aydelotte argued, because individuals must learn on their own terms. As Aydelotte states this point in *College English*,

> [a]n idea must be grasped, digested, made one's own before it can be expressed in an effective manner. In this process, it is sure to undergo change in some way analogous to that in which food is changed when it becomes part of our bodies. When a student undertakes to write about what he is studying he comes sharply face to face with the necessity for personal independent thought. All real power over ideas, all ability to influence the thought of others depends on this intellectual independence and sincerity. (117)

Since "the value and excellence of . . . writing . . . depend[s] on the ideas [the writer] has to express,"Aydelotte continues, all good writing begins with an idea that writers make their own and remain loyal to as they express themselves in prose.

Second, one of the most important assumptions Aydelotte made is that such personal knowledge develops not from lectures but from reading and discussion. In English 2A the process began with reading literature. The purpose of this reading was to offer criticisms of life, and such criticism, Aydelotte assumed, clarified students' personal views. Literature, therefore, became part of the dialectic among students, under the guidance of a Socratic questioner, the teacher, who helped students first develop and then articulate their individual views. After arriving at their individual understandings, students, Aydelotte made clear, worked out their thought in prose, so that it was understandable to a reader.

However, Aydelotte was not thoroughly Platonic in his rhetoric. He did not, for instance, embrace an idealized rhetoric as Plato does in the *Phaedrus* consisting of definition of the subject, dividing it into logical headings, and achieving unity of its parts. Nor did Aydelotte accept Plato's theory that the rhetor needed knowledge of the human soul to fit each speech to the psychology of the audience (Kennedy 42). Nor did he accept Plato's absolutist view of transcendent truth. But what Aydelotte's approach to rhetoric shares with Plato's was the assumption that an effective rhetoric begins not with words but with knowledge of subject matter. Aydelotte advanced the thought approach to make this knowledge, especially the personal knowledge of the student gained through reading and discussion, central to the writing process. Once students have gained that knowledge, they must remain true to their personal understanding and express their views honestly in prose.

Although Aydelotte was suspicious of rhetoric, his teaching methods drew on some rhetorical principles. One of these is invention. This emphasis sharply separates Aydelotte's approach to writing instruction from the Harvard method. As Sharon Crowley argues in *The Methodical Memory* (1990), Harvard rhetoricians such as Wendell and Hill presented in their texts a "collapsed model of invention" (87). Central to this view is the outline in which the individual plans the paper. Once the plan is on paper, invention is largely finished. Aydelotte, on the other hand, viewed invention as a social, dialogic process. All student utterances participate in a conversation about the ideas expressed in the literature, and by so doing, "a communal understanding of that subject grows" (Halasek 5). Through this process students develop a deeper understanding of their own positions concerning the ideas under discussion as they prepare to write. When they write, they write dialogically because their words contain the thought of the literary texts, their fellow students, and their own.

Teachers also play an important role in this process. Aydelotte was familiar with Plato's Socratic method, a method commonly used in Oxford tutorials but less commonly in the United States, which relied more on recitation and lecture. He discussed the method in "The Problem of English in Engineering Schools" and in the introduction to *English and Engineering* (1917; 2nd ed, 1923). As he asserts in the introduction, the teacher's "method must be that of Socrates, that of the 'intellectual midwife,' presiding over the birth of ideas" (xx). His teaching approach encouraged students to explore ideas through teacher-led discussions in which the students challenge each other to clarify their beliefs on issues. As a teacher, Aydelotte spent considerable time helping students discover content for essays by having them discuss ideas expressed in significant literature. Once the discussion is completed, students then turned to writing.

Unlike the Harvard rhetoricians, Aydelotte did not offer students mechanical methods for organizing material. Organization should follow thought, not the other way around. The writing process for Aydelotte was by definition the activity of students working out their thought in prose. As Aydelotte wrote to Charles Robert Gaston, the President of the National Council of Teachers of English, on October 19, 1922, "the fundamental value of English writing is the discipline it gives thinking." By writing essays once a week and by doing more informal journal writing, students learned to think in prose, and this thinking included discovering the formal connections among the elements of their thought.

Aydelotte also demonstrated some interest in another element of rhetoric, the concept of audience, when he occasionally spoke of the teacher serving as an audience for student writers. In "Experiment," for instance, he states that "the business of the teacher is to be a good audience–tactful, interested, widely appreciative, and intellectually critical" (130). He then argues that when teachers function as an audience, they play a necessary role because no writer can write without one (130). His method of evaluating themes was also based on the concept of audience. As did Oxford tutors and Copeland of Harvard, Aydelotte responded to essays orally in conference, giving students immediate feedback.

Aydelotte mentioned the importance of audience in other contexts, especially in discussions of diction and student conferences. In *College English*, echoing Krapp's contextual view of usage, he analyzed the role that audience plays in diction:

> The question of the usage of words is a question of saying exactly what one means in terms which will be intelligible to other people. The choice of words is the choice of audience. The reason for using good English is to make oneself clear and agreeable to educated people. There is no argument against slang if the writer wishes to address an audience whose language is the particular brand of slang he uses, and provided, of course, that he wishes to address them as one of themselves. (120)

But theory did not drive practice. Aydelotte did not require students to write for a variety of audiences to practice diction shifts. He assumed that students working out their thoughts in prose would learn effective diction.

The concept of audience played an equally important role in student conferences. In effective conferences, Aydelotte believed, the instructor should place most emphasis on evaluating the essay's thought. In "Experiment," he advised teachers to ask students questions in conference about essays such as "What did you mean here? What would you say to this idea? Would that other one disprove your point?" (131). These questions encouraged students to see their work from the point of view of educated readers represented by the teacher. These questions suggest that Aydelotte had a notion of rhetoric embedded in his approach, but he did not make rhetoric theoretically explicit.

Aydelotte clarified his position on elements of rhetoric most often when answering critics, especially those who argued the dominant formalist position. In these cases, he often appropriated the language of formalism to his own cause by claiming that formalist concepts actually were modes of thought rather than forms of discourse. For instance, in a 1911 letter to *The Nation* Professor Ada L. F. Snell of Mt. Holyoke College (a college devoted to Harvard formalism) questioned Aydelotte's position in "The Freshman English Course" (*The Nation* [1910]), arguing that freshman English courses should emphasize form. She maintained that even if students possessed ideas, they still would not necessarily have the linguistic and logical forms in which to express them. She continued:

> A knowledge of form is, moreover, the surest guide to the mastery of ideas. Once the student sees that every good writer lays out his ideas according to a pattern, that there is a certain logical plan underlying the whole essay, or poem, or textbook, he is able to grasp ideas, as the writer intended, in the proper relationships. (9)

Her final position is that, since freshmen already have ideas to express, they need no help in developing them; they do, however, need help learning the forms necessary to communicate them. Hers was a clear statement of Harvard formalism.

In an unpublished response entitled "Letter to the Editor of the *Nation*," Aydelotte answered Snell's criticisms by claiming that the two agreed on most issues but disagreed over terms. He claimed, for instance, that Snell used the term "form" ambiguously. In her first use, she wrote that a freshman's early attempt at writing leads to "merely a 'glob' of ideas; a mass of material without a vital organization and innocent of a definite purpose, or of proportion, or of progression" (Snell 9). Aydelotte claimed that his concept of thought included the formal connections that Snell mentions: "By 'form' [Snell]... apparently meant the organization of ideas, the perception of logical relations–in other words thought" (1). He went on to assert that Snell's other sense of form, something like "the 'laws of human expression'" (1), is logically inconsistent with her first definition. These laws, he argues, these principles of Harvard formalism, "have not yet been formulated [so] that they can be made of much use to Freshmen" (2). In other words, some uses of the idea of form mean the same thing as thought, the principal one being the idea of establishing meaning relationships among parts of a discourse. Aydelotte rejected the other uses of the term that identify, abstracted from any particular communication context, rhetorical principles such as the modes of discourse and principles of style. These methods have "accomplished very little" even in the hands of "a very formidable system of teachers, courses and text books, operating in our High Schools and Colleges during the last fifteen or twenty years ..." (2-3). He clearly refers to the Harvard approach in this statement.

The problem with Aydelotte's argument rests in the difficulty of teaching formal matters without some abstraction from context. The quickest way to teach beginning writers to paragraph is to teach them paragraph structures. Without a sense of form, as Snell argues, students will not be able to write coherently. Such discourse structures must first be internalized before students can use them, an assumption that Aydelotte consistently rejects. He assumes that teachers should never isolate form.

For advanced students, however, for those who have mastered the conventions of written English, Aydelotte's approach offers important insight. It encourages such students to make creative connections among elements of discourse. These connections are not based mechanically on conventional form but on the dancing of the writer's thought within generic restraints. These advanced students were the kinds who attended the very selective Oxford. Since they had an excellent preparatory school background and were widely read, they did not need college work on their writing. What help they needed could take place within tutorials.

In a February 11, 1918, letter to Professor R. A. Jelliffe of Oberlin College, Aydelotte again attempted to clarify his position on rhetoric. Jelliffe had written January 31 to congratulate him on the publication of *The Oxford Stamp* and to admit that, even though he (Jelliffe) wrote a text book on expository techniques, he had come to appreciate Aydelotte's views. He went on to argue, correctly I think, that at least some students need special help with mechanics. "Sub-freshmen," what we would now call basic or developmental writers, need a course to "drill in the decencies" of mechanics and usage, and regular freshmen need some of this work, too. He also admitted to using description to train students to write with "precision and accuracy." In his 1918 answer to Jelliffe, Aydelotte found some common ground with his correspondent and made one of his clearest statements on the role of rhetoric in his method of instruction:

> Once you place the emphasis on thought and insist that a man's writing embody real ideas in order to measure up to the standard, you can, I think, profitably devote as much time to the rhetorical aspects as the man needs. I am opposed to rhetoric only when it is made to take the place of thought.

This position has two elements. First, Aydelotte assumes that instruction in developing one's thought and then expressing that thought simply and directly is of prime importance. After students begin to try to think with care, and after they begin to express that thought effectively, then the instructor can teach rhetorical principles as needed. Second, the instruction in rhetoric should be minimal. It should provide freshmen with just enough technique to meet their needs. In effect, Aydelotte's notions of teaching rhetoric mirror current views on teaching mechanics. Rhetoric should be taught within the context of student writing when the writing demonstrates that students need the instruction. Teachers, in Aydelotte's opinion, should not allow instruction in rhetorical principles to overshadow the emphasis on the centrality of thought in the writing process.

## The Bitter End at IU

When Aydelotte left IU in 1915 he could look back on his seven years there with a mixture of satisfaction and regret. In an April 27, 1915, letter to Byran announcing his resignation, Aydelotte expressed both emotions. He first reminded Bryan that he had mentioned "two or three times during the last year or so that I was dissatisfied with my position" as Associate Professor. When an offer from MIT came with "a decided promotion," Aydelotte accepted it. But he also thanked Bryan "for the very good opportunity you gave me here when I returned from Oxford and for the personal encouragement you gave me in working at the problem of the Freshman course." Aydelotte had indeed gained valuable administrative experience serving as the coordinator of English 2A, experience that he would eventually parlay into the presidency of Swarthmore. He had learned how to develop courses. He had gained a modest national reputation as a theorist in composition and literature. He had produced four well-received books: *Elizabethan Rogues and Vagabonds* (1913), a work of impressive scholarship that remained a standard work in the field for several decades; *College English* (1913), a well-written statement of teaching philosophy and methods; *Materials for the Study of English Literature and Composition* (1914; 2nd ed. 1916), his anthology of readings for the thought course; and *The Oxford Stamp, and Other Essays* (1917), his collection of essays on the Oxford educational system. In addition to his teaching and scholarship, he had launched in 1914 the *American Oxonian*, the official magazine of American Rhodes scholars, which he edited for many years. His national reputation was such that MIT, one of the best technical schools in the nation, offered him a full professorship.

But it must have pained him to leave Bloomington and his home state under a cloud. Despite his fine record as a scholar, IU refused to promote him. As Frances Blanshard notes, the only promotion that he received at IU came the first year when the word "Visiting" was removed from his initial title of "Visiting Associate Professor" (110). Part of the problem was that he lacked the Ph.D. But some older, established colleagues disliked his approach to freshman English and therefore disliked him. He never spoke in detail about the problems at IU, not even to his friend and biographer Blanshard, who notes that Aydelotte never discussed "mishaps unless they were funny" (110). The mishaps at IU apparently were not. He received what Blanshard suspects were hints that he should leave. When he returned from Oxford in 1914, the catalog for the following academic year implied that he was still on leave. English 2A was no longer approved for freshman English credit and disappeared. He was assigned to teach only upper division courses even though he had developed a national reputation as a freshman English theorist and wanted to teach on that level (110).

But some good resulted. He learned the importance of solving administrative problems and gaining cooperation, even when colleagues initially disagreed with him. As he sometimes said at Swarthmore, "It is not enough to be right; you must also be persuasive" (qtd. in Blanshard 110). He would sharpen these interpersonal skills throughout his career as he moved up the administrative ladder and developed innovative curriculums at MIT and Swarthmore.

## NOTES

1. Football had become by this time a popular pastime in American colleges, and football players, especially those such as Aydelotte who had distinguished themselves, were campus heros. Aydelotte was later disturbed by the popularity of big-time football on college campuses, and, in an essay entitled "Spectators and Sports" in *The Oxford Stamp*, criticized the effect that the sport had in America. He argues that spectators corrupt college sports because these fans, often alumni, want to win at any cost, including buying professional players for their team. Aydelotte holds up as an ideal Oxford's sports programs, in which all students play for the love of the game.

2. During the early years of the 20$^{th}$ century, British students in the elite public school enjoyed a language-enriched education based partly on the classics in the original languages. This enriched language education was not available to the average student in Indiana, especially those coming from farms and small towns. Many such students needed work on principles of organization and correctness in order to write adequately.

3. While it may be true that Campbell emphasized correctness in his rhetoric, Blair did not. Unlike Aydelotte, Blair was interested in rhetoric and makes that clear in the introductory chapters of his *Lectures* that he wanted to make students think. Even Campbell, for all his emphasis on usage, grammar, and style, attempted to introduce students to sophisticated methods of thought. So Aydelotte offers a skewed vision of the two 18th-century rhetoricians.

4. Aydelotte clearly privileges thought over form, ignoring the fact that ideas do not fully exist publicly until they are expressed in language. Language consists of formal patterns, and these patterns contribute to the thought. Aydelotte was not an important theoretician of the language/form debate; he developed an important approach to teaching writing that avoided the sterility of the formal method that ignored the importance of thought.

5. Aydelotte in part meant by this that the emphasis was placed on the student and his or her interests, not just on the subject matter. The purpose of education became, then, the student developing a response to the material, not merely understanding that material in a particular way.

6. This idea Aydelotte took from Briggs at Harvard. Briggs, however, used the class to discuss college life–an early form of student advising. Aydelotte, on the other hand, used the hour to lecture on a literary issue and to make writing assignments.

7. These were important issues to Aydelotte, and he used these topics in his MIT course and in his AT&T program later in his career. The knowledge/information binary was central to Aydelotte's pedagogy–knowledge grew from discussion and individual thought; information came from lectures and suggested the kind of passive learning that Aydelotte associated with most American college educations of the time.

8. For a critical evaluation of Foerster, see Chapter 7 of Crowley's *Composition in the University*.

# 4: The Oxford Approach at MIT, 1915-1921

After Aydelotte's rejection by IU, he must have found his MIT reception refreshing. President Richard Cockburn Maclaurin hired Aydelotte to revitalize the English Department, which had been under the influence of Arlo Bates, its retiring Chair, for many years.¹ Most importantly, Aydelotte saw at MIT the possibility of applying ideas cultivated at IU to a different student audience, future engineers. Using English 2A as a model, Aydelotte developed English 12,"English (Nineteenth Century Essays)," a freshman course (*Bulletin* 1916-1917), and edited for it *English and Engineering* (1917; 2nd ed., 1923), the earliest technical writing anthology. He became the first outside writing consultant for AT&T and developed an ambitious writing program for its employees during World War I when the company was forced to hire poorly-educated, young employees to replace the men mobilized for military service. Finally, at MIT, President Maclaurin asked Aydelotte to develop an English-History curriculum modeled loosely on the Oxford method of teaching cognate subjects in the same course of study. While the last curriculum was not successful and had critics among the faculty, it laid part of the intellectual groundwork for Aydelotte's honors program at Swarthmore.

In some ways, Aydelotte's move to MIT was surprising. As Perkins notes in "Frank Aydelotte," the move did not appear to advance Aydelotte's career. There were neither English majors nor graduate students there (36), and Aydelotte would have the opportunity to teach few specialized literature courses since MIT subordinated English to technical studies. Originally, as he admitted in a February 24, 1948, letter to John Nason, his successor as president at Swarthmore, Aydelotte did not consider the job desirable. He moved to Cambridge for the libraries, particularly Harvard's, to continue his research on Renaissance literature. "I planned, of course, to do my work at Tech honestly," he confided, "but I intended to make my main activity in the field of Elizabethan scholarship." But that scholarship never progressed because he began working out the role of English studies in engineering education and spent his time "propagating English at MIT."

President Maclaurin first became interested in Aydelotte when an acquaintance, Professor D. C. Jackson, sent him a copy of Aydelotte's 1914 *Atlantic Monthly* essay, "English as Humane Letters." In a November 25 letter, Maclaurin responded enthusiastically to Jackson about Aydelotte's approach: "It seems to me eminently sane and I wish that our colleges could take up the study of English literature from this point of view more generally than they do now." He continued:

> I was brought up on the classical tradition [in New Zealand] and have a great respect for the methods employed by those who believed in it and really understood it. I have never been able to see why the methods that they employed might not be adapted to English literature and why the results should not be quite as satisfactory as with the classical material

It is not hard to see what in Aydelotte's essay attracted Maclaurin. In it, Aydelotte applauded the British approach to the classics, termed *Literae Humaniores*, which combined reading Greek and Roman literature along with ancient and modern history and philosophy to ground the student in ancient and modern culture and thought. This instruction, Aydelotte argued, had prepared Oxford and Cambridge graduates to create England's democracy, to work brilliantly in business and industry, and to establish the commonwealth ("English as Humane" 373). In short, Aydelotte valued the elitism of Oxford that produced leaders who spread Anglo-Saxon values throughout the world, one of Cecil Rhodes's primary aims.

While Aydelotte rejected classical literature and philosophy as the basis for American education, he recommended English literature as the best substitute for Americans to study. As he wrote in "English as Humane Letters,"

> English literature is for us what the classics were to our grandfathers in this country and in England, and as perhaps the greatest modern literature, it has, aside from the questions of language, one obvious advantage over the classics as a means of popular education: it is permeated with the modern spirit, it is a record of modern thought, it deals directly with the intellectual problems and the conditions which face us, with the world as it has been refashioned by Christianity and modern science. (377-78)

Although none of these goals is strictly literary, they do indicate Aydelotte's Arnoldian belief that literature, which included all written discourse, should be read for its thought and criticism of life.

The approach has weaknesses, however, primarily its narrowness. Classical studies at Oxford were broad in that they encompassed not only classical but some modern studies, especially in science and philosophy. Aydelotte, on the other hand, largely limited his student's education to the study of British literature, which included some British philosophy of science, educational theory, and history. But students would complete that program without studying much of the thought of other nations and earlier periods. Even American thought was largely neglected.[2]

Aydelotte did, however, demand more from American students than college work often did at the time. He argued that English studies should teach students to think about the substance of literature, not to appreciate its history and form, and he therefore questioned the worth of the standard methods then used in the United States: *belles lettres*, literary history, philology, and liberal culturalism. In place of these methods he recommended that literature be approached to develop in students "that power of sane, keen thinking which is the distinguishing mark of a liberal education" (378).[3] Students should approach literature as a body of thought so that they come to see "that the poets and novelists and essayists are men who are trying to unify and explain life to us" (378).

Throughout his argument, Aydelotte emphasized ideas that attracted Maclaurin. Literature should teach students to think. Literature should include more than the study of minor poets, novelists, and dramatists; it should emphasize major authors, including essayists on science and technology as well as those who explored contemporary social and educational issues. The intense study of a few good writers, read carefully and in depth, Aydelotte believed, could provide students with a sound liberal education (Moran "Road" 165-66).

Of all his programs, then, the one at MIT placed the most emphasis on "English [studies] as a cultural influence," as Teresa Kynell argues (40). However, while Aydelotte did emphasize culture's importance, his approach continued to emphasize critical thinking, the most significant element in his pedagogy.

Another element that attracted Maclaurin to Aydelotte's approach was the Indiana professor's interest in the education of technical students. English Department Chair Henry G. Pearson, in the 1916 *MIT President's Report*, noted that MIT hired Aydelotte because he was "specifically interested in the problems connected with giving instruction in English to men who are receiving professional training" (111). Aydelotte had first expressed interest in this question at IU. In *College English*, he had identified the relationship between science and literature as a central modern problem. Each student, Aydelotte argued, "after due thought . . . [must] determine his own natural position [in relation to the two systems] and to understand that of one who differs from him" (23). In other words, scientists and humanists must understand each others' positions to communicate. Such understanding would grow from reading essays by Newman, Arnold, and Huxley, which presented both sides of the debate. Aydelotte, following Newman, concluded that art and science, the two major divisions in human thought, used different methods to achieve similar ends. As Aydelotte wrote,

> [t]he purpose of science is the same quest for truth which one finds in literature. It is the expression of man's thought about life and the world around him, the explanation of it, so far as man has been able to go, from its peculiar point of view. Literature is no more and no less than

this, the expression of man's thought about life and the world we live in, only from another point of view, following other methods. The fundamental aims of the two are identical (28).

It is hard to understand fully what Aydelotte means here. Science, especially the hard sciences, seem less to be the study of human life than the study of the physical world in which humans operate. Art, on the other hand, examines human values and beliefs within a social or cultural context. It is difficult to see how the two disciplines share "fundamental aims" beyond the search for knowledge within their very different spheres. While it makes perfect sense to argue that a liberal education should emphasize knowledge of both spheres, it does not make sense to collapse the goals of art and science into one.

Despite the fuzzy thinking, Maclaurin found this position attractive. First, it reflected some of his own ideas about education. Maclaurin, echoing Arnold, had argued that "science and culture must be combined" and that "the root of culture . . . is the possession of an ideal broad enough to form the basis of a sane criticism of life" (qtd. in Blanshard 118). In his inaugural address at MIT in 1909, he commented that "science and culture must be combined; i.e., the two must go hand in hand, science being studied and taught in such a way as to make for that broad and liberal outlook on the world that is the mark of a really cultured man" (qtd. in Pearson 19). Maclaurin found in Aydelotte a kindred soul who shared a belief in liberal education for engineers.

Second, being a scientist himself, Maclaurin wanted an English professor sympathetic to science and engineering. By giving science equal status with literature and the other arts, Aydelotte proved that he recognized science and technology as important contributions to modern life.

Maclaurin also found a third focus of Aydelotte's approach attractive. Aydelotte rejected the notion that education, especially professional education, should create narrow specialists. Professional or useful knowledge has its place, Aydelotte argued in *College English*, because it teaches professionals to "do skillfully certain useful things" (7). True education, however, demands more, for the broad kind of education that Aydelotte advocated created professionals who possessed liberal knowledge. Following Newman's view of education, Aydelotte believed that the university should provide students with a "broader outlook" of the kind provided by liberal studies (6). This broad outlook results from the students' contact with all branches of knowledge so that students understand the limitations of each. Each branch offers one approach to understanding the human condition; consequently, to be fully educated, students must be exposed to all. This broad understanding of human knowledge allows the professional to connect professional knowledge and skills to other disciplines. As Aydelotte wrote,

> [t]he liberally educated man...will view his professional knowledge in the light of a larger whole, will see it not as the whole world of knowledge but as only a part, will understand not merely the facts and

> rules-of-thumb which he uses daily but the underlying principles which link his occupation with the whole world of science, art, and philosophy. The possession of the power of thought which liberal knowledge implies will give him a wisdom and a resource in the practice of his profession and a pleasure in contemplating its relations with the whole world of knowledge unknown to his more narrowly educated associates. (7)

In other words, the engineer who designs a bridge with understandings of physics and art will build a sounder, more aesthetic bridge than the engineer who only understands practical, rule-of-thumb engineering.

In the chapter in *College English* titled "Literature and Economics," which draws on the social and economic ideas of Carlisle and Ruskin, Aydelotte discussed in particular how the study of the liberal arts, especially literature, benefits business and science. As Aydelotte argued, the effect will be subtle but essential:

> The effect of the liberal point of view upon a man's work in any one field is likely, in actual life, to manifest itself in a finer and subtler modification of his achievements, less easy to analyze or point out, but no less valuable in the end. He will not perhaps reorganize the body of knowledge of his profession, nor revolutionize its practice, but he will understand it more fully and practice it more wisely. The physician who is a reader of poetry, the literary man who is likewise a student of science, will have his outlook upon his own profession modified not in any abrupt or violent way: subtly, in ways hardly noticeable even to himself, the one will be restrained from the too implicit faith in science which is the undoing of so many able physicians, will estimate a little more truly the human, the mental factor in each of the perplexing problems daily offered him; and the other will prune out in a more sober and orderly fashion the extravagances which are so often a blot upon the most glorious vision of beauty. By being first a better, a more complete man, each is a better specialist; but the difference is one which only the knowing will perceive, not the difference between the bad and the good, but between the very good and the best. (40)

A broad education would create specialists who also possess humane, liberal knowledge. This background, with its understanding of essential human problems delineated by both literature and the sciences, would cause specialists to become more than competent; it would help them become, Aydelotte believed, the best in their area. After being educated in the best that had been thought and done in the world, engineering students would always compare their endeavors to the highest standards, and this process would encourage them to strive for the highest goals.

One of Aydelotte's aims was to educate engineers who were also leaders. Broad knowledge of the liberal arts, he thought, would prepare them to understand the human condition and the problems inherent to it in ways that those with technical training alone could not. Because of this knowledge, they would be able to understand better the aims and interests of other people so that they could better supervise subordinates, interact with colleagues, and justify their plans to the general public. Such liberal knowledge among leaders, Aydelotte argued in "The Function of the Liberal College" (1921), "is the most crying need for the world today" (4) because it offers insight into "the ends to which technical skills are only a means" (4). Technical knowledge without humane direction was dangerous, Aydelotte assumed, and humanely educated engineers could provide direction. Such engineers, for instance, would enjoy a special leadership position in the modern world as "mediators between labor and capital" to help solve problems between the two groups. Aydelotte's ideal engineers would possess two skills central to all leaders: the ability to identify and solve problems and the ability to communicate those solutions convincingly to others, especially nonspecialists.

When Aydelotte interviewed at MIT, he found in Maclaurin a man with whom he shared much personally. They hailed from pioneer stock, Maclaurin from New Zealand and Aydelotte from Indiana. In addition to sharing a British-style education, they believed that they could adapt the system for American colleges. Both were scholars interested in interdisciplinary studies. Aydelotte's major scholarly work, *Elizabethan Rogues and Vagabonds* (1913), combined literature and history, and Maclaurin was an interdisciplinary scholar in law and mathematical physics (Blanshard 118). Because Aydelotte questioned the value of narrow specialization and the fragmentation of the liberal arts among departments such as philosophy, theology, fine arts, and history, Maclaurin found in Aydelotte a professor with a vision to unify the teaching of English and engineering at MIT. As he outlined his hopes in a April 21, 1915, letter to Aydelotte, Maclaurin wanted him "to train [MIT students] in English so as to enable them to think clearly and express themselves as cultivated engineers, and at the same time to arouse and stimulate their interest in good literature . . . ." He thought that Aydelotte was the person to accomplish these goals and hired the associate professor away from Bloomington with a promotion and a raise. Aydelotte was to become a full professor with a handsome salary of $2,700 per year (Blanshard 118).

## The Writing Program at MIT

MIT's English Department needed redirection. As one of Aydelotte's colleagues, Henry Latimer Seaver, remembered years later, before Aydelotte arrived English was a "service department . . . [whose] function was mainly to scrub up illiterates" (qtd. in Blanshard 123). The department was organized after Harvard's. As Aydelotte wrote in a September 17, 1954, letter to Frances Blanshard, when he arrived at MIT he found English was taught using Harvard's method of "emphasizing correctness of style" (3). Instructors emphasized formal elements of correctness and organization over substance, and composition was taught separately from literature. The required literary survey introduced students to the names of English writers and little more (Blanshard 123).

The *Bulletin of the Massachusetts Institute of Technology* for 1914-1915, the year before Aydelotte arrived, demonstrates that the emphases in composition were on clarity and precision: "While attention is given to [English Composition's] place in general cultivation and to its aesthetic side, the greater stress is placed upon the absolute necessity that every professional man shall be able to express his thoughts *with clearness and accuracy*" (367 italics mine). Students worked to achieve these goals for four years. During the first, they took a "systematic course in Composition"; during the second, they wrote themes "in connection with the study of literature"; during the last two, they wrote in connection with their "regular technical work" (367). The required second-year literature survey course took an historical approach, emphasizing masterpieces (367-68).

Upon assuming his professorship, Aydelotte changed the program to achieve new goals. The *Bulletin* for 1916-17, Aydelotte's second year, shows that the English Department, under his influence, developed thought-approach aims:

> The instruction in English has as its purpose to enlarge the student's acquaintance with general ideas and to broaden his interests by showing him how scientific conceptions are related to other fields of thought. . . . In all the courses literature and composition are studied together. During the first term of the first year relatively greater emphasis, however, is given to writing, and there is some study of the elementary theory and technique of composition. The second term of the first year is given up to the reading of certain Nineteenth Century essayists, with oral and written discussion of their ideas. In the first term of the second year time is devoted to a fairly comprehensive study of a few great representative authors. During the second term of the second year again the chief emphasis is laid on composition, though, as in earlier courses, the material for written work is furnished through reading and class discussion. (324)

The marks of Aydelotte's approach stand out: the emphasis on thought and ideas; the connection between literature and science; the study of 19th-century essayists; the substitution of literature courses that study a few writers in depth for the literary survey; and the connection among reading, writing, and class discussion. In the 1917 *MIT President's Report*, Pearson, the chair of English, announced clumsily the shift in philosophy: "instead of separating composition and literature [as the department had done in the past], the attempt is being made to teach them in conjunction, so that the advantages of progress made by the student in one of these subjects will accrue to his work in the other" (105). Aydelotte had convinced the faculty to adapt his methods for MIT's engineering students.

However, the catalogues and reports to the president suggest that tensions existed between Aydelotte and advocates of utilitarian writing courses. This tension is not surprising given that MIT had a history of such writing instruction. As David

R. Russell explains, in the decades before Aydelotte's arrival, MIT developed an elaborate technical writing program based on utilitarian principles first under George S. Carpenter and then under Robert Grosenver Valentine, both hired from Harvard (*Writing* 108-09). Valentine especially conceived his courses as training the new managerial class in the practical rhetoric needed to advance in industry and government.

MIT's employing Aydelotte therefore indicates a shift, but his hire did not mark the end of utilitarian writing instruction. The same year that Aydelotte arrived, the English Department also hired two new instructors to teach "Report Writing." In the 1916 *MIT President's Report*, Pearson announced the hires of William Green, an MIT graduate with experience in industrial management, and Thomas G. Goodwin, an M.A. from Harvard. The 1916 *Bulletin* describes their course as one that "acquaints the student with the various kinds of writing incidental to an engineer's work, and gives practice in the writing of business letters, interdepartmental memoranda, and reports. The reports embody the results of actual investigations made by the students" (327). This description suggests that, while Aydelotte's thought approach influenced the department, it did not eradicate utilitarian writing. Pearson indicates the tension between the two philosophies when he wrote in the 1916 *President's Report* that the English program had two ends: 1) to train students in professional expression and 2) to "develop in them through the study of English Literature the broader interest in life which they need as a complement of their technical training" (112). The department, he noted, needed to work harder to "correlate" the two goals (112).

It is not clear how cooperative Aydelotte was in this effort, for he flatly rejected utilitarian approaches such as Green and Goodwin's. He was especially suspicious of those approaches that emphasized the mastery of conventional formats and genres. After discussing in "Training in Thought" his thought approach, he argued that it had "more value for strictly technical purposes than a course occupied exclusively with what is called 'technical writing'" (302), a course he considered too narrowly conceived. As he argued in *Suggestions*,

> [i]t is not the aim of all this work [in Aydelotte's thought approach] to teach principles of technical writing; it is rather to lay the foundation upon which good technical writing must be based. The aim is to develop the power of careful expression of thought, to liberalize and broaden the student's outlook so that he will see his profession not as a narrow, isolated specialty but as a part of the great work of civilization. (15)

In "Training in Thought," Aydelotte specifically attacked technical writing courses grounded in formalism. He argued that such courses taught "tricks," by which he meant rules of thumb. But true education should do more than teach such practical rules; it should teach something more important, what he called "general intelligence" (302). This general intelligence would prepare students to produce any writing their profession demanded because properly trained students could think for themselves and write in any situation. A student trained to follow set forms would lack such flexibility, Aydelotte claimed. As he argued in "Training in Thought,"

> [t]here is no "fool-proof" method of writing engineering reports. An engineer who relies on a stereotyped form will turn out a machine-made product, devoid of real vitality. The problem is one of common sense, of perspective, of power of clear thought and clear expression, and of imagination to grasp the point of view of the man who is to read the report. (302)

It is hard to see, though, how Aydelotte's thought approach would give students an accurate sense of real world writing. To write as professionals, engineering students would need some familiarity with letter and report genres and stylistic conventions that the profession valued. Those students would also benefit from writing in the rhetorical contexts they would experience on the job. They would benefit from knowing what the audience of engineers expected from professional discourse. Aydelotte was unwilling to provide MIT students any such practical experience on the grounds that engineering English did not exist as a separate genre. Writing was either good or bad depending on how effectively it expressed the author's thinking. Aydelotte's refusal to recognize the importance of technical writing conventions weakens his approach.

In 1917 Aydelotte addressed the problem of "machine-made" writing by publishing the first edition of *English and Engineering*, an anthology of technical or (as it was then often called) engineering writing. Although Aydelotte originally designed the book for a specific MIT course, English 12, offered second semester of freshman year, it immediately developed a national following and was used in fourteen institutions in the United States. By 1919, it was adopted at McGill in Canada, at the Chinese Government's Institute of Technology, and at Waseda University in Japan. In 1923, it was popular enough to go into a second, expanded edition, and it remained in print for 22 years (Blanshard 125).

The book's approach was an extension of the thought approach Aydelotte had developed at Indiana. As with English 2A, Oxford inspired the method, and Aydelotte modified some parts of the British system to make them appropriate for American engineering students. This book represented an important stage in the development of technical communication: Aydelotte integrated technical writing and the humanities.

Aydelotte thought that engineers were being trained so narrowly that they lacked adequate writing skills and cultural sophistication. These deficiencies, some believed, prevented narrowly-trained technicians from advancing to supervisors. This state of affairs was caused by the explosion of technical knowledge at the turn of the century. Earlier, when relatively little technical knowledge existed, engineering students took a program heavy in humane subjects, particularly rhetoric, languages, and literature (Nelson 494). As technical knowledge advanced, engineering courses proliferated and crowded out the humanities. By the time Aydelotte published his book in 1917, a movement had begun to return humanities to the engineering curriculum to make graduates literate, and Aydelotte's approach was one of the earliest and most important in this movement (see Connors "Technical" 329-32; Hagge 464-65).

As John Hagge argues, many early engineering writing texts published after Aydelotte's did more than emphasize the need for professional literacy. Engineers, these books assumed, needed not only to know the conventions of engineering writing to advance in their professions; they also needed "humanistic enculturation" or, more specifically, "cultural reading" (462) to round off their specialized education and prepare them to interact with nonengineers. Although a tradition existed for this position in essays by engineers, the classical statement in textbooks appeared first in *English and Engineering*. In its introduction Aydelotte stated his goal to enculturate students: "to furnish something of the liberal, humanizing, and broadening element which is more and more felt to be a necessary part of an engineering education" (xiv).[4] While later engineering texts did not discuss readings in the engineering writing class as Aydelotte's did, they echoed his concern for humanistic training by including a chapter or two on the value of independent reading for general information and cultural development. S. A. Harbinger's *English for Engineers* (1923; rev ed 1934), Clyde W. Park's *English Applied to Technical Writing* (1926), Philip B. McDonald's *English and Science* (1929), and Richardson, Becklund, Guthrie, and Haga's *Practical Forms in Exposition* (1934), all argue for the benefits of cultural reading. Such broad reading, these writers argue, not only soothes and entertains but also provides tangible, professional benefits to the engineer. In particular, reading literature, history (especially of science), and cultural analyses prepares students for a successful career. In addition to making one's writing clear and correct, Clyde W. Park argues, reading literature makes possible a "general effectiveness" that interests educated readers in one's writing (252). Such reading also enriches intellectual lives and readies engineers to "participate in the social life of [their] community and [to] meet on equal social terms the men and women with whom [their] profession make[s] [them] acquainted" (Harbarger 287). Perhaps most importantly, these textbook writers argue, such reading, especially in literature, creates "sympathy" for others and "breeds tolerance, humanity, and sophistication" (Mcdonald 153; Richardson et al. 15-16), traits necessary for effective leaders. This sympathy would grow in part from a common core of readings that would function as did the classical education of the old college: it creates a basis for shared knowledge that makes understanding and cooperative action more likely. Most of the textbooks mentioned above provide reading lists that would create this common body of knowledge.

One weakness of this indirect approach, however, was that engineering students were encouraged to read but were given little time to do so. All of the above textbooks recognize that students had insufficient time to read beyond their technical literature. If the students can't read in college, the books argue, they should plan to read in the future, when they had more leisure. But by then they would be involved in a developing career and might still lack time for culture reading. The importance of Aydelotte's approach, from the liberal arts standpoint, grew from his insistence that his students read and discuss in class the broadening essays that he included in *English and Engineering*, making enculturation central to the students' intellectual development. Furthermore, Aydelotte's text emphasized more than cultural reading; it also emphasized a second, related goal, teaching engineers to express themselves thoughtfully in prose in response to the essays (xiv).

*English and Engineering*, especially in its second, expanded 1923 edition, represents a novel approach to technical writing. Rather than emphasizing functional elements, such as mastering correctness, cleaning up one's style, and learning to write using standard organizational strategies (the primary emphasis of all of the texts mentioned above), Aydelotte articulated instruction that began with the assumptions that engineers must think clearly, write effectively, and be cultured as well. As Aydelotte stated in his teacher's manual, *Suggestions for the Use of Aydelotte's English and Engineering*, one of the best discussions of his classroom methods, "The general purpose of the book is to train students to read and write thoughtfully, and to give them some inkling of the broad human significance of literature, its relation to life in general and to engineering in particular" (1). In "The Problem of English in Engineering Schools," he identified three related goals of the course: "Power of clear thought and clear expression, appreciation of refined pleasure, and the possession of a broad and human outlook on life" (199). As Aydelotte argued, these purposes are intimately connected because good writing results not from mastering technique but from becoming cultivated. "The engineering student," as Aydelotte put it, "cannot be taught to write in a cultivated manner by any other method than by making him a cultivated man. The outcry in the practical world for 'better English' is really a call for better and more liberal education" (*Suggestions* 2).

In "The Problem of English in Engineering Schools," Aydelotte argued most directly for a broad approach to technical English. He explicitly stated that MIT did not teach "engineering English" or "business English" (200) because such courses were too narrow (he ignored the report writing course). While he recognized that engineering students want to master business letters and engineering reports, he noted that "we do not assume that they [engineering students] will necessarily prefer a narrow success to a broad one, that just because they have chosen to be engineers, all things human are alien to their interests" (200-01). Aydelotte's method, therefore, required students to read widely so that they learned to think about engineering issues. This kind of education would make students more than proficient technicians; they would be prepared to serve as leaders in the profession. Aydelotte argued this point in "Training in Thought":

> That engineering is an intellectual profession, the mission of which is
> to be one of leadership in working out the problems of the modern

world and in serving its highest interests, is the claim of many of the most distinguished engineers of the day; and these men demand from engineering schools not merely technical proficiency but also that development of character and that liberal cultivation, that capacity for original thought about human as well as material problems, which will enable technical graduates to play a worthy part in the engineering world when the period of their practical apprenticeship is ended and they are ready to take the places vacated by the present leaders. (300)

The broadly-trained engineer, Aydelotte believed, would be a leader, capable of identifying and solving the problems of modern society. Central to this leadership would be the ability to write effectively not just to fellow engineers but also to other, non-technical groups.

The purpose of *English and Engineering* was to prepare students for such leadership positions by covering the following topics: writing and thinking, engineering as a profession, the aims of engineering education, pure and applied science, science and literature, and literature and life. Each topic consisted of two or more essays, usually written by a major intellectual of the period, that addressed some aspect of the theme under discussion. After reading and writing essays on each topic, engineering students, Aydelotte assumed, could attack other modern problems and communicate their findings to a broad audience.

Aydelotte's approach to writing addressed some of the problems of the period's dominant formalist methods. Aydelotte reminded English teachers that they should demand that students think critically. After reading, discussing, and writing about the collected essays, MIT's students would have grasped Aydelotte's assumptions about writing--that thinking and language are connected, that usage is based on the practice of the best writers, and that engineers must learn to write to advance.

The first section of the book addressed questions about writing. The other sections offered students subjects for discussion and writing about their profession and their culture. Section two, "The Engineering Profession," addresses issues of the profession itself and related ethical issues. The third section, "Aims of Engineering Education," contains essays that argue for a broader engineering education. The fourth section, "Pure and Applied Science," argues against a purely practical scientific education. The fifth section, "Science and Literature," introduces engineering students to the humanizing part of their education, the role of sciences and humanities in modern life.[5]

Aydelotte compiled *English and Engineering* to present subject matter first for discussion and then for writing. Discussion was in fact central to the thought approach, and this is one of the innovative elements of this strategy. While the discussion approach was common in Oxford tutorials, it was less common in the US, where teachers tended to lecture to large classes following the German model. For the discussion to be valuable, it had to be free, and Aydelotte insisted that "No orthodox point of view is prescribed" ("Problems of English" 204). He argued that students think through issues on their own, forming individual opinions (204). The instructor's goal was not to offer preformulated opinion; it was "to raise questions which it may take [the student] half a lifetime to answer; our purpose is to give him a thoughtful outlook on life and on his profession" (204).

Aydelotte called his method "Socratic" and referred his readers to Plato's *Theaetetus,* in which Socrates calls himself an intellectual mid-wife (*English and Engineering* 3n). Teachers using the book, Aydelotte advised, should master the Socratic method "of bringing out ideas by discussion" (3) not by lecturing like "the typical German professor" ("Training in Thought" 301). Teachers should not advocate their own ideas but question students to stimulate thought. For the Socratic dialogue to work, teachers must "preserve freedom of thought and expression, to encourage skepticism and sincerity, to cultivate resourcefulness in suggesting various questions and illustrations, and to acquire skill in bringing the discussion to bear upon the important issues" (*English and Engineering* 3-4).

In "College Education and College Life," the unpublished commencement address given at Woorster College in 1922, Aydelotte made the clearest statement of the dialogic nature of his teaching method. He outlined the three "essentials" of classroom discussion. The first was that all participants, students and teacher alike, must "agree for a moment to put themselves on an equality [sic] and to ask for no quarter" (3). Second, participants must have thick skins and be willing to "endure hard knocks without hard feelings" (3). As they question others, they must allow others to question them. And third, students must hold strong convictions but be willing to consider the positions of others. In short, Aydelotte viewed the classroom as an arena for strong-willed students to assert their beliefs on issues raised. The purpose of the class was not to help students gather information but to make them test "ideas in action" (3), one of the benefits Aydelotte found in Oxford conversation. Through this process, students clarified their beliefs as they modified positions in response to sharp questioning and dialogic interactions.

Aydelotte recognized, however, that teachers should not be neutral; they must lead the discussion "to reach the result" desired (3). In other words, teachers must know in advance the main points the discussion must cover. But in the classroom, instructors should distance themselves from the fray (8) and allow students to do intellectual battle. The teachers' main responsibility, according to Aydelotte, was to keep the discussion moving by asking questions. To help guide discussions, Aydelotte recommended that teachers periodically recapitulate the discussion's main points.

Aydelotte suggested two other ways to help students think through complex issues, both of which made connections among reading, thinking, and writing. The first was the student essay itself. Aydelotte believed strongly that students should write regularly but not every day, as the Harvard daily required. As Aydelotte argued, the focus of the course should remain on thought because "less writing and more thinking would result in more solid advancement. A man learns to write by trying to express ideas, not by trying to juggle words" (*Suggestions* 5). Essays, therefore, should grow out of the readings and discussions. Although Aydelotte did not use terms from the rhetorical tradition, he thought of the readings and discussions as a form of invention during which students thought through their positions and differentiated their positions from others'. When they wrote, they drew on knowledge the discussions generated.

After the discussions generated thought, Aydelotte required students to write essays that further clarified that thought. He did not want students to write summaries of the readings. To discourage summary, he assigned papers to respond to precise questions raised in the texts. "The ideal theme subject," he maintained, "will be simply the task of stating fully and carefully and with original illustrations his [the student's] opinion on one of the various questions discussed in the class room" (*Suggestions* 5). Appropriate assignments would ask students to analyze an important sentence, to illustrate a statement with their own experiences, or to refute a position in the reading (*Suggestions* 5). If presented well, these assignments would generate student interest by connecting course material to experience and opinion. As Aydelotte states in "English in Engineering Schools," such writing assignments "are all subjects . . . which involve the expression of intricate and complicated ideas, which demand that he [the student] weigh conflicting considerations and answer arguments; and they are subjects that he [the student] will do his best to treat in a clear and convincing manner" (206).

Another strategy to help students think through complex issues was to ask them to outline essays and discussions. Such outlines ensured teachers that students understood the material and were prepared to write on it. Aydelotte also advocated double outlines that traced contradictory implications of a position. As Aydelotte argued, "One of the best proofs of a student's power of thought is his ability to hold in mind two different points of view in regard to a certain question and to state the implications of each" (*Suggestions* 4).

## Aydelotte's Contributions to Technical Writing

Aydelotte's lasting contribution to technical writing is limited because his influence did not extend beyond the 1930s. Earlier, Aydelotte had enjoyed some national influence. First, he had been an active member of the Society for the Promotion of Engineering Education's Committee on English that Samuel Chandler Earle of Tufts chaired and had advocated actively for his views. Formed in 1914, this committee examined the role of English in an engineer's life (Kynell 31). Aydelotte argued that English should instill in students both culture and a thoughtful view towards engineering as a profession, and these views appeared, along with others, in the committee's surveys and reports.

In addition to the committee work, Aydelotte influenced the field in a second way. I have already discussed Aydelotte's greatest influence on engineering textbooks: *English and Engineering* first articulated the notion, picked up by later textbooks, that engineers needed more than training in their professional discourse; they also needed to be cultured in order to operate in American society along side other professions. Hence textbooks like Harbinger's, MacDonald's, Park's, and Richardson and his colleagues' contained chapters and reading lists designed to enculturate engineers.

Third, his *English and Engineering* (first edition 1917) inspired another thought anthology, Rensselaer's Ray Palmer Baker's *Engineering Education: Essays for English* (1919) (Kynell 41). While Kynell argues that both books shared a "similar theme" and "some" essays (41), in actuality the books, while similar, are also different in their focus and share only one essay in common, John Lyle Harrington's "The Value of English to the Technical Man." The fact that Baker's book appeared was a tribute to the popularity of Aydelotte's. Wiley clearly published *Engineering Education* to compete with Oxford's *English and Engineering*, which had created a market for the thought approach in engineering programs around the world. Baker distinguished his book from the earlier one by asserting that his addressed more contemporary issues. As Baker noted in his introduction, while students should "be familiar" with the Arnold/Huxley debate between "utility and culture," "the specific issues over which they clashed are apparently settled" (vii). Baker's anthology therefore included more specific issues such as the importance of mathematics, physics, and chemistry to engineers and their education. Since Aydelotte ignored these specific issues and continued to include the Arnold/Huxley debate in the second, 1924 edition of *English and Engineering*, he did not agree that the utility/culture issue was dead. His influence on Baker's book was more general. Like Aydelotte, Baker used the thought approach to cluster essays of divergent views on issues to encourage "the clash of opinion which is the strongest incentive to thought" (viii), a conclusion with which Aydelotte agreed.

Both books, however, lost their audiences within a decade. About the time Aydelotte introduced his "broad" approach (Connors "Technical" 331), the field as a whole embraced a more pragmatic one based on Harvard's method or the methods of 18th and 19th-century rhetoricians such as Blair, Campbell, and Whately. Most of the early technical writing books shared an inherent flaw in that they emphasized the modes and correctness at the expense of content, a weakness that Aydelotte's method attempted to correct. The weakness of Aydelotte's approach, though, was that his method did not introduce students to the conventions of technical discourse, a goal that Aydelotte consistently rejected.

One of the earliest textbooks is *The Theory and Practice of Technical Writing* (1911), by Earle of Tufts, the "father" of technical writing (Connors "Technical" 331). As Kynell argues, Earle was the first theorist to recognize that English, if taught well, could function as a "technical tool" rather than as "a means to culture" for engineers (32). Clearly influenced by the Harvard rhetorics, the book emphasized the modes, modified for engineering. Earle renamed these as forms of exposition: descriptive exposition, narrative exposition, and directions. The book departed, however, from the Harvard model by including discussions of audience analysis and an appendix with samples of technical writing, especially reports. A second early book, also published in 1911, is Harwood Frost's *Good Engineering*

*Writing*. Written for professional engineers as well as for engineering students, the text shows little influence of the Harvard rhetorics. Instead, Frost drew on his experience as an editor of *Engineering Digest* to explain how to write engineering articles and books. Although the book is practical in that it teaches the reader to write for engineers, it contains a section on rhetoric based not on the Harvard theorists but on 18th and 19th-century British rhetoricians, Campbell, Blair, and Whately. Since Aydelotte questioned the usefulness of these rhetorics, he must have found Frost's approach deficient.

Another early Harvard-influenced textbook is T. A. Rickard's *Technical Writing*, which began as University of California lectures to engineering classes in 1916 and was published in 1919, two years after Aydelotte's text. Rickard, an engineer himself, emphasized style, grammar, and correctness and cited Adams Sherman Hill's *Principles* several times as a "useful" book (2, 313).

During the 1920's two important books appeared. In 1923 Baker of Rensselaer published *The Preparation of Reports*, which Richard W. Schmelzer considers the first technical writing textbook. As the title suggests, the book discusses report types that students in technical and administrative fields should know. In 1923, the year after the second edition of Aydelotte's anthology, S. A. Harbarger published *English for Engineers*, which Connors considers the first "modern" technical writing text ("Technical" 332). Departing from the Harvard rhetorics, this book provides the range of technical genres engineers needed: letters, reports, reviews, professional papers, and articles. As Kynell argues, the text "espoused a . . . workplace or 'real world' philosophy" that made it possible to connect the study of English to students' "ultimate professional success" (55-56). All of these books used approaches that Aydelotte rejected because all emphasized technique instead of content.

As technical writing as a field came to emphasize work-place writing, Aydelotte's thought approach declined in popularity. It was reduced to an occasional chapter on the necessity of cultural sophistication in some engineering writing texts. By the mid-1930s, the book was out of print. In 1931 J. Raleigh Nelson could comment favorably on Aydelotte's program at MIT, but he pointed to the same general weakness that Joseph M. Thomas had noted about the thought approach to freshman English. The MIT program required an "unusual staff" (497), one broadly trained in both the humanities and the sciences. As American education came to emphasize specialization, and as the ideal of the educated person continued to shift from the generalist to the specialist, the thought course disappeared, along with *English and Engineering*, which was replaced by more practical books in the tradition of Harbarger's that prepared engineering students for real world writing.

## Aydelotte at AT&T

After developing his writing course at MIT, Aydelotte had an opportunity to apply his educational principles in a different arena, the New York headquarters of AT&T (see Moran "Frank Aydelotte: AT&T's First Writing Consultant"). The year was 1917, the height of World War I, when many American men had been mobilized to fight the Great War in Europe. Because of this mobilization, AT&T found itself with a staff of uneducated young women and boys, some in their early teens. Few had college degrees, and many had not finished high school. The company wanted to educate these young people to make them more effective workers. C. R. Mann, who coordinated the writing of the Carnegie Foundation report on engineering writing to which Aydelotte had contributed, recommended Aydelotte to Mr. A. C. Vinal, in charge of the AT&T project, as an ideal person to develop a program for the company. As Mann explained the new program's goals in a letter of August 5 to Aydelotte,

> [t]he American Telegraph and Telephone Co. is considering beginning a new type of educational work among boy employees who are from 16 to 22 years old. They are trying to devise a kind of corporation school that shall give these boys not only technical skill but also some real broadening education. It is their ambition to give a schooling that will rival that of the college in social and cultural lines as well.

Mann went on to note two general advantages of Aydelotte taking on the project. First, it would enhance cooperation between colleges and businesses. Second, it would create a "new kind of consulting specialist" and provide work for English professors like that available to professors of science and technology. Vinal wrote Aydelotte on August 5, 1917, to invite him to participate.

Aydelotte was interested and wrote Maclaurin on August 20, to ask permission to take the job. The English professor explained that he liked the offer because of its "liberal remuneration" but claimed that his real attraction was intellectual. The work offered "extraordinary interest" because it posed "an absolutely new problem, and I think I see the line to take in order to solve it." The "line" was to modify the thought approach for this new environment.

Aydelotte, with the encouragement of Maclaurin, accepted the offer. On August 17, 1917, Vinal wrote Aydelotte explaining the importance of the program to AT&T:

> In discussing this matter with your people at [MIT], you will have in mind that in view of the fact that this is the first time we have undertaken general training work for employees in all departments, and in view of the fact that we are departing from our usual custom in utilizing the services of a person not a member of the Company, we must be especially careful to so plan as to assure the success of

> the work beyond question. When I say the success of the work, I
> have in mind not only its reception on the part of students, but also
> on the part of the officials.

In other words, AT&T was trying a new training method by hiring an outside consultant, and Vinal worried that it might fail. He was especially concerned that the company executives would be unreceptive.

Problems threatened the program in its earliest stages. Aydelotte's modified thought approach must have seemed strange to pragmatic executives. As usual, Aydelotte refused to teach a business or technical writing course emphasizing correctness, form, and on-the-job writing, the very things that many executives thought their employees needed; instead, he designed a program that placed writing within the larger intellectual context of AT&T and its functions within American culture. Aydelotte emphasized "liberal knowledge." As he wrote years later in *Breaking the Academic Lockstep*, "An educational system based on belief in the value of liberal knowledge will infuse a liberal element into all training, even the most technical, while an excessive preoccupation with techniques, with means as opposed to ends, may deprive" even traditional liberal subjects "of any liberal element" (8). Employees, therefore, were not to study techniques alone; instead, they were to study ideas and then apply them to their jobs at AT&T. For the program to work, Aydelotte needed executive support, which he cleverly won by using executives as lecturers in the program.

A second early problem was the amount of time Aydelotte could give to the program. Vinal himself insisted that Aydelotte personally supervise it, and a serious disagreement emerged in their negotiations. Given his continued MIT responsibilities in Cambridge, Aydelotte could only give the AT&T program in New York one day a week, Fridays; he planned to work in Cambridge the other four days. Vinal insisted that Aydelotte be in New York on Thursdays as well. Aydelotte responded in an August 20, 1917, letter promising that, while he could not be in New York two days a week, he would spend "several days, or a week" at the beginning organizing materials and working with executives. When this offer did not satisfy Vinal, Aydelotte wrote a stern letter on September 25, 1917, advising that he would withdraw from the program unless the "arrangements we make be satisfactory to both sides." Vinal finally agreed to the one-day visit, and the program got underway.

Because Aydelotte was AT&T's first outside writing consultant, his program is important for two reasons. First, since Aydelotte was one of the early English professors in technical communication to consult, his program offers insight into at least one kind of work that consultants did then. The particular period in which he worked, World War I, made special demands on the program since it had to train many young, poorly-educated employees. This need in part justified his emphasis on a broad education because he assumed that his students had poor academic foundations. Second, the program demonstrated that Aydelotte's thought approach, with humanistic goals, could work in business and industry. The fact that AT&T,

both the executives and the employees, found the program valuable suggests that it was successful for all involved.

## The AT&T Program

An unpublished company flier entitled "Educational Work–English Courses" that announced the program gives a clear sense of the course's goals. First, the company wanted to help its employees by affording them "every reasonable means . . . to perform their work as effectively as possible and also to prepare them to assume greater responsibilities." In other words, the company wanted not only to train its employees to work efficiently in the present but to prepare them for more rewarding careers later. Second, the Company hoped to improve the verbal facility of its employees. The flier notes that many experienced workers "find difficulty in expressing the results of their work to the best advantage, either orally or in writing, and have voiced a desire for further training in this direction." The flier goes on, however, to make clear that the program had a purpose broader than teaching English skills, and this broader purpose indicates Aydelotte's influence on the course's goals. The course was not only going to "give training in English." It would also teach employees "to think, to analyze, to construct, and to present ideas effectively," all goals that Aydelotte had made central to his MIT writing course. But Aydelotte's plans, at least initially, were even larger. In an August 20, 1917, letter to President Maclaurin explaining the course, Aydelotte noted that his goals would be not only to teach the employees to write, to think, to "broaden their outlook," and to "give them some appreciation of literature," but also to provide participants with an education equivalent to college. As it turned out, this last goal was overly ambitious.

The program immediately attracted the attention of AT&T's employees. According to an unpublished, undated typed summary, 795 employees returned their applications to enroll, a surprisingly large number.[6]

The program needed to meet the needs of a range of ages and educational backgrounds. As the company flier makes clear, AT&T would offer two different courses. The first would be an "elementary course" for boys and girls 14 to 18. Such a course was necessary because the war had forced the company to hire younger workers to replace older, mobilized ones. Many of these employees, some no more than children, had left school, without a high school diploma, and this branch of the course would therefore be more like a high school than a college course. The second course would be "an advanced course for men and women" over 18. Although older, many of these workers had not been able to finish high school or start college. Both groups needed general training in writing and thinking to make them valuable to AT&T as present and future employees. Both groups would benefit from a humanistic education that broadened their outlook on life.

Since the content of the course would be based on AT&T itself, Aydelotte had to learn as much about the company, its operations, and its role in American society as he could. He planned to treat this topic "liberally," by which he meant that he would study the company from various points of view and in various social and intellectual contexts. These points of view ranged from the engineering of the Bell system to AT&T's influences on society. Such a broad approach would help workers understand how their jobs fit into the company and into the context of American culture.

Aydelotte's plan is in many ways admirable, but some ethical problems existed. In many ways, the program as Aydelotte conceived it was less elitist and more democratic than his other programs. His goal was to help a group of young, disadvantaged men and women get the education denied them by the circumstances of the war. Aydelotte insisted that this education be broad rather than narrow. In some ways, Aydelotte wanted to help AT&T workers gain a similar kind of control over their futures that the more politically liberal Bryn Mawr Summer School for Women Workers did when it was founded a few years later, in 1921 (see Hollis). But Aydelotte's program was also designed to form workers to meet the needs of AT&T for educated, docile employees willing to fit into the company hierarchy. While Aydelotte wanted employees to become critical thinkers, problem solvers, and forceful writers, he did not want them to question too deeply the corporate goals and labor policies of AT&T. In other words, he designed assignments for students to learn about AT&T's many roles in American culture, but students were not encouraged to be critical of those roles.

To prepare the course, Aydelotte learned as much as he could about the company. In an August 17 letter to Aydelotte, Vinal mentioned that he had sent him "a carload of literature" about the company so that he could learn the Bell system. In a letter of August 16, Vinal instructed John F. Oderman, District Telephone Chief of Boston AT&T, to allow Aydelotte to study the phone system and "get the atmosphere of the work and a knowledge of the various phases of the business." On top of his teaching responsibilities at MIT, Aydelotte spent hours examining the AT&T papers to select material for the program.

Despite this preparation, Aydelotte could never, in such a short time, become an expert on AT&T, so he devised a plan to draw on executive expertise. While Aydelotte would lecture on writing strategies, design assignments, and oversee the curricular aspects of the program, the executives would lecture on their own areas in the company. By making executives lecturers, Aydelotte accomplished two goals. First, by making the executives part of the program, he gained their support and encouraged them to allow employees to take time off for the course. Second, he made the executives feel important by having them speak before the classes about their own jobs and responsibilities at AT&T. This method had the added advantage of creating interesting subjects for student-worker writing. While he himself could not possibly have spoken authoritatively on technical and business topics, he could draw on executive knowledge to give the course intellectual grounding. The plan of this part of the course was to give students, through a series of overviews, a better understanding of the whole company and their own jobs within it. This knowledge, Aydelotte reasoned, would prepare students to do their own work more efficiently. The knowledge would also prepare them to advance within the company because they would understand the organization comprehensively.

A good example of Aydelotte's interaction with company executives was his relationship with N.C. Kingsbury, one of AT&T's Vice Presidents. In an October 30, 1917, letter Aydelotte invited Kingsbury to talk on "The Bell System as a Public Servant." Aydelotte suggested that he cover the following issues: 1) the value of the telephone in peace and war; 2) the relevance of the Bell system to the public through the Interstate Commerce Commission; and 3) the "publicity, aims, and methods" of the company. The point of the lecture, Aydelotte made clear, should be to give a "bird's-eye-view" of the topic before students were presented with more detailed discussions of writing topics (which would grow from the specialist lecture), Aydelotte's lectures on writing, and students' discussions with tutors. Aydelotte referred to Kingsbury's article "Publicity," which had appeared in a trade journal, as an appropriate basis for the talk. Kingsbury responded on November 2, noting that topics one and three were appropriate but that the second was too technical. After the lecture, Aydelotte wrote Kingsbury on November 10 thanking him for his "frank, broad-gaged talk on the Telephone Company," just the sort of talk the course needed.

A second strategy that Aydelotte developed was to use college-educated employees as tutors, a strategy made necessary by the large number of workers entering the program. This plan made it possible to ensure large numbers of students personal attention without seeing them all himself. On November 12, Vinal wrote to Aydelotte, telling him that the "tutorial work is now completely organized for the advanced" students and that the elementary students would soon all have tutors. The plan divided the elementary students into groups A and B. As Vinal wrote on November 17, he made this division because students varied in abilities. The A group was the better half, group B the weaker. The plan would benefit all concerned. The company would not have to let the elementary groups attend class at the same time, the instruction could be geared to student ability, and Aydelotte's class size would drop. Each group received a letter from Vinal. As the letter to group A makes clear, this group of about 30 students would meet once a week as a whole during their lunch hour for a half-hour discussion of their papers with Aydelotte. At the same time, group B students would meet with employee-tutors in groups of five to do the same.

According to Vinal, tutors devoted four hours per week to the program, all time to be taken from the tutor's work schedule. These hours included two-and-a-half hours tutoring five students each. The tutors also spent one hour attending a lecture by Aydelotte and a half-hour in conference with him. The tutors were responsible for overseeing the students' exercises and papers and were, Vinal made clear to the elementary students, to be treated respectfully:

> We would like to suggest that those who have been good enough to volunteer to act as tutors are doing so at considerable personal inconvenience, and we trust that your appreciation of the help offered you by your tutor will be evident by promptness on your part in forwarding your written work, by punctuality in meeting your weekly appointment, as well as by the interest we know you will take in the work itself.

On October 11, Aydelotte gave a talk, titled "Address," to the AT&T tutors to outline his expectations. It was most important, he argued, that the tutors get to know the students' personalities. This personal connection he considered more important than knowing "principles of [the] English language" (12). He did not expect tutors to be experts in grammar and rhetoric; instead, he wanted them to function as a receptive audience.[7] As he told the tutors,

> [t]he business of a teacher of English composition is to be a good audience. Nobody writes except for an audience. Nobody ought to write, except for an audience. Only crazy people talk to themselves .... The business you have is to be an audience to this particular student. You must also be a sympathetic and eager audience. (13)

He went on to note that the tutors should not be so critical as to hurt students' feelings. Criticism should be "instructive—not destructive" (14). Finally, Aydelotte expected tutors to encourage students to write essays free from self-consciousness and argued that the program could accomplish this by de-emphasizing formal elements. As he put it, stating a basic of the thought approach, "We hope, first of all to lay emphasis on the idea [not on formal elements] .... In my opinion, you cannot teach anyone about form until he has an idea that he wants to express. I do not care if they know rhetoric or not if they can write" (12). The weakness of Aydelotte's position is that he did not know the rhetorical tradition well and limited rhetoric largely to Harvard formalism.

Aydelotte developed different courses for the elementary and advanced groups. In his "Address by Professor Aydelotte to Advanced English Class January 3, 1918," he explained to advanced students his principles. He did not want students to read material superficially. He wanted them to read a few essays thoroughly and apply the ideas to everything else read and encountered. "When I ask you what Ruskin says," Aydelotte commented, "I am asking you to read Ruskin and apply his ideas to other ideas which you have in your head" (5).[8] In other words, ideas discussed in class should be connected to the rest of their lives, in particular, to their jobs. By doing this, he hoped the employees would "relate the thing [they] are doing to the best things that have ever been done" (5). By recognizing this, the students would learn how their jobs fit into larger systems and processes, thereby giving their daily work significance. He wanted them to understand that all work was "to advance civilization," (5) so even the most humble job contributed to an advancement of American culture.

As Aydelotte made clear in the "Address by Professor Aydelotte to Advanced English Class January 24, 1918," he wanted students to connect the various worlds usually considered distinct. He wanted, for instance, the advanced students to find connections between business and other worlds–science, literature, and imagination. In particular, he wanted them to see that business, if viewed correctly, should embrace "spiritual ideals" (5) and that business suffers when separated from other systems of thought.

To achieve this goal, Aydelotte modeled the advanced course on idea courses at Indiana and MIT and used some of the same readings he had in *Materials* and in *English and Engineering*. To this material he added readings about AT&T and the executive lectures. The readings, for instance, included Charles G. Dubois's "The Bell System–Its Constituent Companies and Their Relations to Each Other," an overview of AT&T. Aydelotte soon turned students to two of his favorite Victorian essayists, teaching Arnold's "Culture" and "Hebraism and Hellenism" from *Culture and Anarchy* and a selection from Newman's *The Idea of a University* on knowledge versus information. He used several essays that addressed questions of writing, including George Henry Lewes's "The Principle of Sincerity" and Robert Louis Stevenson's "Truth of Intercourse," both of which emphasized sincere writing. Other readings were on questions of business, such as Louis D. Brandeis's "Business–A Profession" and a section from Ruskin's *Unto This Last* retitled "Ruskin on Business and the Professions." As were the selections in his anthologies, these readings encouraged students to think about important issues and connect those issues with their daily lives.

Aydelotte developed a sequence of writing assignments to encourage advanced students to think about the readings, to reflect on those readings in relation to AT&T, and to learn to express ideas (unpublished list). The earliest assignments required students to write letters about their personal experiences, but Aydelotte soon moved them to more complex work. In one, for instance, students read a brief passage from Newman's *The Idea of a University* distinguishing knowledge from information and asked students to write a letter discussing this issue in relation to their jobs. Another assignment asked them to respond in writing to the following topic: "In what respects does the American Telephone and Telegraph Company seem to you to fulfill Ruskin's ideal as expressed in the essay [on business] handed to you December 20th?" As these assignments suggest, Aydelotte encouraged students to see connections between the ideas in the reading and either their personal experiences, their work, or other systems of ideas.

For the elementary classes, Aydelotte had to devise a curriculum unlike any he had developed previously. These students were young, often only fourteen, and poorly educated. To teach them, Aydelotte began with basic reading and writing. In an address given to the tutors on October 11, he outlined the elementary curriculum. For the first half year, these students would work with their tutors on exercises in English grammar and learn to write in "a straight-forward way" (1). He would teach them to read by giving them a piece entitled "The History of the Telephone," which had the added advantage of teaching them about AT&T.

Aydelotte hoped that, by the middle of the year, they could begin the advanced course.

One of Aydelotte's goals for all employees was to encourage them to read literature. At Oxford, Aydelotte had become convinced that the Oxford system of giving students reading lists that they read on their own, often over holidays, offered the best system to make students responsible for their own learning. To encourage such independence at AT&T, he arranged for the New York Public Library to open a branch at AT&T so that employees had direct access to books. In an April 19, 1918, letter to Aydelotte, Vinal noted with pleasure the success of this part of the program: "You would be delighted to sit in the library day after day and see the people come in and get books. You certainly have accomplished to a large degree your purpose in getting the students, both elementary and advanced, to read real literature." Aydelotte ensured that the library contained books appropriate for the elementary students. He corresponded throughout the winter of 1918 with Mary Frank of the New York Public Library, providing her with lists of juvenile reading for AT&T. Helen Cook, one of the women at AT&T associated with the program, wrote Aydelotte on April 18, 1918, telling him that the books for young readers were so popular that the original books had been "read over many times." She quoted one elementary student, Oscar Hengstler, who had told her of the reading, "Gee, how I do love the Knights and Ladies now," an expression of his interest in *Ivanhoe*. She asked Aydelotte to send a new list of juvenile books and highly recommended the novels of A. Conan Doyle and adventure books. The list that Aydelotte sent Cook includes works by Cooper, Bret Hart, Twain, Kipling, O'Henry, Tarkington, and Dickens (letter of April 30, 1918). As Aydelotte had learned himself at Oxford, a good education required students to read widely on their own, and he succeeded in encouraging his AT&T students, even the youngest, to do so.[9]

By all accounts, Aydelotte's AT&T program was a resounding success. Vinal was delighted with Aydelotte's work, and consulted with him for many years on educational issues. When Aydelotte fell ill in the spring, Vinal wrote a friendly note on April 12 wishing him well and blaming the illness on the stress of Aydelotte's schedule. Meeting his obligations at MIT and traveling once a week to New York City to lecture had taken its toll. A student named H. Euryl Fisher wrote on April 11 to express her concern for his health and to tell him that the employees had "come to look forward to your weekly discourse which entertains while giving instruction so interestingly." At the end of the course, students wrote him letters about how much they learned. Ella A. Waeff, for instance, wrote on May 23: "I feel that the English course which ended today would not be complete for me unless I told you that I thoroughly enjoyed the work, and that the lectures have been a source of inspiration and of great benefit to me." Another student, Josephine V. Thompson, wrote on May 1 of the "great pleasure it has given me to attend the weekly talks given by you .... My only regret has been that so few of us were privileged to hear them."

Aydelotte also found the course rewarding, writing to Mann, then education advisor to the War Department, on May 14, 1918: "We finished in New York yesterday with a grand love fest. I don't know when I have had more fun out of giving a course of lectures" (qtd. in Blanshard 125). The following year, in an unpublished address presented at Dartmouth College, Aydelotte expressed his admiration for his AT&T students: "I was amazed by the eagerness with which they [the young employees] had grasped the fact that it was liberal knowledge rather than merely technical which they needed to make them free" (5). Almost twenty years later, in a letter to former AT&T employee Henry C. Fisher dated October 22, 1937, Aydelotte wrote about his AT&T experience: "I look back on those days at the A.T. and T. as one of the most interesting adventures of my life . . . ."

When he wrote Mann, Aydelotte realized that he could no longer continue his AT&T work. Mann had invited Aydelotte to join him in the War Department to design a training curriculum for the military, a position he eventually accepted. But the AT&T program was an important phase in his career. It gave him an opportunity to demonstrate that his thought approach could work outside the ivory tower, that it could be modified to help businesses train employees to write and think. It provided Aydelotte with direct experience working with business people and a firsthand sense of the work people entering the work force did on the job. Most importantly, perhaps, it convinced him that his humanistic approach to technical communication worked well in a variety of contexts, including business. While these were all valuable lessons, Aydelotte did not develop further his work in technical communication.

## MIT's English and History Program

The last major curriculum that Aydelotte developed at MIT was a combined English and History curriculum. Its main supporter was President Maclaurin, who, being trained like Aydelotte in the British educational system, saw an opportunity to create an Oxford-like curriculum in this country. Since he had hired Aydelotte in part because of his Oxford background, Maclaurin turned to him to oversee the development of the new curriculum by combining English and history into a single department. Unfortunately, the curriculum was not a success. In fact, it was more of a stopgap measure than a reasoned, carefully developed series of courses. The classes were too big, and the program lacked the necessary intimacy of the Oxford tutorial system. The method was foreign to U.S. education, which emphasized discrete, specialized courses. The experience, however, was important for Aydelotte because it introduced him to the pitfalls of creating interdisciplinary courses in the United States. He would find the experience invaluable when developing Swarthmore's Honors Program a few years later.

The impetus for the new program sprang from the health problems of Professor Currier, the man who had for years almost single-handedly taught history at MIT.

The *MIT Report of the President* for 1918 mentioned that Professor Currier had fallen ill during the winter term of 1917-18 and that the English Department had been temporarily assigned the work in history (72). When Currier retired, the English Department was required to take over the history duties permanently. In a long letter to Pearson, still Chair of English, dated June 24, 1918, Maclaurin lent his support to the approach, and quoted a report by the "Corporation of the Visiting Committee on the Department of English," which advocated a new approach combining English and history. Since Maclaurin shared these views, they offer insight into the President's thinking.

The Committee held first that history was an important subject for engineering students. However, it rejected the lecture approach because it did "not meet the special needs of such young men" (1). As did Aydelotte, the Committee believed that informational courses were inferior to courses that emphasized the development of knowledge: "No matter how well conceived, an informational course in History cannot be other than superficial, cannot be tied in with the other work of the students, and, since it cannot be buttressed, as in academic colleges, by a number of attendant, intensive courses in History, cannot be of very lasting influence or benefit in the real education of the student of pure and applied science" (1). In other words, a single history course taught in the lecture format offered students only information; in order to create knowledge, MIT would have to develop other methods. MIT needed a new approach because of its special problems. Students majored in engineering and took relatively few courses in the humanities. These courses therefore needed to be designed to complement the technical work.

A proper education would offer engineering students a general knowledge of Western civilization and the forces that shaped it. While this knowledge would not bear directly on the students' technical information, it would provide humane background knowledge that would contribute to technical success. Engineering students should possess a background that

> presupposes a correct use of the English language, facility of expression, some knowledge of at least one or two other modern tongues, an acquaintance with the main currents of literature and human history, an understanding of the principles of economics and of politics, and some conception of and some definite opinions in philosophy and ethics which lie at the foundation of civilization. (2)

Such a background would permit students to make connections among various branches of "human thought and experience" (3).

The curriculum should be reconceived so that knowledge is not "divided into separate parcels" (3). Instead, the disciplines should be taught together so that students understand the relationships among them. As the Committee argued,

> [a] knowledge of literature without any conception of the historical environment and atmosphere in which that literature was evolved; the

ability to use the English and other languages without association with and knowledge of books; and the study of politics, economics, history and literature without some conception of the philosophical and moral thought fundamental to and accompanying human endeavor, is to leave the student's mind immature and his technical learning of little avail. (3)

The Committee made the British influence on its thinking clear when it noted that MIT should develop a humanities curriculum similar to "a course corresponding, roughly and very partially, to the *Literae Humaniores* [The Greats] of the old [British] universities" (3), especially Oxford.

The Committee recommended that Maclaurin consult the faculty about the "possibility of uniting the work in history with the work in literature and English" to create courses "in which 'English,' English literature, history, ethics and philosophy are related in such a way as to make each of these topics strengthen and illuminate the others" (4).

This program cut across the grain of American educational practice in three ways. First, it questioned the necessity of separate departments for humane disciplines. English and history would no longer be two departments but one. Faculty trained in English would teach both subjects in sequences of related courses. Second, it questioned the elective system popular at the time. Instead of taking a series of discrete, unrelated humanities courses, students would take general courses that emphasized connections among branches of knowledge. Third, the plan redefined the purpose of education. MIT would no longer offer students specialized information through lectures in the humanities. It would instead encourage the development of more general kinds of knowledge.

Maclaurin handed the English Department no small job. As he made clear to Pearson in a June 24, 1918, letter, the department was to meet during the summer to plan a new curriculum that combined English and history for "the immediate future," by which he meant that fall. Pearson was told to consult all members of the department in his deliberations but follow the leadership of Aydelotte, who "is especially interested in the problem and is to be charged with some special responsibilities in the new course" (letter of June 24, 1918). As Aydelotte had confided to Mann in an April 29, 1918, letter, the MIT Corporation had approved the program and dropped the responsibility of designing it in his lap. He was worried about the program because a "superficial mixture" of the two subjects had been thrown together in the spring that would "not do and I am afraid the whole scheme will get a black eye unless I can put it in shape by October."

By June Aydelotte was in Washington, working for Mann in the War Department. Maclaurin had sent him a copy of his June 24 letter, and the President received an enthusiastic response in a letter dated June 26. Aydelotte noted that the Committee had made "a masterly statement of the position I should take in regard to History, English, and Philosophy." The opportunity to reconstitute MIT's humanity offerings "seems to [him] the finest opportunity [he had] ever known." And Aydelotte had big plans. He informed Maclaurin that to do the job right, to create more than what he had called in April a "superficial mixture," would take not several months but several years, and that he would, after the war, take "a year or half-year off" to return to Oxford to work on the curriculum with "[o]ne or two first-class historians and philosophers." No evidence exists that Maclaurin agreed to send Aydelotte to England; Maclaurin felt the prick of necessity to design a curriculum for fall and expected Aydelotte to create a workable series of courses immediately.

An undated, unpublished Aydelotte draft entitled "Proposal for Combining the Work of the Departments of English and History" suggests Aydelotte's thinking. In the proposal's general statement, Aydelotte attacked the typical American notion that education should produce specialists. He argued that the aim of the "Technology curriculum" is "not to produce specialists in either study [English or history] but rather liberally educated men of affairs" (1). Such men involved in the active life did not need specialist understanding in history, literature, and philosophy; instead, they needed broader understandings of major movements within these disciplines and the interconnections among them. To avoid disunity and "superficiality," the program would use one of Aydelotte's IU principles. Students would undergo "a thorough study of a few works of a few of the most important English writers" rather than a broad survey of many works (1). Nor would the curriculum attempt to cover all historical periods. Instead, it would focus first on one, the "Period of Revolution, 1775-1850," and would cover the following events: "the Revival of Romanticism, the American Revolution, the French Revolution, the Oxford Movement, the English Reform Bill of 1832 and the repeal of the Corn Laws in 1846" (2). And the focus of this study would not be the events themselves. Instead, the course would examine "the currents of thought reflected in political institutions, social conditions and in the literature of the day" (2). As this argument made clear, Aydelotte expanded the principles of the thought approach to this new course. Now students were not only to read the great 19th-century essayists; they were also to read 19th-century history, philosophy, economics, and political science to achieve a deeper understanding of English thought. For those historical topics that needed specialized treatment, Aydelotte advocated guest lectures by "specialists outside the department" (2). Where the specialists in history were to come from is not clear. While no trained historian remained at MIT, the school could draw on the resources of Cambridge and Boston. Finally, Aydelotte advocated that class size remain small to allow for "class discussion, [and] written work with individual conferences" (2).

In addition to proposing the combination of English and history, Aydelotte also suggested that the English Department bring other subjects under its jurisdiction. He suggested that the department hire a psychologist to cover "'applied' psychology" (3), such as methods for supervising workers and evaluating types of leaders. He also called for the continuation of a "History of Science" course that should be required of all students because of its importance to a technical education. As the proposal makes clear, Aydelotte attacked the tendency to create loosely-related specialties; in place of such an approach, he advocated a more integrated system that helped students see connections. As he noted, "What is needed is an English equivalent for *Literae Humaniores*" (3), a program based not on ancient but on English language and culture. This language echoes Maclaurin's letter of June 24 and suggests that the two men, both trained in the British system, saw an opportunity to create a similar system at MIT.

Aydelotte's draft proposal was sent to faculty members for responses, and Aydelotte received at least two strongly written criticisms. Professor Robert E. Rogers was willing to use some history to illuminate the literature, but he objected to trying to create a *Literae Humaniores* program at MIT because of dissimilarities between British and American education:

> I should like to point out one grave difference, a difference which, in my opinion, lessens the similarity to a very great extent. In Oxford, the various aspects of the classics are taught by experts in these branches; history, by an historian, economics by an economist, and the like. They are not taught by one department [English] whose members have had no training in the separate branches of the field. There is no one in this Department capable of treating history as an historian, psychology as a psychologist, or philosophy as a trained philosopher. The most we could do would be to do our usual English work, using in a more or less general fashion material drawn from other studies. This, I think, is admirable, if it would be considered the work of the English Department, but I do not see how it could pretend to call itself history, or any other specialized subject. To do so would be misleading and dishonest. (2)

While Rogers would like to see "adequate" training in subjects such as psychology, sociology, and philosophy, "the English Department is no more capable of handling those subjects expertly than it is the subject of history" (2). In short, Rogers recognized a serious flaw in Aydelotte's plan. American English professors were not trained to teach history or philosophy as a discipline and could not do so credibly.

A second criticism, unsigned but titled "Brief of a Devil's Advocate," also rejected the proposal, but on somewhat different grounds. Departmental divisions, the writer argued, are not logical but conventional, and he could think of many possible combinations of subjects, including English and various modern languages such as French and German, for instance. In that case, students would read the literary classics in all modern languages, not just English, an approach in which Aydelotte never expressed interest. He always advocated studying British literature alone. But the critic concluded that combining various subjects into one big department would lead to confusion and therefore questioned the merger's wisdom.

Despite these criticisms, the English Department, under President Maclaurin's direction, developed a plan to teach the combined courses. The undated minutes of a staff meeting that took place sometime during the summer of 1918 indicate how the English teachers shaped the first course in the sequence, "English and History

[EH] 21." They began with this course and developed the others during the academic year. EH 21 was to cover the Age of Revolution. For books, the group decided on Volume III of Tout and Powell's *History of England* and Page's *British Poets of the Nineteenth Century*. In addition to these, the committee decided to assemble a pamphlet of "brief selections" from writers of the period that included Paine, Burke, Rousseau, and Carlyle. It also contained selections from Wordsworth's *Prelude*. Aydelotte was instrumental in compiling this pamphlet even though he was in Washington, DC. On August 1, 1918, Pearson wrote to consult him about the pamphlet's development. On August 10, he wrote again to say that he "hoped that [Aydelotte] will find they [the pamphlet's selections] are satisfactory." In addition to the pamphlet, students would also read some novels as outside, supplementary reading.

Although the minutes do not discuss writing assignments, they do mention that each student was to keep a notebook to record points of discussion and "comments and criticisms" of the selections. "The purpose of the note books," the minutes comment, "is to train the student in assembling material from different sources and in arranging it in an orderly fashion and making it compact and exact in statement." The 1919-1920 catalog description of EH 21 mentions that students also wrote reports, and the *MIT President's Report* for 1918-19 indicates that writing was central. While students studied "the main current of thought in the nineteenth century as interpreted by masterpieces of English Literature," they worked in small classes that encouraged discussion of the readings. These discussions led to writing assignments, which were "integral" to the course (66). As the report makes clear, the course had the stamp of Aydelotte's thought approach: "the student will not be called upon to write until he has ideas which he can express; furthermore, as a result of the class discussions he will be stimulated to put forth his best efforts [in his writing]" (66).

In MIT's 1918-19 annual catalog, the Department of English was renamed the "Department of English and History" (93) after only half a summer's work. Amazingly, within a few months, the faculty had designed under Aydelotte's direction a respectable series of courses that integrated the study of writing, literature, and history. As Pearson commented in the 1919 *MIT President's Report*, the combining of the two disciplines had yielded "satisfactory results . . . in spite of the hurried conditions under which the work was undertaken" (72).

The hurried planning, however, led to problems. There were, for instance, no fewer than six courses, all with their separate numbers, entitled "English and History [EH]." EH 11, 12, and 13 were to cover "European History of the last hundred years" (94), and 12 and 13 were simply a "continuation" of the course during the rest of the year. EH 21, 22, and 23 covered English history from the French Revolution through the 19th century and show the influence of Aydelotte's thinking. EH 21 covered the French Revolution; 22 covered "the conflict of political and economic principles that marked the first half of the Nineteenth Century in England"; and 23 addressed the "influence of the development of science upon English literature and thought" (94). All courses were taught in small classes, and each course required students to meet in conference with the instructor, write reports, and give speeches. Because of Aydelotte's commitment to British studies, American history, literature, and philosophy received no attention.

Although the *MIT President's Report* for 1918-19 notes that English and history were to be taught together permanently, Aydelotte was not to teach long in the program. In 1920, he went on leave to reorganize the selection process of Rhodes Scholars in the United States. In 1921, after much reflection, he accepted the presidency of Swarthmore College and left Cambridge for Pennsylvania and the heavy responsibilities of developing that school into one of the nation's foremost small liberal arts colleges. When he left Bloomington, his departure was hardly noted publicly, except, perhaps, with a sigh of relief on both sides. But his departure from MIT was recorded in the *MIT President's Report* for 1920-21 when Chairman Henry G. Pearson, speaking for the English Department, wrote

> [d]uring the six years in which he has been associated with the Department, Professor Aydelotte has made a marked contribution to it in fresh ideas, enthusiasm, and skill as a teacher.... His loss will be felt by Faculty and students, who cordially wish him success in his presidential duties. (84)

Aydelotte had learned much from his years at MIT. He had developed three major curriculums based on the thought approach, he had worked closely with students majoring in technical disciplines, he had associated closely with people in the business community, and he had taken his first tentative steps towards designing an interdisciplinary curriculum with the English and history courses. Most importantly for this study, he had fashioned new ways to teach writing in various contexts using the thought approach. He would draw on all of these experiences as President of Swarthmore when he expanded this approach to form the nation's most famous Honors Program there.

## NOTES

1. David R. Russell claims that Aydelotte went to MIT as the chair of the English Department (118). This is not the case. The chair throughout Aydelotte's years at the school was Henry G. Pearson. The only administrative position that Aydelotte held in the department was being "[i]n charge" of English 12, titled "English (Nineteenth Century Essays)" (*Bulletin* 1916-17 325). Aydelotte did, however, have an enormous impact on the department, its philosophy, and its course offerings.

2. Partly, Aydelotte's emphasis on British literature reflects the influence of Rhodes and the Rhodes Scholarship. Aydelotte, like Rhodes, wanted to spread British values to other nations. To do this, Aydelotte used that nation's literature in his pedagogy.

3. It is peculiar that as an American he could not place at least some emphasis on American literature, which addresses American problems and American thought.

4. Aydelotte's main goal throughout the text was to emphasize the thinking/writing connection. He wanted engineering students to think about engineering as a profession, to take a more liberal, philosophical view of it.

5. See Michael G. Moran's "The Road Not Taken" for a more detailed discussion of the text's many topics.

6. It's not clear how many students actually enrolled, but the total was less than 795.

7. The statement expresses again Aydelotte's view that knowledge of formal elements of writing is less important than thinking clearly and expressing that thought in prose.

8. This statement echoes Matthew Arnold's famous dictum, the best that has been thought and said.

9. In addition to making books available through the library, Aydelotte encouraged younger students to read by giving them books as prizes in writing contests designed to keep them interested in the work. Part of the purpose of the prizes was to introduce young students to good literature.

# 5: The Oxford Approach and Honors Education at Swarthmore, 1921-1940

In 1921 Aydelotte assumed the presidency of Swarthmore College, a sleepy, old-fashioned Quaker liberal arts school that, unlike Bryn Mawr and Haverford, was better known for its social life and athletics than its academics (Clark 175-77). During his eighteen years as president, he changed Swarthmore into one of the nation's most intellectually rigorous small colleges. Aydelotte accomplished this change by creating Swarthmore's Honors Program, which became the national model for curriculums designed to challenge exceptional students (*Annual Report of the General Education Board, 1929-1930* 14). While achieving this goal, he became the leading spokesperson for honors education in America, writing extensively on the subject himself and inspiring Robert C. Brooks's 1927 *Reading for Honors at Swarthmore* and the Swarthmore College Faculty's 1941 tribute to Aydelotte, *An Adventure in Education*, both of which described the Honors Program at different stages. Aydelotte himself wrote *Honors Courses in American Colleges and Universities* (1924) and *Breaking the Academic Lockstep* (2nd ed. 1944), two books that describe Swarthmore's honors program and survey the various forms such programs took across the nation. As early as 1928, Aydelotte's reputation was such that Fred R. Yoder of the State College of Washington invited him to write an essay on honors education for an edited volume "because you have given far more attention to this [question] than any other man in the country." While Aydelotte admitted that he did not create the Swarthmore program single-handedly, he was the driving force behind it, and the program reflected to a surprising degree his views on education in general and the teaching of English, especially writing, in particular. As Brooks noted in his 1927 book, "To President Aydelotte belongs the credit for the scheme of honors work at Swarthmore as a whole"(9).

In this chapter, I will not discuss all elements of Aydelotte's Honors Program; instead, after examining his educational principles and the development of the program in general, I will concentrate (with a few glances elsewhere) on the English Literature Division, one of the two first honors divisions created, and on the central role that writing played in the program. Ironically, at the same time that Aydelotte made writing an essential part of the honors program, he also oversaw the dismantling of practically all writing courses at Swarthmore. While this evolution was consistent with Aydelotte's thought approach, which questioned the value of instruction in composition apart from reading, some evidence suggests that honors students might have benefitted from more writing instruction, especially in the early years of the program.

## Why Aydelotte Chose Swarthmore

Although Aydelotte had had offers to become president of other colleges, he had turned them down. In 1920, for instance, he had been offered the executive position at Reed College in Oregon but had declined because Reed was located too far from the northeast, the hub of Rhodes scholarship activities in the United States. But when the offer came from Swarthmore's Board of Managers, he grasped the opportunity immediately.

In a letter of February 23, 1921, to his friend Professor Warner Fite of Princeton, Aydelotte wrote that he had been attracted to Swarthmore for both personal and professional reasons. He liked that the school was on a sound financial footing, which he believed would free him from the usual presidential fund raising responsibilities. He thought that, while the school needed work "on the academic side," it had the money to make the changes that he planned.[1] He was impressed by the faculty and thought that he could work with it. He noted in *Breaking* that when he visited, the faculty listened cordially to his ideas and encouraged him to accept the position (30).[2] He also believed, as he wrote in a February 28 letter to Fite, that he would be able to improve the faculty by hiring new members as he developed his honors curriculum.

He was equally impressed by the Quakers serving on the Board of Managers because they seemed receptive. Quakers, he noted in his "Report of the President 1939," were not afraid to consider novel, even unpopular proposals, especially those that appealed to their traditions of perfectionism and idealism (1). As he wrote in *Breaking*, these men and women, being members of a minority group, were willing to listen, without prejudice, to his ideas even though these ideas were not widely held (30). Because of the Board's receptivity to his educational principles, he thought that Swarthmore was one of the few small colleges in the country that would support his efforts to achieve excellence through innovative yet untried methods.

In short, he was convinced that Swarthmore offered him the freedom to accomplish the educational goals that he had been working towards piecemeal since beginning his experimentation at Indiana in 1908. As he remembered in his "Report 1939," he "saw here [at Swarthmore] an opportunity to carry out a long-cherished plan for the improvement of undergraduate work in American colleges" (1). He planned to accomplish this goal by developing an American honors college along the lines of the honors schools at Oxford. Writing to Professor C. R. Bagley at the University of North Carolina on February 15, 1923, he reported that "we are trying here at Swarthmore to put in some honor schools more or less on the analogy of the honor schools at Oxford. We plan to allow students to volunteer at the end of their Sophomore year to read for honors, and if they are accepted they will spend their last two years entirely on honors work." This restructuring of Swarthmore from a typical small liberal arts college that emphasized sports and social life to a college that would make the intellectual life central to its mission was the goal that Aydelotte put before himself, the faculty, and the Board of Managers.

The program he developed, however, had elitist, exclusionary leanings and was designed for white students who had enjoyed educational advantages. While Aydelotte recognized the necessity of educating the masses, he thought that American education had largely achieved this goal.[3] His model for Swarthmore was Oxford, which was highly selective, and his goal was to make this school equally selective. In fact, at Swarthmore his educational theory took a sharp turn. At IU and MIT, he had assumed that the thought approach could educate the average student. Now, he abandoned that notion, and emphasized educating the intellectual elite, the group of students he believed American higher education neglected. This elite would then assume their rightful leadership positions in the American democracy, which, Aydelotte believed, would fail without an elite. In one sense, then, Aydelotte returned to the goals of the 19th-century small college that was designed to prepare a similar elite group of leaders.

As Everett Hunt, Aydelotte's Dean of Men at Swarthmore, has noted, Aydelotte was advanced in his educational views yet "conservative on many social issues" ("Frank Aydelotte" 31). Educationally, he advocated the student-centered classroom that allow unfettered inquiry, at least for the honors student. This kind of inquiry, Aydelotte believed, empowered students to take charge of their own educations, thereby preparing them for leadership positions requiring problem solving and creative thought about social problems. At the same time, however, he believed that a college should be consistent with the mores of the general community in which it functioned. Consequently, Aydelotte was not interested in issues of social justice or racial equality. Hunt gives the example of Aydelotte's refusal to address the issue of huge discrepancies between the salaries of professors and campus workers such as scrub women and night watchmen. Another example was Aydelotte's refusal to admit a qualified African-American student such as George Arnold on the grounds that he would not be comfortable in an intimate, co-educational, all-white environment. This exclusionary, racist tendency in Aydelotte's social thought collides with his liberal educational theory at Swarthmore. He limited his honors program not only to the elite but the white elite.

## Aydelotte's Educational Theory

Aydelotte identified the problems facing American education and his solutions for them in his 1921 "Inaugural Address" delivered at Swarthmore and in the writing he completed during the next twenty years. As did Dewey and other progressive educators, Aydelotte believed that the main problem that education faced was that the social, political, and industrial contexts within which it operated were making new demands on colleges and universities to produce better-educated graduates to function as leaders. "In industry, in government, and in international relations we are entering upon an age which brings new and difficult problems for the minds and souls of man," Aydelotte wrote ("Inaugural" 19), and these new complexities required a better-educated American leadership to solve them. One of the main problems of industrialization, according to Aydelotte, was the danger of confusing ends with means. Industrialization could produce "all the material products of our civilization" (21), but the problem as Aydelotte saw it was the tendency to view the ends of industrialized civilization as only the production of material goods. Such goods should be the means to a greater end, he argued, the improvement of the human spirit. As Aydelotte put it, "The end of all industry is the production of human beings of a finer quality, and unless this end is realized and achieved, no measure, however great, of material success, can redeem it from failure" ("Inaugural" 21). The danger that higher education must avoid, then, was the training of experts who understood the techniques of producing material goods but who lacked the wisdom to realize that these goods were means to spiritual ends. To Aydelotte, the purpose of education must be to educate humanists in the liberal arts tradition who had "vision" ("Inaugural" 21) to understand larger goals, the enhancement of the spiritual side of life.[4] He had tried to train students at Indiana and MIT to understand this point; at Swarthmore, however, he wanted to make this understanding central to the honors curriculum.

The problems with American higher education as Aydelotte understood them were complex. On the one hand, the United States, like all industrialized nations, needed an educated populace. One of the goals of American colleges and universities had to remain mass education, a goal he believed American colleges had partially accomplished. As Aydelotte argued, "[w]e have opened wider the doors to higher education, and it is evident that if democratic government is to be successful, these doors must be opened still wider" ("Inaugural" 20). Without an educated populace, democracy would cease. But educating the masses created educational problems, Aydelotte believed. The curriculum, he feared, became geared to the average student with average results. As Aydelotte noted, "[w]e are educating more students up to a fair average than any country in the world" ("Inaugural" 23). This, he believed, was an important accomplishment, an accomplishment that European nations had been unable to achieve. He expanded on this point in "A Revolution in American Academic Standards": "We are in this country giving a very large group of students of average ability a certain familiarity with intellectual things and a respect for the intellectual life which together constitutes a great intellectual achievement" (2). Yet this goal, important as it was, limited the potential of American higher education to educate fully the above-average student, those students, Aydelotte assumed, who would become leaders. Aydelotte called, therefore, for a kind of tracking in which the elite would enjoy educational advantages such as personal freedom, small classes, and personal attention while the more average, pass student took more typical lecture classes.

Because the standard curriculum of American colleges and universities had been created to educate the average, American educators had come to assume that students were uninterested in learning. Colleges therefore established methods to make certain that all students mastered at least a basic amount of information. To ensure this, American higher education had developed the course and credit system, a system that Aydelotte questioned. Each course taught students a set amount of material by requiring them to read textbooks and attend lectures. To make certain that students memorized enough, professors assigned them exercises, quizzes, examinations, and papers. If students passed these various tests and assignments for enough courses, the college or university certified this fact by granting a degree. As Aydelotte wrote critically of the system in "Honors Work and Graduate Study,"

> [t]he methods of mass education, the academic lockstep, the spoonfeeding, the elaborate machinery of courses and credits, exercises and petty tests, . . . are thought to be necessary to insure that a million students in our colleges and universities shall not spend all their time on football and fraternities, but shall pay some attention to their studies and do some work for their degrees . . . . (102)

In short, Aydelotte argued in *Honors Courses*, the traditional college curriculum was organized "along the lines of secondary schools" (5). Such a system was necessary, the argument went, because of human nature and the large numbers that American colleges must educate, a position with which Aydelotte and his faculty partially concurred. As Robert E. Spiller, a member of Swarthmore's English Department, argued in the *English Journal*, "the majority of students admitted to college should continue with the traditional approach because they needed guidance and drill to progress intellectually" ("Pre-Honors Courses" 503). But as Aydelotte noted in "The Honors Idea," if traditional instruction remained the only kind, the United States faced the problem of mediocrity, because "[a]s the numbers increase the average standard of excellence is inevitably lowered" (1). Traditional instruction prevented students "from ever getting into any long intellectual stride. They learn some tidbit of knowledge, are examined in it, and forget it, and by repeating this process a sufficient number of times are supposed to have acquired an education" (*Honors Courses* 5).

While Aydelotte admitted that the traditional system suited the average student, especially the student who either lacked the interest, drive, or ability to strive for excellence or needed firm guidance to do any work, it did not educate effectively the more able and ambitious.[5] The system, in fact, limited the achievements of bright students who, if they were freed from what Aydelotte termed the "academic lockstep" of American higher education, would work harder and achieve more academically. Instead of encouraging independence, the system encouraged "the school-boy virtue of docility in the performance of daily tasks" that discouraged initiative (*Honors Courses* 6). These more gifted students needed a system that on the one hand demanded more of them and on the other gave them more freedom to educate themselves. As Aydelotte argued in his "Report 1939," which reviewed his presidential achievements at Swarthmore,

> [s]trenuous effort is essential to the development of sturdy character. Our best undergraduates tended [before Aydelotte arrived at Swarthmore], in my opinion, to deteriorate for lack of stimulus to do their best, or they tended to use surplus time and energy in extracurricular activities of various kinds which, while blameless in themselves, were inferior in intellectual and moral value to the experience of grappling with the great central problems of our civilization, which are the subject matter of our different departments of knowledge. (1)

The best students, Aydelotte believed, did not need simply more education. It was not a matter of giving them more textbooks to read or more tests to take. Instead, they needed an education that was "qualitatively" different—one that gave them freedom from the drudgery of the traditional curriculum (Blanshard 103). As the Swarthmore College Faculty wrote in *Adventure*, echoing Aydelotte's own ideas,

> [t]he aim [of honors education] is to release from the academic lockstep the student whose natural pace is faster, to single out from the mass those whose absorptive capacity is greater and give them more to cover, to discover those who, whether of outstanding gifts or not, would profit by a harder argument and give them problems that are more advanced, and to free from academic red tape those who can carry responsibility. (17)

Instead of being held back by courses developed for their more average comrades, these students, whether they be brighter, harder working, or more ambitious than their fellows, needed an entirely different curriculum.

These students required an Honors Program designed specifically to meet their needs. Aydelotte planned the program to work in the following way. All Swarthmore undergraduates would take a fairly standard college curriculum for two years. Aydelotte found this system necessary because American high schools were at least one to two years behind their European counterparts, and American undergraduates needed a general education before doing more specialized work. While students were in these freshman and sophomore courses, instructors identified the exceptional ones with the intelligence, ambition, and independence for honors work. These students were invited to make an application to the chairs of the various honors divisions. Instructors in each division would meet to discuss the candidates and select those they thought would benefit from honors work. Those admitted then spent their last two years taking honors seminars that released them from regular course work. They read largely on their own and met once a week in a small seminar to discuss that reading and papers based on it. Those students who did not do well in the program could be returned to regular class work. Successful honors students completed the program by taking comprehensive examinations at the end of their two years to determine what honors degree, if any, they deserved.

The keys to the program were, first, to allow honors students to work at their own pace without being held back; second, to allow students to educate themselves through their own reading; and, third, to hold these students to a higher standard than most undergraduates. Aydelotte conceived of the undergraduate honors degree as similar in difficulty to the M.A.

Proof that such a method worked Aydelotte found among the American Rhodes Scholars at Oxford. As a former Rhodes Scholar himself and as the current American representative to the Rhodes Trust, he witnessed firsthand the intellectual development of these American students. They entered an educational system that was more demanding than their own and that produced British counterparts who "were one or two years ahead of American college students of the same age in academic attainments" ("Report 1939" 1). But American students had fallen behind their English colleagues not because the Americans were intellectually inferior or less able. They were behind because of weaknesses in the American system, which did not challenge them to work to their full potential. In fact, the Rhodes Scholarship program proved to Aydelotte that when Americans matriculated in the more demanding Oxford honors schools and faced the higher standards there, the Rhodes scholars "speedily made up the lost ground and [found] no difficulty in holding their own with their English mates in the final examinations in the Oxford honors schools" ("Report 1939" 1). The problem, therefore, lay not in the native abilities of American students; it lay instead in the nature of the American system that limited itself to educating the average student to an average level. As Oxford proved to Aydelotte, American colleges and universities needed honors schools for brighter, more ambitious students, those students with the abilities to achieve more than the average student could.

Aydelotte recognized that his arguments raised questions about democracy in education. He especially recognized that honors work was open to criticism because it did not treat all students alike. But he rejected what he considered misguided attempts to apply democratic principles to education (Swarthmore

College Faculty 12). He held that all students should not be treated alike because not all students possessed the same abilities. Just as some were better athletes, some were better students. Because of this fact of nature, he argued, "we must learn to see the error in that superficial interpretation of democracy which assumes that all men are equal in intellectual ability. We must understand that in recognizing individual differences we are paying the truest homage to the worth of all individuals" (*Breaking* 11). To Aydelotte's way of thinking, then, it was undemocratic to treat all students the same. If education was to be effective, colleges must design programs that met the needs of all students while recognizing differences. "The end of democracy," he wrote in *Breaking*, "should not be to make men uniform, but rather to give them freedom to be individuals" (19). Therefore, the purpose of education in a democracy should not be to make students the same by taking the same courses and doing the same work; it should be to make students different by allowing them to follow their own interests, to develop their own powers, and to work to achieve their full potential. Aydelotte considered all education personal.

Aydelotte, however, conflated two issues. On the one hand, most progressive educators would agree that any curriculum should take individual interests of students into consideration. On the other, however, a program such as Aydelotte's gave such consideration primarily to a carefully selected social and intellectual elite by offering this group educational resources not available to their fellows. These resources included smaller classes, more attention, more interesting courses, more time to do their work. A more democratic approach would have been to give all students some of these benefits, a position that he rejected because he worked on the Oxford honors model which separated students into pass and honors.[6]

While he recognized the need to educate students of all ability levels, his primary interest as an administrator was in educating this elite, those that the current system, he believed, neglected. This goal was essential because bright students were future leaders. As he argued, echoing John Dewey, American democracy would work only if American education trained its "ablest young men and women...for ... leadership without which democracy cannot survive" (*Breaking* 11). In his "Inaugural Address" he alluded to De Tocqueville's "skepticism" concerning education in America. Because the nation was a democracy, it would be incapable, according to de Tocqueville, of "reaching ... the same high level of education and culture which is the glory of the older nations on the other side of the Atlantic" (*Breaking* 20). While Aydelotte feared that this weakness was a danger, he thought a solution existed: create more demanding programs for the ablest in order to produce leaders trained in the liberal arts and sciences and capable of solving the problems confronting the nation. All citizens would benefit from such leadership. If Aydelotte believed that one of the problems with American education was its assumption that all students were the same and should be treated so, he also saw two other, related problems. The first was the assumption that all college courses were of equal value, no matter what the subject matters, and the second, that the best way to organize knowledge was by means of the departmental system, a system that Aydelotte believed fragmented knowledge.

Regarding the first of these problems, Aydelotte rejected the notion that all courses were equal. This assumption had its birth to a large extent in the Harvard elective system developed by President Eliot. A reaction in part against the old, set curriculum of the 19th century, the elective system in its purest form did away with almost all requirements and allowed students to take whatever courses they wanted, no matter how incoherent their final programs of study might appear. At one point at Harvard, the only requirement was English A, freshman English. To graduate, students merely compiled enough course credits. While not all colleges adopted Harvard's elective system in its pure form, the system influenced the curriculums of most American colleges.

Aydelotte interpreted this tendency as asserting that all courses, no matter what their natures, were equally important. He rejected this assumption, especially for the small, liberal arts college. Instead of teaching all possible subjects, such colleges should teach the fundamental courses in the arts and sciences– English literature, philosophy, psychology, political science, the natural sciences, etc.– because these courses served as the basis for a liberal education. Having been influenced by Newman's views, Aydelotte believed that each discipline of the liberal arts provided a separate way to understand the world. Each one offered solutions to basic human problems and therefore performed an essential function in higher education. By taking these courses of study, students not only understood human problems but also learned methods for analyzing and writing about them.

Liberal arts courses therefore developed minds and characters while teaching students to think. These courses developed knowledge as opposed to information. They prepared students for a variety of careers rather than a particular one. Such courses Aydelotte opposed to practical ones, those that prepared students for a particular career by emphasizing what he dismissed as "useful technique." As he wrote in *Breaking*,

> [t]he essence of liberal education is the development of mental power and moral responsibility in each individual. It is based on the theory that each person is unique, that each deserves to have his own powers developed to the fullest possible extent–his intellect, his character, and his sensitiveness to beauty--as against merely learning some useful technique. (7-8)

If the goal of higher education was to educate each student liberally, Aydelotte assumed, colleges, especially small, liberal arts colleges, needed to offer only courses that contributed to the students' understanding of, to echo Arnold's famous phrase, the best that had been thought and said.[7]

Related closely to Aydelotte's suspicion of the elective system was his suspicion of the departmental system, which to him reflected the American college's view of knowledge. To Aydelotte, this system divided knowledge into arbitrary chunks that did not encourage students to connect subjects studied to other bodies of knowledge. During a typical semester, especially during their first two years, students normally took five different courses, which might range from English to history to biology to French to physical education. While each might be valuable in itself, no mechanism existed to help students see connections among them. In *Breaking*, Aydelotte compared this system of organizing knowledge to the Federal Reserve in that it assumed credits earned could be deposited in an academic bank to be saved for graduation; the process of accumulating credits mirrored the process of intellectual development. Aydelotte disagreed. "Intellectual values," he argued, "cannot be correctly represented by this system" (13). Actual learning took place within individuals as they made connections among bodies of knowledge, and effective educational systems, such as Oxford's, recognize that.[8]

Aydelotte proposed two related solutions. First, since each discipline, as Newman had argued, was a method of approaching reality, students needed to study a major discipline in depth to understand its methods and findings. Once they knew how to read on their own in one area by identifying the central texts and mastering them, they would be able to educate themselves in other areas. Aydelotte was adamant about this. Shirley Davis, a student of the class of 1935, remembers complaining to him that, because she could take only eight set honors seminars during her last two years, she could not explore other subjects in which she was interested as could students in an elective system. Aydelotte responded by reminding her that "[e]ducation does not end with college; you have your whole life ahead of you to broaden your horizons on your own. If you do not, then we have failed you in some general way" (Davis 138-39).

Second, not only did undergraduates need to understand a major subject in depth; they also needed to understand the relationship between the nature and methods of a primary discipline and those of other, closely-related disciplines. The student who majored in English literature would benefit from seeing connections among the primary field and other fields. Under the Swarthmore system, English majors usually studied English history and philosophy, taking most of their honors work in literature but supplementing that with work in two cognate fields.

The American course-and-credit system failed students, Aydelotte believed. It encouraged students to think that learning was a matter of following certain procedures of taking and passing courses. "Our academic requirements," Aydelotte argued in *Breaking*, "are too much concerned with processes, assuming that if the student goes through the motions [of compiling credits], he will get an education" (15). Such a system encouraged students to be passive learners who came to believe that learning is a matter of attending lectures and reading textbooks and taking examinations that often tested memory alone. For Aydelotte, actual learning was different. It was a matter of reading the essential works of a discipline on one's own and discussing them, not taking information in wholesale from a lecture or a textbook. A form of the great books approach therefore became central to the Swarthmore honors method. Swarthmore students read the classic texts of their disciplines to ground themselves in the field's fundamentals. They then supplemented this essential reading with collateral reading, much done on their own, at their own pace, following their own inclinations.

Aydelotte believed that American education had enormous problems. He also believed, however, that Oxford had found solutions. Instead of telling students how many credits they needed to graduate, Oxford told students what intellectual ground to cover (*Breaking* 15). Oxford accomplished this by asking students to read independently under a tutor to prepare for comprehensives. Students did not take courses to compile credits; they read a body of material, often during holidays, and used the time during terms to live the Oxford social and athletic life and to collect materials for more serious study on vacations. Students did not study a lone subject. Instead, if they were bright, they studied in one of the honors schools, such as the Modern Greats, which combined the fields of economics, history, political science, and modern languages. This combination of subjects, designed to prepare students for careers as teachers, administrators, and diplomats, helped the Oxford undergraduate see connections among disciplines. Each subject gave students a different way of understanding the world, and the combination of subjects provided students the liberal background needed to work in various careers.

Though Aydelotte himself had not taken a B.A. at Oxford, he had experienced the Oxford method while studying for his B.Litt. under Raleigh and Firth. The result of this collaboration had been his thesis, *Elizabethan Rogues and Vagabonds*, which combined historical and literary analysis to examine the degree to which Renaissance drama accurately reflected the reality of tramps and sharpers in Elizabethan life. Aydelotte wanted Swarthmore undergraduates to benefit from an education similar to the one he enjoyed at Oxford.

## Swarthmore's Honors Program

While Aydelotte modeled the Swarthmore Honors Program on the Oxford honors schools, he recognized that the Oxford system needed modification to meet American needs. He did not, therefore, dismantle the Swarthmore departments, which remained those one would normally find in a small liberal arts college, nor did he jettison for all students the course-and-credit system. In fact, students at Swarthmore took a fairly standard freshman and sophomore curriculum, and students not in the honors program, the "pass" students, continued a traditional American undergraduate education based on the course-and-credit method. However, Aydelotte developed a junior-senior honors program that introduced fundamental changes to the American college. This system, especially the honors seminar, became the model for American honors programs across the nation.

The first major change was to create "honors divisions" that combined at least three related subjects from three different departments into a program of study. This concept became central to the Swarthmore method (Swarthmore College Faculty 29). Honors students majoring in English literature, for instance, normally studied in that Division which combined the study of literature with the study of English history and philosophy. As literature majors, students would concentrate most heavily, about half their time, on English literature while spending about a quarter of their time each on history and philosophy. In terms of seminars, students would take four literature seminars during their last two years. They would also take two history and two philosophy seminars coordinated with the literature seminars. An unpublished typescript entitled "Required Work for Students Reading for Honors in English" for 1924-25 outlines the relationship between the three subjects. That year, students were to read English literature, history, and philosophy from the late 18th to the end of the 19th century. During the junior year, students in the English section would take two seminars in which they read a general survey of English literature of the period, studied selected works by about 30 major British authors, and did intensive work on individual writers to link their work "with the history and philosophy of the period." Meanwhile, students also took a history seminar that included the reading of Trevelyan's *British History of the Nineteenth Century* and other such standard works plus "intensive study" of major historical movements, such as the French and Industrial Revolutions, for presentation and discussion. The philosophy seminar, which students would take after finishing the one on history, covered the same period, emphasizing a survey of philosophical thought and a study of major philosophical movements "with reports and discussions." These movements included rationalism, empiricism, utilitarianism, pragmatism, evolution, German Idealism, and relativity. By studying these three areas, students would develop a sophisticated understanding of 19th-century British literature and thought, the same goal that Aydelotte had tried to achieve through MIT's English-History program.

This system addressed one of Aydelotte's major criticisms of American education, its tendency to fragment knowledge through unrelated courses. By concentrating the lion's share of their time on their primary area, they came to understand the methods of that discipline. By concentrating on three related liberal disciplines, a student mastered their methods but also made connections among the major area and the two secondary ones. In 1922-23, the first two honors divisions were established, Political Science and English Literature.

Second, Aydelotte rejected for honors students the traditional course-and-credit system to measure a student's progress. Oxford accomplished this measurement through the tutorial system, in which each student worked through reading lists with and wrote papers for a tutor. The tutor's responsibility was to prepare students for the comprehensive examination and to keep track of their intellectual progress. While Aydelotte admired the tutorial system, he rejected it at Swarthmore for two reasons. First, like many effective teaching methods, it was too expensive. While the most prestigious British universities were highly selective, educating a small percentage of the population, Aydelotte realized that American schools must continue educating a larger group. Since the same instructors who taught honors students would continue lecturing to regular students, it was financially unfeasible to institute tutorials. Second, American professors lacked experience with the tutorial system and were not prepared to use it.[9] They were, however, familiar with the graduate seminar, which they could modify for the undergraduate.

The seminar placed a small group of students, as few as three and as many as ten, with a faculty member to study a particular issue in a field.[10] Since these seminars met just once a week, students had ample time to read on their own. Since the seminars were small, instructors could track progress and give each student individual attention. The seminar had the additional advantage of encouraging discussion, an element central to all of Aydelotte's programs.

Third, Aydelotte rejected the traditional methods of testing knowledge with quizzes and examinations. These methods, he believed, encouraged students to memorize "tidbits of knowledge which they immediately forget" (*Honors Courses* 5). Students never transformed information into knowledge. In place of the quiz-and-test system, Aydelotte set up a more open system of teaching and testing students. In the seminars, instructors usually gave students a reading list of the material the seminar would cover. Students were expected to read this material largely on their own; they were also expected to read additional material as they had time. But they were freed from the "lockstep" of attending regular courses and lectures (unless they wanted to) and completing daily class work, including quizzes and examinations. At the end of their two years of honors work, they took a series of comprehensive examinations that tested their knowledge of the seminar material. As at Oxford, these examinations were given by outside examiners, experts in the areas who taught at other colleges and universities.

Writing played a central role in both the honors seminars and the comprehensive examinations. In the classic liberal arts seminars, in fact, student essays formed the basis of the entire method (science seminars were handled differently since students spent time in the laboratory conducting experiments). In the examinations, the outside examiners based their judgments of students first on written answers before giving them follow-up orals. Consequently, to be successful, honors students had to write well. To understand the role of writing in the seminar and the examination, it is necessary to understand in more detail how the two worked.

## The Honors Seminar

One of Swarthmore's contributions to American education was the honors seminar, a method that has become standard in many honors programs. Aydelotte did not develop this method alone; it grew out of consultations with the faculty.

During his first year, Aydelotte met with a group of Swarthmore members of the American Association of University Professors who agreed with the educational principles he had articulated in his inaugural address and wanted to implement them immediately. Aydelotte set up the necessary committees and initiated the process of designing the Honors Program. The idea of the honors seminar came out of the committees. Two excellent teachers, Professors Robert C. Brooks from Political Science and Jesse Holmes from Philosophy, ran trial seminars during the spring semester of 1922. They discovered that the seminars had an important advantage over the tutorial: the seminars, which functioned as peer groups, encouraged student discussion and the critique of papers. In other words, the seminars, unlike the traditional Oxford tutorial, added a social dimension to the instruction which Aydelotte and the Swarthmore faculty viewed as essential. These first two seminars were successful and functioned as the models for the actual honors seminars when they began in 1922-23 (Blanshard 189).

In some ways, the Swarthmore honors seminars were similar to the Princeton preceptorial system that Woodrow Wilson developed around 1905. As Wilson described it in 1910, this system, like Swarthmore's, placed a small group of students with a faculty member to work through a body of reading so that students could experience methods "as direct, as simple, as individual as those long employed in the laboratories of the sciences" (385). Like the Swarthmore seminars, students met in preceptorials not to be tested but to discuss and develop a deeper understanding of the reading (386). The Princeton system threw students and teachers together in "close association," which, according to Wilson, "is the only means of intellectual contagion" (386). The major difference between the preceptorial and the honors seminar was the emphasis placed on writing, which was not an important component of Wilson's program.

In 1915 Charles G. Osgood, a Princeton English professor, also discussed the preceptorials but expressed the liberal culturalists' suspicion of teaching writing. The preceptorials on English literature, Osgood argued, attempt to make "a living connection between the literature and the student" (233-34). The purpose was to use literature to work a change in the student's character. Osgood allowed writing to play only a subordinate role in the preceptorial when he asserted that composition at most should be used to "supplement" the method because composition can "serve to define impressions, to make occasions for the student to pursue some inquiry or subject of special interest, to formulate or test [the student's] ideas more deliberately than can be done in conference, to seize and appropriate what he has gained by the discussion" (234). The major difference, then, between Wilson's preceptorial and Aydelotte's honors seminar was that Aydelotte made writing central, not subordinate, to the learning process. The seminar made student writing the basis of discussion.

While the Swarthmore honors seminar also shared some similarities to Columbia's Great Books program John Erskine started in 1920, the two programs had different aims. In his Columbia program, Erskine had students read the great books, mostly works of literature considered world classics, and meet on Wednesday nights for small group discussions. According to Erskine, the purpose was not to give students a scholarly knowledge of the books but a "reading acquaintance" with them (*My Life* 166). Erskine in fact claimed that the classics were once best sellers and that students should read them as such (166). The purpose of the program was a liberal culture one, as Erskine made clear in *The*

*Memory of Certain Persons*. By reading a common body of classic work students would come to share "the true scholarly and culture basis of human understanding and communication" (343). Aydelotte, on the other hand, introduced honors students to the intellectual life and to the fundamentals of their academic disciplines. While English majors read classic literature, they also read the seminal scholarly works in their fields, and then by supplementing that basic reading with more recent scholarship, students grounded themselves intellectually and academically in their professional literature. As did the Princeton preceptorial method, the Columbia program differed from the Swarthmore program in one final important way. Erskine required no writing, only discussion; Aydelotte, on the other hand, made writing essays the center of the honors method.

The honors seminar gradually evolved. By 1939, Aydelotte's last year on campus at Swarthmore, it had, according to the Swarthmore College Faculty, the following general characteristics. It met once a week for fourteen weeks with only occasional additional meetings, usually near the end of the semester if the seminar fell behind in its work. Each seminar met for three to five hours, depending on the quality of the discussion. Generally seminars with more "brilliant" honors students met longer than seminars with more average students. Meetings lasted as long as the discussion did. The seminars did not meet at scheduled times but met at a time mutually convenient to the professor and participants. The number of students varied from about three to ten, with the ideal number being four to six. To avoid overcrowding, most divisions preferred to open a second seminar on a topic if the first one filled up. This was done to keep the group small enough to encourage discussion. For the first few years, two faculty members from different departments conducted the seminars. After the system had been firmly established and the faculty familiar with it, a single faculty member taught the seminar. The seminars were always opened to visitors, including observers from other schools, Swarthmore students considering honors, other faculty members, and any other groups interested in witnessing the method. In the early days of the program, seminars often met not on campus but at professors' houses, where refreshments were served (82-84).

In terms of technique, professors handled seminars differently. Dorothy Canfield Fisher, a visiting writer, sat in on three honors seminars in the late 1920s and described each. In the first, an older professor working with four or five students ran the session as a "glorified bull session" (53) with little set form. In the second, which discussed the Sherman Antitrust Act, the teacher provided more direction by starting with a brief lecture before opening the seminar for discussion. Fisher was impressed by the way the professor handled a student question concerning how the professor could claim knowledge about what the Supreme Court thought on the issue. The professor answered by quoting from court decisions but then remarked that he realized he had biases and encouraged students to read opposing arguments. This strategy encouraged students to think independently and to question all positions, including the professor's. The third seminar, on ethics, brought a few students together with a nationally-known philosopher. Instead of lecturing, the professor, despite his depth of knowledge, led a discussion. Fisher commented in purple prose on the importance of the experience:

> After half an hour of listening to the intimate intellectual give-and-take between the mature, experienced mind of the professor and the questing young spirits I had an almost mystical vision of those conventionally dressed young people, not as faces and hands and collars and silk stockings but as living fires. I saw them flickering and smoking, flaring up in brilliant flashes of intuition, their boldest, richest flames blown about helplessly by their inexperience, while with care and patience the older man went about the business of trimming and shaping them into clarity and steadiness. (56)

Fisher concluded that the seminar system was "one of the greatest forward steps ever taken by education in this country—equally great . . . for students and professors" (56).

While different instructors used different strategies, there existed what the Swarthmore College Faculty termed "the typical humanities seminar," which made student writing central. In order to generate and sustain discussion, the instructor assigned for each meeting a "minimum [amount] of required reading." This common reading provided the necessary background knowledge for the meeting's discussion. In addition to this reading list, students were often given a list of extra "collateral reading" which they could do as time permitted. Along with the reading lists, the instructor gave out a list of paper topics, which would develop "the most significant aspects of the material under consideration" (96). Depending on the size of the seminar and the desires of the instructor, students prepared papers either once a week or once every two weeks. While the instructor might make opening comments, the bulk of the meeting was spent discussing the papers, which the student authors usually read aloud, often after providing seminar members with outlines or copies. The instructor usually encouraged all students to critique the papers and discuss the issues raised (96).

As Aydelotte makes clear in his "Honors Courses in American Colleges and Universities," like the papers at Oxford, the Swarthmore papers were an essential part of the honors method. As at Oxford, where the only set requirement was for students to meet once a week with their tutor to read a paper, at Swarthmore the "only instruction that is absolutely ironclad" was that students attend their seminars once a week and "write a paper or some kind of a report on the work . . . done during the week" (60). Again following the Oxford system, Aydelotte insisted that honors students enjoy complete "freedom in the preparation of their papers" (60). The instructor referred students to the reading material and assigned them a general topic, but the student decided what to emphasize and how much ground to cover. Despite this freedom, Aydelotte was convinced that students invariably worked hard and made the right decisions on coverage, emphasis, and focus. He was "perfectly amazed at the trustworthiness of these students" (60) to write strong papers without specific guidance.

Since the papers reflected the students' interests and efforts, Aydelotte viewed them as the most accurate sign of intellectual progress. He writes in *Honors Courses*, "we know from these papers, week by week, far more accurately how they [the students] are progressing intellectually than we do about ordinary students" (60) who take quizzes and examinations. The papers also benefitted students. By writing them, the students crystalized "ideas in [their] own mind[s]," becoming in the process more precise thinkers. The papers also developed the students' "powers of expression," helping them become better writers (15). For Aydelotte, then, the importance of the papers was to help students develop intellectually and rhetorically, and to provide an accurate measure of that development.

Few listings of paper assignments are extant, but these few give a good idea of the papers that the English faculty assigned and the roles these papers played in the seminars. In the fall semester of 1923, a seminar meeting on October 22 covered Chaucer's *Troilus and Criseyde*. In addition to reading the work, students did "supplementary reading": Boccaccio's "Philostrata," Shakespeare's *Troilus and Cressida*, and either George Lyman Kittridge's *Chaucer and His Poetry* or William George Dodd's *Courtly Love in Chaucer and Gower*. The instructor designed the supplementary reading to do two things. The two literary works were treatments of Troilus and Criseyde in later literature to compare with Chaucer's. The Kittridge and Dodd books, both standard discussions of Chaucer, provided critical backgrounds. Students were to read more critical work of their choosing.

The papers written for the meeting drew in different ways on this supplementary reading. Miss Knapp presented "The System of Courtly Love in Medieval Literature," an overview of its topic. Mr. Muth read a similarly broad paper, "The Background and Setting of 'Troilus and Criseyde.'" Miss Liberton wrote a comparative paper on Troilus in Boccaccio, Chaucer, and Shakespeare, and Miss Swartzlander wrote a parallel paper on Criseyde as did Miss Gowing on Pandarus. Miss Krusen wrote an evaluation entitled "Is 'Troilus and Criseyde' the Greatest Narrative Poem in the English Language?" and Mr. Abell wrote on the poem's contribution to English literature.

In the spring semester of 1924, these same students took another seminar, which included a January 7 meeting covering Thomas More's *Utopia* and Sidney's *An Apology for Poetry* ("Honors Readings"). The instructor required the students to read these works (no supplementary reading is listed on the typescript for the class) and then write on central issues. As the paper titles show, the seven essays discussed the works in light of other fields, especially philosophy. Miss Muth wrote "Theories of Education in the *Utopia* and in Plato's *Republic*"; Mr. Abell, "Theories of Government in the *Utopia* and in Plato's *Republic*"; Miss Swartzlander, "Theories of Communism in the *Utopia* and in Plato's *Republic*"; Miss Kruzer, "Family Life in the *Utopia* and the *Republic*"; Miss Liberton, "Social Abuses and their Remedies in the *Utopia* (Part I)"; Miss Knapp, "Tragedy and Comedy in Sidney, Horace and Aristotle"; and Miss Cowing, "The Problems of Versification in Sidney, Horace and Aristotle." The titles suggest that papers varied in method and approach. The first four papers connect various elements of More's work with *The Republic* and suggest that the students were more than passingly familiar with Plato. They had probably read Plato in a coordinated philosophy seminar. The assignments required students to use comparison/contrast to address four central ideas in the *Utopia* as they relate to *The Republic*. The last two papers, those on tragedy and comedy and on versification, are more traditional literary papers, although both required students to apply Horace's and Aristotle's literary theories to Sidney. The fifth paper, which was on social abuses and remedies in the *Utopia*, seems less a study in either the history of ideas or the history of literary theory than a close reading of More.

Three elements are worth noting about the seminar method. First, because students had read a common body of background material, and had taken a philosophy seminar together, there existed in the meetings common ground for discussing papers. Sometimes this material consisted of other pieces of literature which the writers could compare for discussion. Other times the material was critical theory, literary history, or philosophy. The theory was either classic works such as Aristotle's *Poetics* or Plato's *Republic* that influenced the work at hand or contemporary criticism, such as Kittridge and Dodd, which provided a contemporary critical perspective. In either case, all students had read the core material that provided a common body of knowledge from which to discuss the literature.

Second, many of the paper topics required specific rhetorical strategies. The most common was comparison/contrast that Miss Liberton applied to her discussion of Troilus in Boccaccio, Chaucer, and Shakespeare or Miss Swartzlander to communism in Plato and More. In all such assignments, students brought together two or more bodies of material to illuminate both. Students practiced other strategies. In her paper on courtly love, Miss Knapp must have defined and exemplified this concept. When arguing whether or not *Troilus and Criseyde* was the greatest narrative poem in English, Miss Krusen evaluated the poem's effectiveness in achieving its end and compared it with other poems of its type.

Third, most of the papers required students to address significant ideas in the works. Few topics permitted writers to analyze the work's form without addressing content. Even Miss Gowing's paper on problems of versification in Sidney, Horace, and Aristotle required comparison and critique of the theories of versification. And the character analyses of Troilus, Criseyde, and Pandarus required the students to compare the significance of the three characters in their three works.

Although Aydelotte did not encourage explicit instruction in rhetoric, the seminar method itself was based on sound rhetorical principles. First, since students read a common body of material, they had a clear intellectual context from which to write. This context, along with the instructor's help, provided writers with a set of rhetorical problems that their papers explored. Second, students had a clear reason for writing. They were to research a central issue and write a paper to inform the seminar about the results. Since the findings were important to the education of all seminar members, the papers received careful scrutiny, and students read the papers later to study for the comprehensive examinations. Third, the student writers had a clearly defined audience—the other members of the seminar, as well as the instructor. Because of the clear rhetorical situation, students must have found the papers rewarding to write and present, and the audience must have found them valuable, if for no other reason than papers prepared students for the comprehensive examinations. Thus, even though Aydelotte rejected explicit instruction in rhetoric, rhetoric was built into the instruction.

## The Examinations for Honors

Writing also played a crucial role in the honors examinations. Aydelotte modeled these on Oxford's final examinations, which furnished "the real moral force behind the informal methods of undergraduate instruction" (Crosby "Oxford System" 51). In the Oxford honors schools, students took the examination at the end of two or three years of work. As L. A. Crosby comments, "The standard character of the examinations is such as to promote a thoroughness and accuracy in preparation and study which is often absent from undergraduate work in American universities" (51). Since the first part of the examinations were written, they valued effective writing. While at Oxford, Aydelotte came to see the value of such examinations for undergraduates.

Aydelotte viewed the comprehensive examination as a method to bring intellectual rigor to the honors program. In his 1923-24 "Report of the President," he justified the new examination to the students, alumni, and Board of Managers as a break from traditional college life, which overemphasized the social. In the past, seniors had been excused from June examinations so that they could partake of the Senior Play and other commencement activities. This system, Aydelotte believed, privileged the social over the intellectual and contributed to Swarthmore's anti-intellectualism. His compromise was to require seniors to take examinations but to hold these examinations earlier so that students could still participate in commencement (8).

The primary curricular purpose of the examinations was to make certain that students mastered the seminar material. As Aydelotte wrote, the examinations and the seminars, the two major elements of the program, provided respectively "the severity and the freedom" and were "the heart of the thing" ("Honors Courses in American Colleges" 64). The examinations added the discipline to encourage students to work regularly because they knew they would be rigorously tested at the end. In the Commencement Number of the *Swarthmore College Bulletin* for 1924, Aydelotte argued that the examinations by outside examiners provided "the strongest proof of the sincerity of the standards by which our honors work is measured" (20). As Brooks put it succinctly, the examinations made the work "*more dangerous*" and thus more significant (*Reading* 54; italics in original). It was dangerous because students were responsible for organizing large bodies of information in three different areas in preparation for the examinations.

One of Swarthmore's primary innovations was the outside examiners. Standard in England for many years, they had rarely if ever been used in the United States. Aydelotte had originally proposed that each division employ three examiners, two outsiders and one Swarthmore faculty member. The faculty decided, however, to engage three outside examiners because having an examiner who knows neither the students nor their work had advantages ("Honors Courses in American Colleges and Universities" 60). First, the student could not flatter the professor to get a better grade. Since the professor no longer possessed the power of grading, students developed a different relationship with teachers, who became coaches preparing their charges for examinations. Second, the students did not worry that the professor might have formed a "preconceived idea" of a student. Since the outside examiner had not met the students before the oral examination, they could be assured their work would receive an unbiased review (Swarthmore College Faculty 109).

The honors faculty enjoyed benefits but also shouldered new responsibilities. Since they no longer held the power of the grade, their relationship with the students and the atmosphere of the honors seminar changed. As a Swarthmore faculty member wrote in *Adventure*, "Student and instructor can work together for a single end: the best method of mastering a given field of knowledge" (110). As Dean John Clark Jordon of the University of Arkansas concluded in a 1926 letter to that school's president, J. C. Futrall, after observing the examinations, the process shifted emphasis from the instructor to the subject matter. The faculty member becomes an older, more experienced scholar (Jordon calls him a "companion") there to "stimulate and guide" students (Swarthmore College Faculty 110). This new relationship created an atmosphere of informality and openness of discussion and work upon which visitors such as Jordon often commented (110).

Faculty members also felt the responsibility to design seminars that prepared students for the examinations. Faculty could neither teach only their pet interests nor cover material partially. They felt obligated to prepare students by exploring the seminar reading thoroughly and fairly. In a sense, the outside examiner tested the faculty as well as the students because students' doing poorly on the examinations reflected on the professors' knowledge and methods (111). The examination system also encouraged the professors to keep up with their fields so that they could train their students in recent research (111).

Swarthmore chose its outside examiners carefully. While the examiners should be specialists in their fields, they should not be so highly specialized or so committed to graduate education that they had lost touch with undergraduate instruction (111). This requirement was necessary because the purpose of the honors program was not to train research specialists but "to encourage high quality college work" (111). In order to prevent the outside examiners from going stale, Swarthmore rotated them systematically to introduce fresh points of view. No examiner was invited more than three years in a row, and each Division invited one new examiner each year to replace one who had served for a year or two (112).

Typically, for each student the examiners received from the heads of departments a syllabus and reading list of the material covered in each seminar taken. The examiners used these lists to create the questions for the writtens (113). The examiners usually framed about seven to ten questions designed to test the students' knowledge of material covered. A few examples from the 1925 examination gives a sense of the kinds of questions asked ("Honors Examinations–1925"). One group of questions requires students to address the relationship among literature, history, and philosophy, as this question shows: "In what respects are literature, philosophy, and history similar disciplines? In what respects dissimilar?" Other questions are on literary topics, such as "What seems to have been Shakespeare's concept of tragedy and the tragic hero?" A representative question for a seminar on ancient and medieval philosophy is "'Socrates was the greatest of the Sophists.' What truth and what error do you find in this statement?" Finally, a sample history question is "What part was played by the middle classes in the Wars of the Roses?" Even this small sample suggests that the questions were demanding and required students to understand the seminar material in depth. Most questions, however, do not require simple restatement of fact; they require students to write an answer that contains original thought.

Examiners then forwarded the questions to Swarthmore, where the students sat for the examinations, writing seven to eight three-hour papers over a week's time (Spiller "Ten Years" 313). Consistent with Aydelotte's commitment to stimulating thought, the best questions demanded that students provide more than factual information. Swarthmore faculty members viewed "those questions most successful which call[ed] for a use of facts to form deductions or syntheses, and not mere statements of fact" (Swarthmore College Faculty 114). As Aydelotte put it in his 1923-24 "Report of the President," these examinations should be a "more flexible, less pedantic" measurement of the "ability and grasp of the subject as well as [one's] memory for details" (7). A student could not slip through the examination by restating an instructor's opinions; instead, the student must demonstrate independent thought and mastery of material (Aydelotte "Honors Work and Graduate Study" [104]). Only occasionally did Swarthmore ask an examiner to revise examination questions; this usually only happened when an inexperienced examiner misunderstood the nature of the seminar material (Swarthmore College Faculty 114).

After the written examinations, the student took an oral examination given by the same outside examiners. This phase allowed the examiners to gain a deeper understanding of the students' knowledge. In the oral, the student "should demonstrate an ability to discuss the subject [of the written examination] in such a way as to show that this knowledge had become a vital part of his intellectual equipment" (115). The oral examination and the preparation for it also encouraged students to develop the "power of graceful cogent discourse," an art most American undergraduates never master (Brooks *Reading* 60). In some departments, panels of examiners conducted the orals; in others, students met with individual examiners (Swarthmore College Faculty 116). After the orals, the examiners in different fields met to discuss the students' performances in all areas and the degree that each student should receive. Students could receive, according to the 1931 *Catalogue of Swarthmore College*, either "honors, high honors, or highest honors" (44). If a set of papers was not good enough for honors, it was returned to the student's division, where the papers were read and the student was given an oral examination to determine if he could receive a "degree in course," a regular B.A. (44), or if he should do more work over the summer and be retested (Aydelotte *Breaking* 41). The determinations of the external examiners had never been overturned even when the Swarthmore faculty disagreed with the decisions (Swarthmore College Faculty 117), although starting in 1927, members of the Swarthmore faculty could meet with the examiners to discuss decisions (Brooks *Reading* 62n).

Swarthmore carefully prepared its honors students for the examinations. The seminar method, with its emphasis on extensive reading, regular writing, and rhetorical critique, went far in readying students for writtens. Honors students in their junior year also took practice examinations, which their Swarthmore instructors critiqued rigorously. The give-and-take of discussion in the seminars prepared students to take the orals, and, starting in 1927, juniors sat in on the oral examinations of seniors to prepare for their own (Brooks *Reading* 50-51).

## Changes in Writing Instruction, 1922-1939

The role of writing instruction at Swarthmore gradually changed under Aydelotte. In *Breaking*, he noted that as the honors program developed, "formal training in English composition has come to have a smaller and smaller place, and many students get none at all" (171). To understand the changes in writing instruction at Swarthmore, we must first understand what writing courses the English Department offered before Aydelotte arrived in 1922. As the 1921 *Swarthmore College Bulletin* demonstrates, the Department considered writing courses important. According to the Department's purpose statement, which remained in the bulletin for several years after Aydelotte arrived, "The purpose of the work in English is to impart the ability to write clear, forceful, idiomatic English, and to arouse and foster love of good literature" (53). The language implies that the Department assumed writing instruction should emphasize control of the elements of Harvard formalism—especially clarity and diction. Since the *Bulletin* does not mention the importance of thought or content, it is safe to assume that Aydelotte, with his commitment to teaching students to think in prose about significant issues, would have found at least some of the English Department assumptions debatable. It is also worth noting that Aydelotte probably would have objected to the Department's assumptions about literature instruction. The description emphasizes that students should learn to appreciate, not to think about, literature.

The pre-Aydelotte department emphasized writing and offered five writing courses of various kinds. The first was a standard freshman English course, English 1, "Composition," a course "[p]rescribed in the Freshman year, for all candidates for graduation. Short and long themes and regular conferences throughout the Freshman year, emphasis being placed upon expository writing" (53). English 2, the more advanced sophomore course, had two versions. Version A, titled "Second Year Composition," taught expository writing, and version B was a journalism course (53). The next course in the sequence, English 3, also had two versions. English 3(a), "Narrative Writing," taught the short story to students who had received As or Bs in their previous writing classes. English 3(b), "Poetics and Literary Criticism," emphasized the theory and practice of critical method (54). Students studied a few key literary texts and learned to write critical papers.

Thus, prior to Aydelotte's arrival, the English Department taught expository, creative, and critical writing. However, Aydelotte soon began effecting changes in the writing courses. The first of these appeared in the third year he was at Swarthmore. The *Swarthmore College Catalogue* for 1923-24 shows a course paralleling English 1(b) (the old "Composition") entitled English 1(a) "English and Engineering." As the description makes clear, this course was modeled on Aydelotte's second semester freshman course from MIT:

> A course in composition for engineering students in the Freshman year based upon the theory that the function of English in technical education is two-fold: To train the student to write by first training him to think; to stimulate his thought by directing his attention to problems of the profession of engineering and the relation between engineering and literature. (58)

It is hard to fathom why Aydelotte started revamping the writing courses by introducing the engineering writing course. It looks out of place in the listing since Swarthmore was not a technical but a liberal arts college (although it did have a small engineering program). Unlike all the other courses, "English and Engineering" lists no instructor, suggesting that nobody on the English faculty was qualified to teach it. Aydelotte was qualified, of course, but as a new president, he had little time to teach, especially during his first few years when he had to sell the honors course to students, alumni/ae, and funding agencies. The fact that the course disappeared from the *Bulletin* in one year suggests that Aydelotte's first attempt to introduce the thought approach at Swarthmore sputtered.

By 1928, however, Aydelotte began making more substantive though no more permanent changes in the writing offerings. The most significant of these was his revamping of the old English 1 course. That course now became "Freshman English," a course similar to his English 2A at IU. As he had at that school, he combined two courses, the freshman composition course and the Department's old required freshman survey of English literature, which had for years been titled

"General Introduction to English Literature," a year-long "rapid survey" (54). "Freshman English," now redefined tersely in the 1928 *Bulletin* as "A general introduction to literature and composition" (73), used Aydelotte's thought approach to teach students to think and write about significant pieces of literature. The new literary survey course, now English 4, "Survey of English Literature," also reflected the thought approach, as its description shows: "A review of the history of English *thought* and literature from Anglo-Saxon times to the present. Required of English majors and a prerequisite to honors work in English; elective for all others"(74) (italics mine) . Two elements are important in this change. First, the course no longer surveyed the literary genres by means of "rapid" reading; it was now a review of English "thought," a key Aydelotte term. Second, it was no longer a course required of all freshmen, but only of students hoping to enter the honors course in English or to major in the subject. These two elements suggest that the course was more demanding and more thorough than the previous freshman course in its attempt to ground students in literature, philosophy, and history, the three related elements in the English Literature Division.

In 1928, students could still take a significant number of additional writing courses. English 2(a) and 2(b) were a creative writing course and a journalism course respectively. English 3(a) (oddly no 3[b] existed) remained a course in writing short stories. Starting in 1929, however, writing courses began disappearing from the course listings. In that year, English 3 was dropped, and the purpose statement emphasizing the teaching of writing as an important departmental function appeared for the last time. In the *Bulletin* for 1930-31, English 1 became an introduction-to-English course with no stated emphasis on writing, and English 4, the survey of English thought course, was renumbered English 2. By 1933, all writing courses had been expunged from the curriculum. English 1, now retitled "Representative Writers," became the introductory freshman course. This course consisted of a list of period courses–the Renaissance, the Eighteenth Century, American Literature, etc.–from which freshmen were required to take two for the year. Although students wrote papers in the courses, no mention of writing instruction appeared in the description. This absence suggests the degree to which writing instruction had been displaced from the freshman sequence. The representative-writers approach remained the freshman requirement for the remainder of Aydelotte's tenure at Swarthmore.

Under Aydelotte, then, Swarthmore's English Department went through three distinct shifts in its writing offerings. First, when Aydelotte arrived, the Department defined the teaching of writing–expository, creative, and critical–as central to its mission and offered courses in all. Second, the Department integrated Aydelotte's thought approach into its curriculum, developing the short-lived "English and Engineering" and then the IU-like "Freshman English." Third, the Department expunged all writing courses from the curriculum. A member of the class of 1929, James A. Michener, the best-selling novelist, pointed to one justification for this. "Swarthmore in those days," he noted, "held, and rightly so I now think, that it was not the College's responsibility to teach specific skills, either typewriting or fancy writing" (84). Michener might be misremembering or perhaps exaggerating because some writing courses remained on the books during the 1920s, but he certainly accurately identified the trend of dismantling the writing program that was underway. The second justification was that the honors seminars, which required students to write and critique papers, and the writing in regular classes as well, took the place of writing courses, especially on the advanced level (*Bulletin* 1936-37, 77).

In *Breaking the Academic Lockstep*, Aydelotte addressed the question of writing instruction, justifying the dropping of writing courses because students no longer needed them. The honors students were "picked students, and superior individuals" who used "better English, on the whole, whether specifically trained in it or not" (171). In other words, these students were from the social elite and could already write well. But his main justification was that the students wrote extensively for their seminars, and the papers were critiqued by all participants "for style as well as content" (171). He went on to note, however, that these papers were written to be read, and consequently sounded good when presented. "They are natural, spontaneous, and not self-conscious," Aydelotte claimed. But, he continued, they were "sometimes careless as to structure; they have the strength and weakness of writing which is intended to be read aloud" (171). While Aydelotte concluded that the seminar method allowed the professors to improve student writing more effectively than did "'pure' composition" courses, one has to wonder what kind of specific rhetorical criticisms students received (171).

That depended on how individual professors used papers in the seminars. At least four distinct methods existed. The first and probably most common was to ask students to read their papers aloud to the group, which then critiqued the papers for content and style. Because papers were read aloud and listeners had no copy to read, this method allowed for little minute textual analysis. But since the students had read a shared body of work upon which all papers were based, these discussions could be specific, at least about the argument and content. After student critiques, the professor, Brooks noted in *Reading for Honors*, could then critique papers and require revisions "in whole or in part" for content, expression, or both (37). The second method, which was used especially in seminars that required many papers, was to have students circulate copies of papers among seminar participants before or in place of formal delivery (Swarthmore College Faculty 98). This method would allow for more specific critiques of the prose. The third method, recommended by Professor Frederick Manning of the History Department, was to require students to turn papers in to the professor for evaluation before delivery (4), a method that would also allow for the teacher's detailed critiquing of prose. The fourth and least common method, developed by the Department of Philosophy, did not require students to read their papers to their fellows for discussion at all but to turn in the papers to the professor for individual critiques (Swarthmore College Faculty 98). This method, unlike the first three, diminished the importance of the papers to the discussions themselves.[11]

The most detailed discussion of the role writing played in the seminars and how it was critiqued appears in Robert C. Brooks's 1926 essay published in the *Association of American Colleges Bulletin*. A political science professor, one of the two instructors who taught the initial honors seminars, and a vocal supporter of Aydelotte's reforms, Brooks played a major role in developing Swarthmore's Honors Program. As his essay makes clear, he viewed writing, especially writing about the assigned reading, as one of the central activities of honors. Students did not read textbooks, which would give them pre-digested information. Instead, honors students read classic, book-length studies in their fields. Since these classic studies were usually dated, the purpose of students' papers was to update these studies through "collateral" reading of newer books and journal articles. Each paper, therefore, "would represent from three to four weeks' work.... In this way the habit of dealing with books as a whole is one which is cultivated in honest work" (195). As Brooks makes clear, the papers were critiqued carefully in the seminars. Read aloud, the paper must "be written in good English" (195) and follow the conventions of academic logic. Both students and instructor critiqued the paper for its expression. "We are continually on the lookout," Brooks comments, "for generalizations that are too sweeping, for rhetoric that is too fine, for vague, ambiguous, question-begging words or phrases like 'higher,' 'lower,' 'more democratic,' 'less democratic,' and our old friend, 'to a certain extent'" (195). Brooks particularly emphasized that he required students to define all terms, especially unusual words (195).

Brooks also argued that the papers helped teach students to think critically. One skill they learned, since they could not include all of their research in the paper, was to distinguish "between details and general principles" (195). While the papers of juniors were usually too long, by the time students were seniors, they had learned "to subordinate details and to deal with the broader principles involved" (195). They also learned "to constantly make comparisons" between systems of thought and subjects of study, this ability to compare being one of Aydelotte's valued methods of thought. Finally, students learned to "draw conclusions," and these conclusions formed the basis of most of the discussion during seminar meetings. As did Aydelotte, Brooks appreciated the fact that these discussions continued in the dormitories, often drawing in "ordinary undergraduates who hear[d] the honor students discussing these fascinating and elusive topics" (195).

Whichever method of evaluation was most common, indications exist that all was not well with student writing, even in the honors program. A steady trickle of criticism can be found about its quality from a variety of sources, including Aydelotte himself. In a December 5, 1925, critique of honors work in general, Manning, formerly of Yale but by then a member of Swarthmore's History Department, lambasted the quality of writing in the honors seminars. After criticizing the honors students for not doing their work adequately, he turned to their writing:

> Much of their present work, moreover, is made almost worthless in consequence of their misunderstanding of the purpose of written papers.

Each student writes a paper once a month in history, three other papers being written in other subjects [in other seminars] in the intervening weeks. I find that they [the students] invariably leave this work for the two or three days preceding the meeting at which they are to read the paper, which is often written that morning; and that despite all their good resolutions they do not read history in the other three weeks. This means that they attempt the impossible, absurd task of studying history in seven or eight crams a year at four week intervals. They take the special assignments for papers, given to help them focus their own work, as mysteriously efficacious substitutes for the work itself. They assume that they can learn history by listening to other papers, an assumption that an indifferently written ten-minute paper can accomplish the task for which a well-written volume may be inadequate. They make fetishes out of these papers. They regard them as conventional "assignments" covering the greater part of what they need to do, and I suspect that they come to regard the system as giving them a vested right of monthly accountability only, in philosophy and history at least. But two years of monthly crams culminating in a nerve-racking grand cram for examinations will never teach them history and philosophy, not if they had an hour with Thucydides and Socrates themselves every fortnight! ... I can only conclude that they have not been compelled to form habits of consistent work, and consistent expression of that work in writing. (1-2)

While Manning's criticisms are leveled as much at the honors system as at the quality of student writing, he does make some points about the writing itself suggesting that the students needed more instruction. First of all, they left the papers to the last minute rather than working on them over a period of time. Second, probably because of the first reason, the papers themselves were "indifferently written" (1), in part, Manning claims, because students had not been trained to express their work "in writing" (2). Manning suggests that the writing could be improved by requiring students to write more often and show the papers to the teacher "for informal and individual criticism and advice" before presentation (4). Apparently he had in mind that the professor would read the paper and critique it for its rhetorical effectiveness, including its organization and mechanics as well as its content. His recommendation also questioned the effectiveness of the seminar system in helping students develop as writers. He thought that tutorials, the method of instruction Swarthmore had rejected, would be more effective.

A second piece of evidence that the honors students did not write well comes from a critique written by Professor Helen Darbishire, an outside examiner from Oxford who was a visiting professor of English at Wellesley College. She agreed to be an outside examiner in part because she and Aydelotte had a connection: they shared the same tutor at Oxford, the over-worked Ernest de Selincourt. Everyone at Swarthmore, including Aydelotte and the students being examined, were excited about having an Oxford don administer the examination. When the results came in, though, that excitement turned to dismay when she determined that only five of the twelve students in English literature should receive any kind of honors pass at all. Six of the others deserved pass degrees, and one an outright failure (Blanshard 216-17). The main reason that she gave such low evaluations was the poor writing on the examinations, which she found weak for four reasons. First, students tended to make "cocksure statements" that they could not support with evidence. She gave the example of the student trying to write on Chaucer's views of predestination who began by writing, "I don't know much about Chaucer's views on predestination but as I'm interested in the subject I will see what I can do" (Darbishire 1). Second, the students failed "to argue a point out clearly" (1). Students not only failed to read the question carefully but also "rambled around" the issues that they did address. "The few answers which started with a thorough understanding of the question and answered it constructively, stood out very conspicuously" (1), Darbishire wrote pointedly. Third, students violated what Darbishire termed the "decorum" of the examination "by personal statement, excuse, or explanation" (1). Fourth, Darbishire criticized many of the papers for their style, which "was in some cases slangy and careless to the point of illiteracy" (1). All of these criticisms, it should be noted, could be due to students' writing prose designed to be heard rather than read. It might be that the Honors Program, at that time at least, did not teach students to write the kind of formal, tightly argued paper that the Oxford don expected after reading British examinations. But another source of her criticism might well be a basic problem in the honors program itself, that it was lightweight compared to Oxford's (Brereton, personal correspondence). British students entered Oxford with a rigorous secondary school education and extensive experience writing examinations. American students lacked such thorough preparation and the Swarthmore program was not training its students up to Oxford's level, a fact that Darbishire recognized.

A third piece of evidence that student writing needed work appears in the Swarthmore College Faculty's book, *An Adventure in Education*. The unnamed faculty writer notes that professors criticized early papers for their "errors of composition," but also admits that "[i]t is probably true that the need for this type of criticism is more generally acknowledged than adequately met" (100). This suggests that student writing received less criticism than it needed.

The final piece of evidence suggesting that at least some honors students had trouble writing comes indirectly from Aydelotte himself. Beginning in 1926, after the honors program had been in place for four years, Aydelotte started to survey honors graduates to determine the value of the Swarthmore honors experience. Over the years, many former students wrote letters in response. While not horribly written, the prose was average, a fact that Aydelotte apparently noticed because many of the letters were corrected, in his hand, for grammar, spelling, punctuation, and style. Although it is impossible to determine what was going through his mind as he edited the letters, his marks prove that he, as did I, noticed that some Swarthmore honors graduates edited poorly.

His response, however, was not to require students to take a writing course; it was instead to coordinate the removal of these courses from the curriculum. But the problem of writing did not go unaddressed, for in 1933 the *Bulletin of Swarthmore College* indicates that the English Department attempted to teach writing informally in two ways. First, the Department started what would now be called a writing center for "[s]tudents who are reported by any member of the College faculty as deficient in written English . . . [for] tutorial guidance for the removal of this deficiency" (*Bulletin* 1936-37, 77). As at IU, such students would attend the center for as much remediation as necessary to raise their writing to an adequate level. Second, in keeping with the view that Swarthmore should not teach skills, the *Bulletin* for 1936-37 noted that groups of students interested in writing and speaking could meet as "student organizations and informal groups" with members of the English faculty to practice their craft (77).[12] Writing, especially journalism and creative writing, therefore became an extracurricular activity.

## Responses to the Honors Program

The response to Aydelotte's work at Swarthmore was almost universally positive. Because of that work, Swarthmore became associated in the public mind with excellence. In 1924, the National Research Council published Aydelotte's first survey of honors courses, entitled *Honors Courses in American Colleges and Universities*. In the preface, Vernon Kellogg writes that Aydelotte's "name gives the report a special prestige because of his well-known large personal knowledge of both English and American honors systems and his devoted efforts to introduce into American colleges and universities practice that gives more particular attention to the individual student" (2). Three years later, William S. Learned wrote a report for the Carnegie Foundation that favorably compared Swarthmore with Harvard because both colleges, by stressing honors work, avoided the pitfalls of traditional college life. "Study is actually 'the major sport' in these institutions," Learned writes approvingly, "and it is so understood by those who are not, as well as by those who are, honors students" (120). Abraham Flexner, at the time one of the nation's experts on the reform of higher education and a member of the General Education Board, wrote the following letter in 1928 about Aydelotte's work:

> I am firmly convinced that the most important thing we can now do is to establish a few institutions devoted not to the handling of numbers, not to the winning of athletic renown, but to the promotion of sound scholarship and to the selection and training of unusual intellectual ability. Toward this end you have in seven or eight years done more at Swarthmore that [sic] I with my knowledge of American education and of Swarthmore could have believed possible.

In its annual reports, the General Education Board often applauded Aydelotte's work, as it did in 1926: "Swarthmore College, under the leadership of one of the early Rhodes Scholars, is . . . experimenting with honors courses, which endeavor to adapt the English system to American conditions" (7). To encourage Aydelotte's work, Flexner convinced the Board to pledge $250,000 to Swarthmore over a five-year period to develop honors work. In its 1927-1928 report, the Board commented that the "Swarthmore experiment has already had a perceptible influence on raising the standards and ideals of undergraduate work in the country at large" (11). In its 1929-1930 report, the Board pledged to contribute $675,000 to Swarthmore's endowment, commenting that the "demonstration of honors work at Swarthmore College is so widely known as to need no detailed comment" and that over the past eight years officials of other colleges had studied the Swarthmore honors system and adapted it to suit their own institutions (14). In a 1928 letter to Aydelotte, Henry S. Pritchett of the Carnegie Foundation wrote that in his "judgment Swarthmore College has assumed a position of leadership among American colleges by its action in [developing honors courses for] students who show the preparation and the spirit to do scholarly work." At a time when colleges were under pressure to admit more students, he continued, Swarthmore had done important work "in setting forth the ideal of the intellectual life as the true work of the college." In 1941, in a review of *An Adventure in Education* in *The Saturday Review*, Edwin R. Embree wrote that "it has been no simple matter to turn a college in these days of mass education and rote learning into a place where students and faculty alike are interested not in courses and credits but in learning and ideas. This is what has been achieved at Swarthmore under Aydelotte" (11). In 1951, John W. Nason, Aydelotte's successor as president at the college, could look back on Aydelotte's influence on American education and claim that Swarthmore during those twenty years had "had the influence of a major university upon American education and had added to the prestige of every College of Liberal Arts in the country" (8). During his years as its president, Aydelotte had managed to draw the eyes of the nation's academic leaders to Swarthmore through his experiment in honors education.

Other colleges followed Swarthmore's lead in raising academic standards by instituting many of Aydelotte's innovations such as "honors courses, tutorials, seminars, and comprehensive or general examinations" (Kimball 191). For instance, according to the *American Association of Colleges Bulletin*, by 1931 Wells College instituted "special honors courses" for "gifted students" during their last two years, and Franklin and Marshall College required its honors students to take comprehensive examinations at the end of senior year ("Some Progressive College Projects" 317-18). Southwestern College at Memphis developed honors courses in 1927 on the Swarthmore model to "encourage intensive, individual work" ("Some Progressive College Projects II" 485). Colgate College added the "seminar-tutorial method" to allow more intellectual students to work independently during their junior and senior years; the college also required seniors to take a comprehensive examination in their major field (Cutler 466). During the 1920s and 1930s, other colleges across the nation made similar changes in their curriculums in response to the Swarthmore experiment (see Aydelotte's two surveys, *Honors Courses* and *Breaking*, for more details).

Aydelotte also attracted the attention of the general public because the popular press responded enthusiastically to his reforms. As Clark writes, "*The New York Times* was a veritable storehouse of information and praise [of Swarthmore under Aydelotte]. The East Coast business or professional man reading his *Times* on the commuting train . . . could not have failed to have made the acquaintance of Swarthmore" (203). The college became well known among the general public in part, Clark notes, because of the number of articles on it that the *Times* printed. From 1913 to 1919, the *Times* published only three non-sports articles about the school; from 1920 to 1930, it published sixty; and from 1930 to 1940, over 150 (203). The *Times* reported any event of note that occurred there, ranging from a new gift, a new building, a new faculty hire, a new wrinkle in the curriculum. On October 23, 1921, for instance, the *Times* announced Aydelotte's inauguration and stated starkly that Swarthmore planned a new program to separate "brilliant" from "mediocre" students ("Seek to Classify" 1).[13] Starting in 1925 and continuing every year thereafter, the *Times* announced the winners of the Open Scholarships. In May of 1930, the *Times* published Aydelotte's essay entitled "Lifting College Standards," which articulated for a general readership his philosophy of honors education. Starting in 1934, the *Times* published Aydelotte's annual president's report. The paper took note every time Swarthmore modified its honors program. On January 15, 1939, the *Times* commented that Swarthmore had widened its honors plan so that students could take four rather than three related subjects ("Swarthmore Widens"), and on May 14, 1939, it reported that thirty-six outside examiners, the largest group ever, were involved in examining the senior honors students ("Outsiders"). When Aydelotte announced his retirement, the *Times* reported Swarthmore's loss, noting his accomplishments: that he had increased the endowment from $3 million to $8 million; that he had instituted the honors program for "advanced seminar students"; that one third of the juniors and seniors took honors; and that Aydelotte had helped "spread [the idea of honors] widely among other colleges" ("Adventure to Aydelotte" 8). No one who regularly read the *Times* could not have recognized that Aydelotte was remaking Swarthmore into one of the noteworthy colleges in the country.

Major magazines also recognized Swarthmore with laudatory articles. Writing in the *Atlantic Monthly* for June 1935, Edwin R. Embree, in a review of American colleges, placed Swarthmore "at the head of the list" among small colleges (662). He pointed to its "culturally-rich" location near Philadelphia, its "tolerant and intelligent Quaker background," its appointment of distinguished professors, its focus on "stimulating teaching [as] the first duty of a college," and its "able" director, Aydelotte (662). That same year Evelyn Sheeley wrote an appreciative article in *The Literary Digest* praising the progressive innovations carried out by Swarthmore and its students. Gone were the days of the traditional college social life where students valued frivolous social and athletic activities. Swarthmore students, Sheeley reported, valued equality. Many of these students, influenced by the Depression, expressed sympathy for the plight of workers by taking summer jobs digging ditches and working in mines "to learn by experience the worker's problems" (22).[14] Women students broke with tradition by rejecting the sorority system and encouraging equality in social life (22). Sheeley portrayed a college that had achieved one of Aydelotte's primary goals: the development of a rich intellectual life among the student body.

Historians of higher education have recognized Aydelotte's importance as an educational reformer. Flexner, in his 1930 *Universities: American, English, German*, argues that three centrally important innovations occurred in American higher education in recent history: the founding of Johns Hopkins University, the introduction of advanced work at the California Institute of Technology, and "the reorganization of Swarthmore" under Aydelotte (152). George P. Schmidt considers Aydelotte the "pioneer" of honors work. At Swarthmore "the honors idea was carefully thought out, and a higher percentage of students enrolled in the program than in most other institutions" (234). Frederick Rudolph views Aydelotte's success in raising college standards and emphasizing the intellectual development of the individual student as a major contribution to American education. Aydelotte was instrumental in changing the traditional American assumption that the average student was "superior to the notable man" (*American College* 457), an assumption that dominated much educational thought early in the 20th century. Aydelotte also, Rudolph argues, returned Swarthmore to some of the more healthy values of the old, 19th-century college by establishing close relationships between students and professors; by making possible small, intimate seminars; and by attending "to oral and written communication" (*American College* 457).[15] All three of these changes signified Aydelotte's "revolt against the impersonalization, the machinelike quality of the university-oriented education" (457) that was on the ascent at the time. By spreading the honors idea across the nation, Rudolph argues, Aydelotte "spoke for the recognition and encouragement of talent and for the return to intimacy and humane considerations, even the return to the student, to the teaching-learning experience" (457-58) that was being eroded in American higher education. Educational historian Burton R. Clark notes that by 1940, the year that Aydelotte resigned, "Swarthmore had raised its head so clearly out of and above the mass of liberal arts colleges that it had one of the most distinct identities on the American scene. Honors was everywhere a symbol of excellence, and Swarthmore had become a symbol of honors" (207), thanks to Aydelotte's work. Bruce A. Kimball points to the "rigorous academic standards [that Aydelotte] instituted through an honors program, open scholarships, more selective admissions, and competitive final exams" (190-91).

Although the role of written work has received, surprisingly, scant attention, especially given its importance to the program, a group of international students enrolled in the International Institute of Teacher's College of Columbia University visited Swarthmore in 1926 and wrote a report that recognized its significance. As the report notes, "[s]pecial reference was made to the weekly written papers required of all honors students. To this device the students ascribed the incentive for accuracy of statement, clearness of expression and comprehensiveness of treatment. In other words they must crystallize their ideas. The fact that the paper must be presented orally and is critically discussed by professors and students was also referred to as a merit. Perhaps this happy innovation at Swarthmore, more than any other single item, marks the honors work here as outstanding" (qtd. in Brooks *Reading* 45).

But what did Swarthmore students think? Many honors graduates wrote to Aydelotte over the years to discuss their Swarthmore experiences, and most remembered honors work as central to their intellectual development. While few mentioned writing papers as significant in themselves, almost all found that the program's intellectual rigor influenced them for the better.

Students commented that honors work gave them intellectual independence, including good work habits. Agnes Gowing wrote in 1926 that it was only in honors that she "learned that since all though[t] is right, all thought is therefore wrong, that I approached any intellectual independence. No course can give one initiative or originality–but it can, and the Honors Course does, give one sufficient self-confidence to express such originality and initiative as he has." Also writing in 1926, Herbert E. Cliff noted that honors "teaches the student to read and to study by himself, which is an invaluable accomplishment." And Margaret E. Way made a similar point when she wrote that honors work "gives one self-reliance and a more tolerant and searching attitude of mind." Florence C. Creer claimed that honors work encouraged "independent thinking": "In [a regular] class, the best way to cover the course is to stick to the beaten track, and frown upon any attempt to stray into delicious bypaths. In honors, for most of us, was our first taste of individual effort, of being allowed to follow whatever mental urge seemed strongest and worthwhile, and it brought a glow of satisfaction and an interest in learning I had never known before" (3). In 1935, John Seybold commented on the emphasis Swarthmore placed "on exact thinking." He went on to argue that the college encouraged him to think independently and "to view all issues objectively and intelligently" rather than to rely on vague notions (qtd. in Sheeley 22). David E. Davis, a student in the natural sciences who attended graduate school at Harvard, wrote in the same year that the Honors Program had given him the freedom to do intellectual work. He complained that his

> main objection to Honors work is that one is spoiled for work at other universities! The freedom from hindrances to study is not found, even at such progressive schools as Harvard. By hindrances, I mean such things as weekly, senseless quizzes, notebooks, superficial lectures, unintelligent examinations . . . . I even find myself [at Harvard] degenerating into the attitude of trying to get by with as little work as possible!

Stephen Laird, a Washington correspondent for *Time*, wrote in 1939 of his years at Swarthmore that the school "couldn't make me bright or polish me into a diamond. But it did make me curious, and perpetually so. And it did make me want to function as intelligently as possible. For this, I shall always be grateful to you [Aydelotte]. I feel that it is your labor that created the Swarthmore I know and am proud of." Writing in 1964, Michener, the novelist, noted that the honors program taught him essential intellectual strategies that he used throughout his writing career:

> My life since college has consisted pretty much of giving myself one Honors course after another, in one field after another, and it is interesting to recall that not one course I took in college has ever been of much practical use to me, but that the systems of attack I learned there have been invaluable. I learned what a library was, how to use an index, and the steps required for reaching an intellectual conclusion. (82)

He applied the honors techniques as he researched and wrote each of his novels. All of these comments from former honors students point in the same direction: that Swarthmore's Honors Program had instilled in them a life-long love of learning and hard work, a value for precise thought, and an appreciation of the intellectual life.

While most student commentaries do not mention writing, implicit in them is the assumption that the research and thought that went into the regular preparation of papers contributed to the students' intellectual development. Mary H. Fairbanks made this point explicitly when she wrote in 1936 that the Honors Program taught her to write. "The values of training in writing," she wrote, "are so obvious that we tend to forget until we go to graduate school how little chance other students have to acquire this technique." Students from other colleges entering graduate school lacked the abilities to write papers of the kind that she had mastered at Swarthmore and therefore had trouble in their courses. She did not. In one of the most eloquent statements about the benefits of Swarthmore honors, she continued that

> Honors work seems to me to obtain with more precision and fullness the aims of a truly liberal education–the capacity for sustained and directed critical thinking coupled with a genuine enthusiasm for intellectual endeavor. It teaches the pleasure of writing and stimulates a love of the printed page. I cannot believe that any honors student will grow to a middle age of reading only stock market reports and Time! We are too acutely conscious of the joys of learning as a way of life.

## NOTES

1. This assumption proved to be false; he soon discovered that honors education of the type he envisioned was expensive and required external funds and a large endowment. He was forced to raise money to support his program's development.

2. It is interesting to note that Aydelotte expressed such empathy for white minority groups while he showed little for African Americans.

3. Aydelotte asserted this position several times in his writing. While it is true that more students went to college, the percentage of the population that did so remained small. The United States had not figured ways to educate the masses, only part of the wealthy and middle classes.

4. This position echoes liberal culturalists such as Hiram Corson, but Aydelotte was more pragmatic than they were in that he developed curriculums that emphasized writing skills. He was not interested in the spiritual.

5. Aydelotte objected to the "one-size-fits-all" approach of American colleges where all students, be they average or bright, ambitious or lazy, took the same courses. Oxford had solved the problem of differing abilities and interests with Pass and Honors degrees.

6. Swarthmore has more recently opened the honors seminars to the general student population. On a recent visit there, an honors student confided to me that this change was not working as far as she was concerned because regular students did not always take the seminar work seriously.

7. Aydelotte was therefore skeptical of pragmatic courses of study such as business; he was more supportive of engineering as long as students spent some time studying the discipline liberally. He valued most the liberal arts program.

8. Aydelotte ignored the possibility that the elective system allowed students to take a large number of related courses that gave them a depth of understanding of many fields.

9. Oxford tutors, for instance, had developed skills for following papers presented orally that American professors lacked. One of my colleagues, Professor Simon Gattrell, who was educated during the last days of the old Oxford system, remembered how remarkably able his professors were at listening to papers orally and then commenting intelligently on them

10. During the first few years of the honors program, each seminar was run by two professors from different disciplines. This was done to establish the multi-disciplinary nature of the program and to help develop teaching skills needed for the seminar approach. A less experienced teacher could sit in with an old hand.

11. These methods were used primarily in humanities courses. Science courses were based more on lab work, not discussions, and had less writing.

12. Interestingly, Aydelotte returned Swarthmore to a method similar to the old 19th-century student debating societies, then one of the few places on campus where students could work on their writing and speaking in the vernacular.

13. This distinction represents Aydelotte's goals as I understand them. He did not divide students into the brilliant and mediocre but into honors and pass students, recognizing that some pass students were intelligent enough to do honors work but chose not to. On the other hand, he encouraged successful students, those at the B level or above or those who wanted to be challenged, to try to work for honors.

14. I have found no evidence that Aydelotte himself encouraged this kind of social experimentation.

15. Aydelotte did this indirectly, not through writing courses but through writing and critiquing seminar papers.

# 6: Conclusion

In 1939 Aydelotte accepted the directorship of Princeton's Institute of Advanced Study but could not be relieved of his Swarthmore duties until the following year. In 1940 Aydelotte officially resigned as Swarthmore's President and assumed his new responsibilities, replacing Abraham Flexner, Aydelotte's "old friend and companion at arms against mediocrity in education" (Blanshard 295), who had founded the Institute. With this last career move, Aydelotte left undergraduate education, the arena in which he had worked for more than thirty years as a teacher and administrator. He could look back with pride on the courses and programs that he had developed. While the work in honors education has remained a vital influence in American colleges, his earlier work in freshman English and technical communication is not as well known but historically significant. Any assessment of Aydelotte's contributions, however, must take this work into consideration if only because it raises important questions about and offers innovative solutions to issues still central to English studies. For Aydelotte, all of these questions and their solutions began with his experiences at Oxford.

When Aydelotte accepted his Rhodes scholarship in 1905, he had recently completed his M.A. in English at Harvard, which at the time was widely recognized as having the most influential English program in the nation, especially in composition. He knew that composition program well, having taken English 2A and having worked as the assistant to Professor Charles Townsend Copeland, the program's director at the time. Aydelotte must have considered himself a strong writer, well trained in English, and ready to launch a college teaching career. Upon arriving at Oxford, however, he discovered an educational system that forced him to reconceive both his approach to teaching English and his philosophy of education. He became convinced that Oxford had worked out educational methods that solved many of the problems that he had witnessed in American colleges and universities. Upon returning to Indiana University to begin his college teaching career, he initiated a campaign to introduce Oxford methods in this country in order to improve higher education, especially in English studies. During the more than three decades that he worked with the undergraduate curriculums at IU, MIT, and Swarthmore, he used the Oxford model to reform the American system to make it more responsive to the individual student and more demanding intellectually. As he worked through his reforms, he produced a body of research that justified them. This body of work, though no longer widely read, is impressive in its scope and purpose, and his career as a progressive teacher and administrator represents one of the academic successes of the first half of the 20th century.

From Oxford, Aydelotte borrowed four principles that he made central to his reforms. First, by experiencing the Oxford tutorial system and small seminars, he came to understand the importance of personalizing education to meet the abilities and interests of the individual student. Instead of taking large lecture courses, students met with a tutor, who, after assessing the student's current state of knowledge, compiled reading lists to prepare the student for the Oxford examinations. Oxford individualized education, especially in the liberal arts. As Sir Walter Raleigh, Oxford's first modern English professor and Aydelotte's mentor and tutor, told Aydelotte, the liberal arts professor has to "look at the way [the student is] looking," not just at the subject (Aydelotte "Universities" 1). The instructor's duty, therefore, was not to communicate a body of research through lectures but to guide students to that research and assist them in mastering it. Consequently, Aydelotte left Oxford believing that all education is self-education that results from students working out their thoughts through reading seminal texts and scholarship about those texts. He shared with progressive educators such as John Dewey the conviction that education should be responsive enough to the individual so that all students could progress at their own pace and follow their own interests.

To reform American education, Aydelotte placed students and their responses to readings at the center of his curriculums. The thought approach, first developed at IU for the general student and then modified at MIT for the engineering student, assumed the centrality of the students' individual, intellectual reactions to a set of readings. The responsibility of teachers was to serve as intellectual midwives to help the student give birth to ideas during class discussions while withholding their own positions. The classroom method was dialectical in that students worked out their responses to the readings by discussing them with each other. At Swarthmore, Aydelotte developed this method to its fullest extent in the liberal arts honors seminar. Composed of three to ten participants, the seminar encouraged all students to participate in the exploration of the seminar's topic by researching central issues, presenting their research in the form of papers, and then discussing the papers as a group.

The second principle that Aydelotte borrowed from Oxford was that literature and writing should be taught not in separate courses, as Harvard's freshman English course did, but in the same course. While Harvard's English A assumed that learning to write was a matter of mastering formal conventions, Oxford made writing central to the learning process. Oxford allowed students the freedom to read on their own, but it also set one weekly requirement–that students meet with their tutors to present a paper over an assigned topic. The tutor critiqued the paper for both content and rhetorical effectiveness, sometimes requiring students to revise or do additional reading. Even though he had completed his Harvard M.A., taking English A and writing essays under some of the most famous English professors in the United States, Aydelotte found that the Oxford system did a better job improving his academic prose, raising it to a professional level. In Raleigh's seminar in Elizabethan literature, for instance, Aydelotte wrote a paper on Robert Greene and the pamphlets on Renaissance sharpers and confidence men that he eventually revised, under Raleigh's guidance, into *Elizabethan Rogues and Vagabonds*, a major study of its subject. Because he saw his own writing improve under the Oxford system, he became suspicious of any method of writing instruction, such as Harvard's, that separated instruction in form from instruction in content.

The thought approach assumed that writing begins with thought, with ideas and positions to communicate. Writing instruction that starts with rules of organization and correctness, Aydelotte believed, produces artificial prose at best. Student writers must first engage a subject by reading through it to clarify their own thought in relation to that reading. Once students have a point to make and the desire to make it, they will then, Aydelotte believed, be motivated to write well. They will also be willing to learn what they need to know about organization and correctness in order to communicate their thoughts clearly and forcefully to a reader. At this point the teacher, in conference, can teach the compositional principles that students lack because they will feel the need to know them. This method reached its apex in the Swarthmore honors seminar in which the teacher and the other participants critiqued the seminar papers for both content and expression.

A third educational principle that Aydelotte took from Oxford was his conviction that students should study in depth more than a single subject and that they should come to understand the relationships among those subjects. The traditional Oxford curriculum was *Literae Humaniores*, known informally as The Greats. Based on the study of Greek and Latin, this curriculum required that students read widely in ancient literature, history, and philosophy (including some science and modern philosophy) in order to prepare for gentlemanly careers in medicine, the law, and the church. Aydelotte, however, did not advocate The Greats; instead, he was more impressed with Oxford's modern curriculums, including the Modern Greats and Raleigh's English Language and Literature. The Modern Greats required students to study modern history, political science, economics, and languages in preparation for a variety of careers in professions such as teaching, banking, and the foreign service. Aydelotte himself studied in the School of English Language and Literature, which required students to read primarily in British literature, history, and philosophy. The combination of history and literary criticism became known at the time as the Oxford approach to literature, and Aydelotte's *Elizabethan Rogues and Vagabonds* is a significant example of that critical approach.

## Conclusion

The main problem that Aydelotte saw in American colleges and universities was the lack of such purposeful exploration of related disciplines. Aydelotte believed that because of the influence of Harvard's elective system, which in its pure form allowed students to take whatever courses they chose, American higher education often did not provide students with a depth of understanding of any discipline. The elective system, Aydelotte argued, did not measure learning because it assumed that students advanced intellectually by accumulating credits, not by developing knowledge. The credit system assumed that students were educated after they had accumulated a set number of credit hours, no matter what quality of courses those credit hours represented. Oxford, on the other hand, did not tell students how many courses to take; instead, it told them, through their tutors, what they should know about their subject areas and then allowed them the freedom to learn the material by means of individual reading.

All of the courses and curriculums that Aydelotte developed in America followed the Oxford model by casting two or more subjects in relationship. Two of his early book titles suggest this tendency in his thought for individual courses. *College English*, for instance, before Yale's George Phillip Krapp convinced him to change the title, was originally called *English and Education* to suggest its dual emphases. *English and Engineering* points to a similar double focus. At Swarthmore Aydelotte modeled the Honors program on the Oxford schools by requiring students to study three related subjects during their two years of seminar work. Students majoring in English, for instance, took most of their two years of honors work in English (four seminars) but also took two seminars each in two minor areas, English history and philosophy. By constructing the curriculum this way, Aydelotte encouraged students to learn the methodologies of three related areas so that they could, by comparing these methodologies, come to understand the differing assumptions of each.

Finally, Aydelotte returned from Oxford with the conviction that American education did not demand enough from its brightest students. Oxford had solved the problem of different ability levels by establishing two degrees, Pass and Honors. The Pass students could earn a B.A. through a course of study that was easier than its American equivalent. Oxford assumed that such students, not greatly interested in things intellectual, would benefit from the academics and the Oxford athletic and social life. Much of the emphasis of the Pass degree was to create gentlemen. For the brighter, more ambitious students, however, Oxford established its Honors Schools, which demanded that such students do their best work in order to pass a rigorous set of examinations. To pass these examinations, students needed to spend an extra year or two reading in preparation for them. Oxford therefore, Aydelotte argued, met the needs of both groups. American colleges, on the other hand, offered at the time one curriculum for both types so that bright students, Aydelotte believed, fell into an "academic lockstep" that made it impossible for them to do their best work because they were forced to do the same work at the same pace as the average student. Unchallenged by the academic system, bright students often spent their extra time not in additional reading but in extracurricular activities that developed them socially rather than intellectually.

Because of his exposure to the Oxford system, Aydelotte returned from England determined to increase the intellectual demands of American undergraduate education. The thought approach at IU and MIT attempted to accomplish this goal by requiring original thought from students, but these programs were hampered by the fact that they existed within traditional American colleges. At Swarthmore, however, Aydelotte found the opportunity to reform from the ground up one college that he hoped would become a model for others. He developed the Honors Program to challenge the brighter students, and initiated Open Scholarships to attract excellent students from across the nation who would benefit from such work. Modeled directly on the Oxford Honor Schools, the program gave students the freedom to work on their own in small seminars (tutorials proved too expensive) to prepare for a series of written and oral examinations at the end of two years of study.

Those of us in English studies therefore should recognize Aydelotte for making three major contributions to our discipline. First, at Indiana in 1908, he developed the thought course, an approach to freshman English that emphasized the relationship between writing and thinking. All good writing, Aydelotte argued in *College English*, begins with original thought that the writer feels the need to communicate to a reader. Viewing literature as the expression of thought, Aydelotte established a new relationship between literature and writing. Students in Indiana's English 2A read literature to clarify their thinking on central issues of the human condition and then wrote essays on those issues. As major authors such as Shakespeare, Milton, Pope, and Wordsworth had done, student writers worked out in writing their thoughts on the human condition.

Second, on moving to MIT in 1915, Aydelotte modified the thought course to make it appropriate to engineering students. The textbook for his freshman course, *English and Engineering*, was the first anthology of readings in technical or engineering writing and expressed his assumption that engineers must learn to think about their profession in relation to other disciplines, especially literature, to broaden their understanding of their civic responsibilities as professionals. While this "broad" approach (to use Connors's term in "Technical Writing") to engineering writing quickly faded as technical writing courses and the textbooks written for them became more concerned with utilitarian writing, Aydelotte's philosophical approach to the course remains historically important.

Finally, beginning in 1921, Aydelotte developed Swarthmore's Honors Program, which became the model for such programs across the nation. He oversaw the evolution of the honors seminar, which set a small group of bright students to work under the guidance of a professor to explore a topic. Recognizing its importance in the learning process, Aydelotte placed writing at the center of the that process by requiring participants to research, write, and present papers to the seminar on topics important to the material under discussion.

Given Aydelotte's many contributions to English studies, it is hard to fathom why he is not considered a significant theorist in the discipline, especially in composition and rhetoric. His work deserves to be better known than it is.

# Bibliography

NOTE: I identify the three archives from which I used unpublished and rare materials with the following abbreviations:
(IU) University Archives at Indiana University
(MIT) Institute Archives and Special Collections at M.I.T.
(S) Friends Historical Library of Swarthmore College

Adams, J. Donald. *Copey of Harvard: A Biography of Charles Townsend Copeland.* Boston: Houghton Mifflin, 1960.
Adams, Katherine H. *A History of Writing Instruction in American Colleges: Years of Acceptance, Growth, and Doubt.* Dallas: Southern Methodist UP, 1993.
—. *Progressive Politics and the Training of America's Persuaders.* Mahwah, NJ: Erlbaum, 1999.
"Adventure to Aydelotte." *New York Times* 16 Oct. 1939: 8.
Applebee, Arthur N. *Tradition and Reform in the Teaching of English: A History.* Urbana: National Council of Teachers of English, 1974.
Anon. Untitled handwritten set of notes describing English 2A. Unpublished manuscript. (S)
*Annual Catalogue of Indiana University.* [Title varies] (IU)
*Arbutus* 1900. [IU's yearbook] (IU)
Arnold, Benjamin A. Unpublished letter to Frank Aydelotte. 5 July 1933. (S)
Arnold, Matthew. "The Function of Criticism at the Present Time." *Poetry and Criticism of Matthew Arnold.* Ed. A. Dwight Culler. Boston: Houghton Mifflin, 1961. 237-38.
AT&T, "Educational Work–English Courses." Unpublished AT&T Flier. September 1917. (S)
AT&T, unpublished list of applicants. (S)
Aydelotte, Frank. "Address." Unpublished transcript. 11 Oct. 1917. (S)
—. "Address by Professor Aydelotte to Advanced English Class January 3, 1918." Unpublished typescript. (S)
—. "Address by Professor Aydelotte to Advanced English Class January 24, 1918." Unpublished typescript. (S)
—. "Bloomington Indiana, 1896-1900." Unpublished typescript. (S)
—. *Breaking the Academic Lockstep: The Development of Honors Work in American Colleges and Universities.* 2nd ed. New York: Harper Brothers, 1944.
—. "College Education and College Life." Commencement Address, Wooster College, June 14, 1922. Unpublished typescript. (S)
—. *College English: A Manual for the Study of English Literature and Composition.* New York: Oxford UP, 1913.
—. "The Correlation of Literature and Composition." *The Oxford Stamp, and Other Essays.* 135-48.
—. "The Correlation of English Literature and Composition in the College Course." *English Journal* 3.9 (1914): 568-74.
—. *Elizabethan Rogues and Vagabonds.* Vol. I. Oxford Historical and Literary Studies. Oxford: Clarendon, 1913.
—. "Elizabethan Seamen in Mexico and Parts of the Spanish Main." *American History Review* October 1942: 1-19.
—. *English and Engineering.* 2nd ed. New York: McGraw-Hill, 1923.
—. "English as Humane Letters." *Atlantic Monthly* Sept. 1914: 377-80.
—. "English as Humane Letters." *The Oxford Stamp, and Other Essays.* 72-85.
—. "English as Training in Thought." *Educational Review* 43 (1912): 354-77.

—. "English in Engineering Schools." *The Oxford Stamp, and Other Essays*. 199-19.
—. "Eng. 2A--Fall term, 1911." Unpublished typescript. (S)
—. "English 2A, Program of work, Spring term, 1912." Unpublished typescript. (S)
—. "English 2A. Winter 1912." Unpublished typescript. (S)
—. "English versus American Universities." Unpublished typescript. (S)
—. "An Experiment with the Freshman Course." *The Oxford Stamp, and Other Essays*. 86-134.
—. "The Freshman English Course." *Nation* 1 Dec. 1910: 519-20.
—. "The Function of the Liberal College." Unpublished typescript of Address at the Friends Summer School, June 30, 1921. (S)
—. "Harvard University 1902-1903." Unpublished typescript. (S)
—. "The History of English as a College Subject in the United States." *The Oxford Stamp, and Other Essays*. 174-98. Also reprinted in *The Origins of Composition Studies in the American College, 1875-1925: A Documentary History*. Ed. John C. Brereton. Pittsburgh: U of Pittsburgh P, 1995. 300-311.
—. "History of the Operation of the Rhodes Scholarships in the United States." *Oxford of Today*. 211-26.
—. "Honors Courses in American Colleges and Universities." *Transactions and Proceedings of the National Association of State Universities in the United States of America* 23 (1925): 51-65.
—. *Honors Courses in American Colleges and Universities. Bulletin of the National Research Council* 7.40 (1924): 3-57.
—. "Honors Courses: history, aims, and adaptations with specification of types and types best suited to American conditions." Unpublished typescript. (S)
—. "Honors Examinations--1925." Undated, unpublished typescript.(S)
—. "The Honors Idea." Unpublished typescript. (S)
—. "Honors Work and Graduate Study." *Journal of the Proceedings and Addresses of the Association of American Universities* Nov. 1935: 102-119.
—. "Inaugural Address of President Aydelotte." *Swarthmore College Bulletin* 1921: 19-25. (S)
—. "Letter to the Editor of the NATION [in Answer to Ada L.F. Snell]." [1911]. Unpublished typescript. (S)
—. "Lifting College Standards." *New York Times* 4 May 1930, sec. III: 8-9.
—. List of advanced course assignments. Unpublished typescript. (S)
—, ed. *Materials for the Study of English Literature and Composition*. 2nd. ed. New York: Oxford UP, 1916.
—. "Notes." Unpublished typescript. Dec. 22 [no year]. (S)
—. "On Teaching English." Dartmouth College Address. Unpublished typescript,1919. (S)
—. "Oxford 1905-07." Unpublished typescript. (S)
—. *The Oxford Stamp, and Other Essays: Articles from the Educational Creed of an American Oxonian*. New York: Oxford UP, 1917.
—. "The Problem of English in Engineering Schools." *The Oxford Stamp, and Other Essays*. 199-219.
[—]. "Proposal for Combining the Work of the Departments of English and History." Unpublished typescript. (S)
—. "Report of the President 1939." Bulletin of Swarthmore College. 1940. 1-20. (S)
—. "A Revolution in American Academic Standards." 13 Nov.1925. Unpublished typescript. (S)
—. "The Rhodes Scholarships." *Nation* 90.2345 (1910): 581-82.

—. "Robert Louis Stevenson[:] Darkening Counsel." *The Oxford Stamp, and Other Essays*. 149-73.
—. "Spectators and Sport." *The Oxford Stamp, and Other Essays*. 22-40.
—. *Suggestions for the Use of Aydelotte's English and Engineering*. New York: McGraw-Hill, 1917. (S)
—. *Swarthmore College Bulletin: Report of the President*. 1923-24. (S)
—. *Swarthmore College Bulletin: Commencement Number*. 1924. (S)
—. "Training in Thought Is the Aim of Elementary English Course as Taught at M.I.T." *Engineering Record* 75.8 (1917): 300-02
—. "Universities." Unpublished typescript of paper delivered on 25 April 1926 at the American Philosophical Society Meeting. (S)
—. Unpublished letter to C. R. Bagley. 15 Feb. 1923. (S)
—. Unpublished letter to Frances Blanshard. 1 July 1954. (S)
—. Unpublished letter to Frances Blanshard. 17 Sept. 1954. (S)
—. Unpublished letter to William L. Bryan. 1 May 1907. (S)
—. Unpublished letter to William L. Bryan. 3 May 1908. (IU)
—. Unpublished letter to William L. Bryan. 12 Sept. 1908. (IU)
—. Unpublished letter to William L. Bryan. 11 Mar. 1913. (IU)
—. Unpublished letter to William L. Bryan. 25 May 1913. (IU)
—. Unpublished letter to William L. Bryan. 21 Apr. 1913. (S)
—. Unpublished letter to William L. Bryan. 30 Apr. 1913. (IU)
—. Unpublished letter to William L. Bryan. 27 Apr. 1915. (IU)
—. Unpublished letter to Helen Cook. 30 Apr. 1918. (S)
—. Unpublished letter to Henry C. Fisher. 22 Oct. 1937. (S)
—. Unpublished letter to Warner Fite. 23 Feb. 1921. (S)
—. Unpublished letter to Warner Fite. 28 Feb. 1921. (S)
—. Unpublished letters to Mary Frank. 10 Jan., 21 Feb., and 28 Feb., 1918. (S)
—. Unpublished letter to Charles Robert Gaston. 19 Oct. 1922. (S)
—. Unpublished letter to D.O.W. Holmes. 28 Jan.1934. (S)
—. Unpublished letter to R. A. Jelliffe. 11 Feb. 1918. (S)
—. Unpublished letter to N. C. Kingsbury. 30 Oct. 1917. (S)
—. Unpublished letter to N. C. Kingsbury. 10 Nov. 1917. (S)
—. Unpublished letter to Floyd L. Logan. 2 Nov. 1936. (S)
—. Unpublished letter to R. C. Maclaurin. 20 Aug. 1917. (S)
—. Unpublished letter to R. C. Maclaurin. 26 June 1918. (S)
—. Unpublished letter to R. C. Mann. 29 April 1918. (S)
—. Unpublished letter to John Nason. 24 February 1948. (S)
—. Unpublished letter to A. C. Vinal. 20 Aug. 1917. (S)
—. Unpublished letter to A. C. Vinal. 25 Sept. 1917. (S)
—. Unpublished letter to A. C. Vinal. 25 Sept. 1917. (S)
—. Untitled, handwritten notes on freshman English enrollment figures at IU for 1909. Unpublished manuscript. (S)
—. Untitled, undated biographical typescript. (S)
—. "What the American Rhodes Scholar Gets Out of Oxford." *Scribner's Magazine* 73.6 (1923): 677-88.
Babbitt, Irving. *Literature and the American College: Essays in Defense of the Humanities*. Boston: Houghton, Mifflin, 1908.
Bailey, Cyril. "The Tutorial System." *Handbook to the University of Oxford*. Oxford: Clarendon, 1932. 125-32.

Baker, Ray Palmer. *Engineering Education: Essays for English.* New York: Wiley, 1919.
—. *The Preparation of Reports: Engineering, Scientific, Administrative.* New York: Ronald Press, 1923.
Baldwin, Charles Sears. *Specimens of Prose Description.* New York: Holt, 1895.
Bates, Arlo. *Talks on Writing English.* 2 vols. Boston: Houghton, Mifflin and Co., 1896.
Bates, Herbert. "The Spirit of the Western University." *Outlook* 55.9 (1897): 604-06.
Beardsley, Monroe C., James A. Field, Jr., Charles E. Gilbert, Kermit Gordon, Mark A. Head, Samuel Hynes, Winnifred Poland Pierce, and Robert Sproull. *Report of the Commission on Educational Policy: Swarthmore College: Report on a College.* Swarthmore, PA: Swarthmore College, 1967.
Beirne, Frank F. "The Inadequate Rhodes Scholar: A Defense." *Atlantic Monthly* 125.5 (1919): 665-69.
Berlin, James A. "Contemporary Composition: The Major Pedagogical Theories." *College English* 44.8 (1982): 765-77.
—. *Rhetoric and Reality: Writing Instruction in American Colleges, 1900-1985.* Carbondale: Southern Illinois UP, 1987.
—. *Rhetorics, Poetics, and Cultures: Refiguring College English Studies.* Urbana: National Council of Teachers of English, 1996.
—. *Writing Instruction in Nineteenth-Century American Colleges.* Carbondale: Southern Illinois UP, 1984.
Blanshard, Frances. *Frank Aydelotte of Swarthmore.* Ed. Brand Blanshard. Middletown, CT: Wesleyan UP, 1970.
Blauvelt, Mary Taylor. "Oxford, Past and Present." *Educational Review* 24 (1902): 358-74.
Bowman, James Cloyd, Louis I. Bredvold, Leroy Bethuel Greenfield, and Bruce Weirick, eds. *Essays for College English.* Boston: D.C. Heath, 1915.
Bradley, Henry. *The Making of English.* New York: Macmillan, 1904.
Brereton, John C., ed. *The Origins of Composition Studies in the American College, 1875-1925.* Pittsburgh: U of Pittsburgh P, 1995.
—. Personal correspondence. 1997.
Brewster, William T., ed. *Specimens of Narration.* New York: Holt, 1895.
"Brief of a Devil's Advocate on the 'Proposal for Combining the Work of the Departments of History and English.'" Unpublished typescript. (S)
Brooks, Alfred. "Comments by Alfred Brooks on letter of September 17 [1954] to Frances Blanshard." Unpublished typescript. (S) This is a typescript of Brooks's handwritten comments on a letter from Aydelotte to Blanshard. (S)
Brooks, Robert C. "Honors Courses in an Effective College: Swarthmore College." *Association of American Colleges Bulletin* 12.3 (1926): 190-92.
—. *Reading for Honors at Swarthmore: A Record of the First Five Years, 1922-1927.* New York: Oxford UP, 1927.
Brown, Cynthia Stokes. *Alexander Meiklejohn: Teacher of Freedom.* Berkeley: Meiklejohn Civil Liberties Institute, 1981.
Brown, Rollo Walter. *Dean Briggs.* New York: Harper & Brothers, 1926.
Bryan, William L. Unpublished letter to Frank Aydelotte. 27 Apr.1908. (IU)
—. Unpublished letter to the Principal and Fellows of Brasenose College. 28 Apr. 1913. (S)
—. Unpublished letter to Frank Aydelotte. 30 Apr. 1913. (S)
—. Unpublished letter to Frank Aydelotte. 9 June 1913. (S)
*Bulletin of the Massachusetts Institute of Technology.* (MIT)
*Catalogue of Swarthmore College.* [Title varies.] (S)
Carl, Murphy. Unpublished letter to Frank Aydelotte. 14 Sept. 1933. (S)

Clapp, Margaret. Unpublished letter to Frank Aydelotte. 22 Apr. 1918. (S)
Clark, Burton R. *The Distinctive College. With a New Introduction by the Author.* 1970; New Brunswick: Transaction Publishers, 1992.
Cliff, Herbert E. Unpublished letter to Robert C. Brooks. 13 Nov. 1926. (S)
Connors, Robert J. *Composition-Rhetoric: Backgrounds, Theory, and Pedagogy.* Pittsburgh, PA: U of Pittsburgh P, 1977.
—. "Handbooks: History of a Genre." *Rhetoric Society Quarterly* 8.2 (1983): 87-98.
—. "Technical Writing Instruction in America." *Journal of Technical Writing and Communication* 12.4 (1982): 329-52.
Cook, Helen. Unpublished letter to Frank Aydelotte. 18 Apr. 1918. (S)
Copeland, C. T., and H. M. Rideout. *Freshman English and Theme-Correcting in Harvard College.* New York: Silver, Burdett, 1901.
"Corporation of the Visiting Committee on the Department of English [at M.I.T.]." Unpublished typescript. 1918. (S)
Corson, Hiram. *The Aims of Literary Study.* London: Macmillan, 1910.
—. *The Voice and Spiritual Education.* New York: Macmillan, 1923.
Creer, Florence C. "Honors Work." Unpublished typescript. 1927. (S)
Cremin, Lawrence A. *The Transformation of the School: Progressivism in American Education, 1876-1957.* New York: Knopf, 1961.
Crosby, L. A. "Courses of Study: The B.A. Degree and the Honour Schools." *Oxford of Today.* 53-101.
Crosby, L.A. "The Oxford System of Education." *Oxford of Today.* 48-52.
Crosby, Laurence A., Frank Aydelotte, and Alan C. Valentine, eds. *Oxford of Today: A Manual for Prospective Rhodes Scholars.* New York: Oxford UP, 1927.
Crowley, Sharon. *Composition in the University: Historical and Polemical Essays.* Pittsburgh, PA: U of Pittsburgh P, 1998.
—. *The Methodical Memory: Invention in Current-Traditional Rhetoric.* Carbondale: Southern Illinois UP, 1990.
Cutler, George B. "The Colgate Plan to the Student as a Whole." *American Association of Colleges Bulletin* 17.4 (1931): 463-66.
"The Daily Theme Eye." *Atlantic Monthly* 99 (1907): 427-29.
Darbishire, Helen. "English Honours. Swarthmore College." Unpublished typescript. May 1926. (S)
Davidson, Frank. *English Department Newsletter.* III. 1-4. Unpublished typescript. (IU)
Davis, David E. Unpublished letter to Frank Aydelotte. 1934. (S)
Davis, Shirley. "An Impetus." *Swarthmore Remembered.* Ed. Marilyn Orbison Gillespie. New York: Swarthmore College, 1964. 137-42.
Dewey, John. *Democracy and Education: An Introduction to the Philosophy of Education.* New York: Macmillan, 1930.
Duffus, R. L. *Democracy Enters College: A Study of the Rise and Decline of the Academic Lockstep.* New York: Scribner's, 1936.
Earle, Samuel Chandler. *The Theory and Practice of Technical Writing.* New York: Macmillan, 1911.
Earnest, Ernest. *Academic Procession: An Informal History of the American College 1636 to 1953.* Indianapolis: Bobbs-Merrill, 1953.
Eliot, Charles William. *Educational Reform: Essays and Addresses.* New York: Century, 1900.
—. "Harvard." *Four American Universities: Harvard, Yale, Princeton, Columbia.* New York: Harper, 1895. 3-43.

—. "Inaugural Address as President of Harvard College." *Educational Reform*. 1-38.
—. "The Unity of Educational Reform." *Educational Reform*. 315-39.
—. "What Is a Liberal Education?" *Educational Reform*. 89-122.
Embree, Edwin R. "Aydelotte in Action." Rev. of *An Adventure in Education*, by Swarthmore College Faculty. *Saturday Review* 20 Sept. 1941: 11.
—. "In Order of Their Eminence: An Appraisal of American Universities." *Atlantic Monthly* 144.6 (1935): 652-64.
Erskine, John. *The Memory of Certain Persons*. Philadelphia: Lippincourt, 1947.
—. *My Life as a Teacher*. Philadelphia: Lippincourt, 1948.
Fairbanks, Mary H. Unpublished letter to Frank Aydelotte. 27 May 1936.
Fisher, Dorothy Canfield. "Melting the Faculty Ice." *World's Work* 58.5 (1929): 52-56.
Fisher, H. Euryl. Unpublished letter to Frank Aydelotte. 11 Apr. 1918. (S)
Flexner, Abraham. *I Remember: The Autobiography of Abraham Flexner*. New York: Simon, Schuster, 1940.
—. *Universities: American, English, German.1930*. New Brunswick: Transaction Publishers, 1994.
—. Unpublished letter to Frank Aydelotte. 14 Sept. 1928. (S)
Foerster, Norman. "The 'Idea Course' for Freshmen." *English Journal* 5.7 (1916): 458-66.
—. Unpublished letter to Frank Aydelotte. 28 Oct. 1912. (S)
—. Unpublished letter to Frank Aydelotte. 5 Feb. 1913. (S)
—. Unpublished letter to Frank Aydelotte. 9 Mar. 1917. (S)
Foerster, Norman, Frederick A. Manchester, and Karl Young, eds. *Essays for College Men: Education, Science, and Art*. New York: Holt, 1913.
Foerster, Norman, and J. M. Steadman, Jr. *Writing and Thinking: A Handbook of Composition and Revision*. Boston: Houghton Mifflin, 1931.
Frost, Harwood. *Good Engineering Writing: What to Read and How to Write with Suggested Information on Allied Topics*. Chicago: Chicago Book, 1911.
Fulton, Maurice Garland, ed. *College Life: Its Conditions and Problems*. New York: Macmillan, 1915.
Gardiner, J. H. "Our Infant Critics." *Nation* 19 March 1908. 257-58.
Garrod, H. W. "Walter Raleigh." *The Profession of Poetry and Other Essays*. Oxford: Clarendon, 1929. 266-70.
General Education Board. *Annual Report of the General Education Board, 1924-1925*. New York: General Education Board, 1926.
—. *Annual Report of the General Education Board, 1927-1928*. New York: General Education Board, 1929.
—. *Annual Report of the General Education Board, 1929-1930*. New York: General Education Board, 1931.
Goggin, Maureen Dowd. *Writing a Discipline: Scholarly Journals and the Post-World War II Emergence of Rhetoric and Composition*. Mahwah, NJ: Erlbaum, 2000.
Gowing, Agnes. Unpublished letter to Frank Aydelotte. 11 Oct. 1926. (S)
Graff, Gerald. *Professing Literature: An Institutional History*. Chicago: U of Chicago P, 1987.
Gray, Donald J. "The Department of English, 1893-1920." *The Department of English at Indiana University Bloomington 1868-1970*. Bloomington, IN: Indiana U Publications, 1970. 55-85. (IU)
Hagge, John. "Early Engineering Writing Textbooks and the Anthropological Complexity of Disciplinary Discourse." *Written Communication* 12.4 (1995): 439-91.

Halasek, Kay. *A Pedagogy of Possibility: Bakhtinian Perspectives on Composition Studies.* Carbondale, IL: Southern Illinois UP, 1999.

Harbarger, S. A. *English for Engineers.* 1923. 3rd ed. New York: McGraw-Hill, 1934.

Hardegree, Maureen Byrnes. "The Thought Movement: A History of the Ideas Course." M.A. Thesis. U of Georgia, 1991.

Harris, William T. "The Rhodes Scholarships." *Educational Review* 26 (1903): 1-21.

Hill, Adams Sherman. "English in Newspapers and Novels." *Scribner's* 2 (1887): 371-77.

—. "English in Our Colleges." *Scribner's* 1 (1887): 507-12.

—. *The Principles of Rhetoric.* New ed. New York: Harpers, 1898.

Hill, A. S. "Colloquial English." *Harper's Monthly Magazine.* Jan. 1889: 272-79.

—. "English in the Schools." *Harper's Monthly Magazine* June 1885: 122- 33.

Hingham, John. "The Matrix of Specialization." *The Organization of Knowledge in Modern America, 1860-1920.* Ed. Alexandra Oleson and John Voss. Baltimore, MD: Johns Hopkins UP, 1979. 3-18.

Holmes, D. O. W. Unpublished letter to Frank Aydelotte. 22 Jan. 1934. (S)

—. Unpublished letter to Frank Aydelotte. 6 March 1934. (S)

"Honors Readings. Division of English Literature. January 7, 1924." Unpublished typescript. (S)

"Honors Readings. Division of English Literature." Unpublished typescript. October 22, 1923. (S)

Howe, Will D. Unpublished letter to William L. Bryan. 15 Aug. 1909. (IU)

Hudson, Hoyt H. "An External Examiner Looks at External Examinations." *An Adventure in Education: Swarthmore College Under Frank Aydelotte.* [Ed. Swarthmore College Faculty]. New York: Macmillan, 1941. 125-35.

Hunt, Everett. "Frank Aydelotte." *Swarthmore College Bulletin* 5.4 (1957): 5, 28-31.

—. Unpublished letter to Frank Aydelotte. 8 March 1933. (S)

Hunt, Everett Lee. *The Revolt of the Intellectual.* New York: Human Relations Aids, 1963.

*Indiana University President's Report 1908.* Unpublished typescript. (IU)

*Indiana University President's Report 1910.* Unpublished typescript. (IU)

Jelliffe, R. A. Unpublished letter to Frank Aydelotte. 31 Jan. 1918. (S)

Jordon, John Clark. Unpublished letter to President J. C. Futrall [of the University of Arkansas]. 12 Mar. 1926. (S)

Kates, Susan. *Activist Rhetorics and American Higher Education, 1885-1937.* Carbondale, IL: Southern Illinois UP, 2001.

Kellogg, Vernon. Preface. *Honors Courses in American Colleges and Universities.* By Frank Aydelotte. *Bulletin of the National Research Council* 7.40 (1924): 1-2.

Kennedy, George A. *A New History of Classical Rhetoric.* Princeton, NJ: Princeton UP, 1994.

Kimball, Bruce A. *Orators and Philosophers: A History of the Idea of Liberal Education.* New York: Teachers College Press, 1986.

Kingsbury, N. C. Unpublished letter to Frank Aydelotte. 2 Nov. 1917. (S)

Kitzhaber, Albert R. *Rhetoric in American Colleges, 1850-1900.* Dallas: Southern Methodist UP: 1990.

Krapp, George Philip. *A Comprehensive Guide to Good English.* New York: Rand McNally, 1927.

—. *Modern English: Its Growth and Present Use.* 1909. Rpt. New York: Ungar, 1966.

—. Unpublished letter to Frank Aydelotte. 27 May 1912. (S)

—. Unpublished letter to Frank Aydelotte. 6 Aug. 1912. (S)

—. Unpublished letter to Frank Aydelotte. 23 Aug. 1912. (S)

—. Unpublished letter to Frank Aydelotte. 27 Feb. 1913. (S)
Kurtz, Benjamin P., Herbert E. Cory, Frederick T. Blanshard, and George R. MacMinn, eds. *Essays in Exposition*. Boston: Ginn, 1914.
Kynell, Teresa C. *Writing in the Milieu of Utility: The Move to Technical Communication in American Engineering Programs*. Norwood, NJ: Ablex. 1996
Laird, Stephen. Unpublished letter to Frank Aydelotte. 16 Oct. 1939. (S)
Lamont, Hammond. *Specimens of Exposition*. New York: Holt, 1894.
Lang, Andrew. *Oxford*. London: Seeley Service, 1922.
Learned, William S. *The Quality of the Educational Process in the United States and in Europe. Bulletin No. 20*. New York: Carnegie Foundation for the Advancement of Learning, 1927.
Lounsbury, Thomas R. *The Standard of Usage in English*. New York: Harper, 1908.
—. "Compulsory Composition in Colleges." *Harper's Monthly Magazine* 123.738 (1911): 866-80.
McDonald, Philip B. *Engineering and Science*. New York: Van Nostrand, 1929.
Maclaurin, R. C. Unpublished letter to Frank Aydelotte. 21 April 1915. (S)
—. Unpublished letter to H. G. Pearson. 24 June 1918. (S)
Maclaurin, Richard. Unpublished letter to D. C. Jackson. 25 Nov. 1914. (S)
Mann, C. R. Unpublished letter to Frank Aydelotte. 5 August 1917. (S)
Manning, Frederick. "Some Observations on Honors Teaching at Swarthmore." Unpublished typescript. 5 Dec. 1925.(S)
March, Francis A. *Method of Philological Study of the English Language*. New York: Harper & Brothers, 1868.
*Massachusetts Institute of Technology* [Annual Catalog]. [Title varies.] (MIT)
Matthews, Brander. "Columbia." *Four American Universities: Harvard, Yale, Princeton, Columbia*. New York: Harper, 1895. 157-202.
Meiklejohn, Alexander. "Inaugural Address." *The Freshman and His College*. Ed. Francis Cummins Lockwood. Boston: Heath, 1913. 113-27.
Merrill, William A. "The Practical Value of a Liberal Education." *Education* 10.7 (1890): 440-42.
Michener, James A. "Swat'more Collitch." *Swarthmore Remembered*. Ed.Marilyn Orbison Gillespie. New York: Swarthmore College, 1964. 79-85.
Miller, Susan. *Textual Carnivals: The Politics of Composition*. Carbondale, IL: Southern Illinois UP, 1991.
Minutes of summer 1918 M.I.T. English Department staff meeting. Unpublished typescript. (S)
*MIT Report of the President*. [Title varies]. Unpublished typescript. (MIT)
Moran, Michael. "The Concept of Thoroughness in Freshman English." *Notes on Teaching English* 18.1 (1990): 1-4.
Moran, Michael G. "Frank Aydelotte." *Twentieth-Century Rhetorics and Rhetoricians: Critical Studies and Sources*. Ed. Michael G. Moran and Michelle Ballif. Westport, CT: Greenwood P, 2000. 1-6.
— "Frank Aydelotte: AT&T's First Outside Writing Consultant, 1917-1918." *Journal of Technical Writing and Communication* 25.3 (1995): 231-41.
—. "Frank Aydelotte, Social Criticism, and Freshman English." *Notes on Teaching English* 18.2 (1991): 13-19.
—. "The Road Not Taken: Frank Aydelotte and the Thought Approach to Engineering Writing." *Technical Communication Quarterly* 2.2 (1993): 161-75.

Moran, Michael G., and Maureen Byrnes Hardegree. "Frank Aydelotte (1880-1956): A Bibliography." *Bulletin of Bibliography* 50.1 (1993): 19-25.

More, Paul E. Unpublished letter to Frank Aydelotte. 9 Feb. 1911. (S)

Nason, John W. "For Frank Aydelotte." *American Oxonian* 38.1 (1951): 8-11.

Nelson, J. Raleigh. "English, Engineering, and Technical Schools." *English Journal* 20.6 (1931): 494-502.

Notestein, Wallace. Rev. of *Elizabethan Rogues and Vagabonds*, by Frank Aydelotte. *American Historical Review* 19.4 (1914): 886-87.

Nutter, Charles Read, Frank Wilson Cheney Hersey, and Chester Noyes Greenough, eds. *Specimens of Prose Composition*. Boston: Ginn, 1907.

Osgood, Charles G. "No Set Requirements of English Composition in the Freshman Year." *English Journal* 4.4 (1915): 231-35.

"Our Infant Critics." *Nation* 27 Feb. 1908, 188.

"Outsiders to Hold Quiz at Swarthmore." *New York Times* 14 May 1939, sec. III: 1.

Palmer, D. J. *The Rise of English Studies*. London: Oxford UP, 1965.

Palmer, Glenn E. "Culture and Efficiency through Composition." *English Journal* 1.8 (1912): 488-92.

Park, Clyde W. *English Applied to Technical Writing*. New York: F. S. Croft, 1926.

Pearson, Henry Greenleaf. *Richard Cockburn Maclaurin: President of the Massachusetts Institute of Technology 1909-1920*. New York: Macmillan, 1937.

Pearson, Henry G. Unpublished letter to Frank Aydelotte. 1 Aug. 1918. (S)

—. Unpublished letter to Frank Aydelotte. 10 Aug. 1918. (S)

Perkins, C. "Mini Biography: Frank Aydelotte (1880-1956)." Unpublished typescript. (S)

Perry, Bliss. *The Amateur Spirit*. Boston: Houghton, Mifflin, 1904.

—. *And Gladly Teach: Reminiscences*. Boston: Houghton, Mifflin, 1935.

Phelps, William Lyon. *Autobiography with Letters*. New York: Oxford UP, 1939.

"Postgraduates." *Time* 9 Aug. 1943: 56-60.

Potter, Stephen. *The Muse in Chains: A Study in Education*. London: Jonathan Cape, 1937.

Pritchett, Henry S. Unpublished letter to Frank Aydelotte. 10 Oct. 1928. (S)

Raleigh, Walter. *The English Novel: A Short Sketch of Its History from the Earliest Times to the Appearance of Waverley*. London: Murray, 1919.

—. "Letter to George W. Prothero." *The Letters of Sir Walter Raleigh*. 2 vols. Ed. Lady Raleigh. New York: Macmillan, 1926. II 298.

—. *The Meaning of the University*. Oxford: Clarendon Press, 1911.

—. *Milton*. London: Arnold, 1922.

—. "Professor Raleigh's Letter [in Support of the School of English Language and Literature]." *The School of English and Literature*, by C. H. Firth. Oxford: Blackwell, 1909. 48-51.

—. *Shakespeare*. London: Macmillan, 1928.

—. *Style*. London: Arnold, 1923.

—. *Wordsworth*. London: Arnold, 1915.

—. Unpublished letter to Frank Aydelotte. 22 December 1907. (S)

"Required Work for Students Reading for Honors in English Literature, 1924-25." Unpublished, undated typescript. (S)

Rev. of *Elizabethan Rogues and Vagabonds*, by Frank Aydelotte. *English Historical Review* 29.116 (1914): 792.

Rev. of *Elizabethan Rogues and Vagabonds*, by Frank Aydelotte. *Nation* 16 April 1914: 437.

Rev. of *Elizabethan Rogues and Vagabonds*, by Frank Aydelotte. *Saturday Review* 15 Nov. 1913: 624.

Rev. of *Elizabethan Rogues and Vagabonds*, by Frank Aydelotte. *Scottish Historical Review* 11.42 (1914): 220-21.

[Rhodes, Cecil John]. *Last Will and Testament of Cecil John Rhodes.* Ed. W.T. Stead. London: "Review of Reviews" Office, 1902.

"Rhodesmen at Swarthmore." *Time.* 5 June 1933: 45-48.

Rice, Jr., Richard, ed. *College and the Future: Essays for the Undergraduate on Problems of Character and Intellect.* New York: Scribner's, 1915.

Rice, Richard Ashley. *Learning to Write.* New York: Scribner's, 1917.

Richardson, H.C., L. N. Becklund, L. O. Guthrie, and C. I. Haga. *Practical Forms in Exposition: A Manual Designed to Assist Technical Students with Papers, Letters, Reports, and Reading.* New York: Macmillan, 1934.

Rickard, T. A. *Technical Writing.* 3rd ed. New York: American Institute of Mining and Metallurgical Engineers, 1939.

Rogers, Robert E. Untitled response to the M.I.T. English-History course. (S)

Rudolph, Frederick. *The American College and University: A History.* Introductory Essay and Supplemental Bibliography by John R. Thelin. Athens: U of Georgia P, 1990.

—. *Curriculum: A History of the American Undergraduate Course of Study Since 1636.* San Francisco: Jossey-Boss, 1977.

Russell, David R. *Writing in the Academic Disciplines, 1870-1990: A Curricular History.* Carbondale: Southern Illinois UP, 1991.

Sampson, Martin W. "English at Indiana University." *Dial* July 1, 1894: 5-7.

Sampson, Martin Wright, and Ernest O. Holland. *Written and Oral Composition.* New York: American Book Co., 1907.

Schmelzer, Richard W. "The First Textbook on Technical Writing." *Journal of Technical Writing and Communication* 7.1 (1977): 51-54.

Schmidt, George P. *The Liberal Arts College: A Chapter in American Cultural History.* New Brunswick: Rutgers UP, 1957.

Scott, Fred Newton, and Joseph Villiers Denney. *Paragraph-Writing: A Rhetoric for Colleges.* New Edition. Boston: Allyn and Bacon, 1909.

"Seek to Classify Mediocre Students." *New York Times* 23 Oct. 1921, sec. II: 1.

Sheeley, Evelyn. "Student-Trends at Swarthmore and Princeton." *Literary Digest* 20 April 1935: 22-23.

Sherman, L.A. "English and English Literature in Our Colleges." *Educational Review* 10 (1895): 42-56.

Shaughnessy, Mina P. *Errors and Expectations: A Guide for the Teaching of Basic Writing.* New York: Oxford UP, 1977.

Smith, David Nichol. Preface. *The Letters of Sir Walter Raleigh.* By Sir Walter Raleigh. Ed. Lady Raleigh. 2 vols. New York: Macmillan, 1926.

Smith, D. Nichol. "Raleigh, Sir Walter." *DNB* (1922-30).

Snell, Ada L. F. "Freshman Composition." *Nation* 5 Jan. 1911: 9.

"Some Progressive College Projects: Curriculum Reorganization, Orientation, and Survey Courses." *American Association of Colleges Bulletin* 17.3 (1931): 317-19.

"Some Progressive College Projects II: Academic Tenure and Promotion." *American Association of Colleges Bulletin* 17.4 (1931): 485

Spiller, Robert E. "Pre-Honors Courses." *English Journal* 15.7 (1926): 499-506.

—. "Ten Years of Outside Examiners." *English Journal* 22.4 (1933): 310- 19.

Steeves, Harrison Ross. "The Cultivation of Ideas in the College Writing Course." *Educational Review* 44 (1912): 45-54.
Steeves, Harrison Ross, and Frank Humphrey Ristine, eds. *Representative Essays in Modern Thought: A Basis for Composition*. New York: American Book Company, 1913.
*Swarthmore College Bulletin* [title varies]. (S)
The Swarthmore College Faculty. *An Adventure in Education: Swarthmore College under Frank Aydelotte*. New York: Macmillan, 1941.
"Swarthmore's Aydelotte." *Time* 12 June 1939: 57.
"Swarthmore Widens Honors Plan of Study." *New York Times* 15 Jan. 1939, sec. II: 8.
Thomas, Joseph M. "Do Thought-Courses Produce Thinking?" *English Journal* 5.2 (1916): 79-88.
Thompson, Josephine V. Unpublished letter to Frank Aydelotte. 31 May 1918. (S)
Thwing, Charles Franklin. *A History of Education in the United States Since the Civil War*. Boston: Houghton, Mifflin, 1910.
*Time*. 5 June 1933. [Drawing of Aydelotte on cover.]
Van Dyke, Henry. *The Spirit of America*. New York: Macmillan, 1910.
Veysey, Laurence R. *The Emergence of the American University*. Chicago: U of Chicago P, 1965.
Vinal, A. C. Unpublished letter to Frank Aydelotte. 6 Aug. 1917. (S)
—. Unpublished letter to Frank Aydelotte. 17 Aug. 1917. (S)
—. Unpublished letter to Frank Aydelotte. 20 Aug. 1917. (S)
—. Unpublished letter to Frank Aydelotte. 24 Sept. 1917. (S)
—. Unpublished letter to Frank Aydelotte. 12 Nov. 1917. (S)
—. Unpublished letter to Frank Aydelotte. 17 Nov. 1917. (S)
—. Unpublished letter to Frank Aydelotte. 12 Apr. 1918. (S)
—. Unpublished letter to Frank Aydelotte. 19 Apr. 1918. (S)
—. Unpublished letter to Group A Students. 10 Nov. 1917. (S)
—. Unpublished letter to Group B Students. 10 Nov. 1917. (S)
—. Unpublished letter to John F. Oderman. 16 Aug. 1917. (S)
—. Unpublished letter to Tutors. 12 Nov. 1917. (S)
—. Unpublished letters to elementary groups A and B, 10 Nov. 1917. (S)
Waeff, Ella A. Unpublished letter to Frank Aydelotte. 23 May 1918. (S)
Walton, Richard S. *Swarthmore College: An Informal History*. Swarthmore, PA: Swarthmore College, 1986.
Way, Margaret E. Unpublished letter to Frank Aydelotte. 24 June 1927. (S)
Wendell, Barrett. *English Composition*. New York: Scribner. 1901.
Wenley, R. M. "Can We Stem the Tide?" *Educational Review* 34 (1907): 241-58.
—. "Transition or What?" *Educational Review* 33 (1907): 433-51.
Wilson, Woodrow. "The Preceptorial System at Princeton." *Educational Review* 39 (1910): 385-90.
Woolley, Edwin C. *Handbook of Composition: A Compendium of Rules Regarding Good English, Grammar, Sentence Structure, Paragraphing, Manuscript Arrangement, Punctuation, Spelling, Essay Writing, and Letter Writing*. Boston: Heath, 1907.
Wozniak, John Michael. *English Composition in Eastern Colleges, 1850-1940*. Washington, D.C.: University Press of America, 1978.
Yoder, Fred R. Unpublished letter to Frank Aydelotte. 23 Feb. 1928. (S)
Young, Karl. Unpublished letter to Frank Aydelotte. 20 Nov. 1913. (S)

# Index

## A

ability levels 18, 130, 162
academic lockstep 25, 108, 123, 128, 147, 162
advanced course 32, 55, 109, 113, 114
advanced students 2, 4, 5, 10, 18, 23, 112, 113
ambitious students 43, 86, 129, 162
American Association of University Professors 136
American course-and-credit system 132
American education 29, 44, 55, 67, 92, 106, 119, 125, 126, 130, 133-135, 151, 152, 154
American higher education 1, 2, 125-128, 154, 162
Amherst College 9, 76
Aristotle's *Poetics* 140
Arnold, Benjamin A. 21
Arnold, George 21-23, 25, 125
Arnold, Matthew 16-18, 21, 31, 58, 59, 61, 63, 65, 66, 69, 80, 92, 93, 94, 105, 121, 125, 131
Arnold/Huxley debate 105
AT&T 27, 89, 91, 107-110, 112-115; employees 109; program 89, 108, 109, 114, 115
audience, concept of 8, 45, 76, 83-85, 91, 100, 102, 105, 112, 141
average in education 1, 2, 9, 15, 21, 26, 43, 51, 55, 89, 125, 127-129, 137, 150, 154, 157, 162; ability 127; student 9, 89, 125, 127-129, 154, 162
Aydelotte, Frank
  American Secretary of the Rhodes Trust 42; Arnoldian beliefs 92; knighted by Queen Elizabeth 40; neglect of technique and rhetoric 25; national following 74, 99; national influence 6, 74, 104; problems at IU 72, 81, 88; progressive educator 17, 18; racism 21, 23, 24; Rhodes Scholar 2, 29, 40, 42-44, 50, 51, 53, 129; views on rhetoric 82

*Breaking the Academic Lockstep* 25, 108, 123, 147

*College English* 2, 8, 11, 14, 24, 55, 58-60, 70, 71, 73, 76-79, 82, 83, 85, 88, 93-95, 162, 163
*Elizabethan Rogues and Vagabonds* 11, 29, 40, 50, 51, 88, 96, 133, 161
*English and Engineering* 15, 25, 27, 84, 91, 96, 99-106, 113, 145, 146, 162, 163
*Honors Courses in American Colleges and Universities* 25, 123, 138, 142, 151
*Oxford Stamp* 15, 16, 24, 30, 46, 55, 63, 87, 88

## B

Babbitt, Irving 11, 14, 15, 75
Bacon, Francis 56, 83
Baker, Ray Palmer 105-106
Baldwin, Charles Sears 33
Bates, Arlo 63, 91
Bates, Herbert 9, 11
Beirne, Frank F. 42
*belles lettres* 56, 93
Bennington 20
Blair, Hugh 55, 56, 89, 105, 106
B.Litt. degree 29, 49
Board of Managers (of Swarthmore) 1, 21-23, 124, 125, 141
Bradley, A.C. 47
Brasenose College 29, 49
Bredvold, Louis I. 79
Brewster, William T. 33
Briggs, LeBaron Russell 6, 34, 36, 38, 39, 61, 68, 89
broad approach to technical communication 101, 110
broad education 95, 108
broadly-trained engineer 102
Brooks, Alfred 68, 72
Brooks, Robert C. 25, 26, 123, 136, 142, 144, 147, 148
Brown, Rollo 36, 38, 61
Bryan, William Lowe 33, 42, 53, 64, 65, 72-74, 75
Bryn Mawr 110, 123

## C

California Institute of Technology 154

Campbell, George 55, 89, 105
Carlyle, Thomas 65, 69, 75, 120
Carnegie Foundation 107, 151, 152
Carpenter, E.R. 76
Carpenter, George S. 98
Civil Rights Movement 23
Civil War 3
classical studies 6, 92
classics 14, 56, 63, 66, 89, 92, 119, 136, 137
Colgate College 153
Columbia's idea course 19
Columbia University 8, 9, 19, 20, 27, 33, 75, 76, 136, 137, 154
composition theory 2, 7, 13
comprehensive examinations 5, 25, 43, 45, 51, 129, 135, 141, 152
consultants 108
conventions (of written discourse) 6, 25, 56, 60, 61, 86, 99, 100, 105, 148, 160
conversation 19, 46, 47, 58, 84, 103
Copeland, Charles Townsend 20, 30, 34, 36-37, 38-39, 71, 85
Cornell, Ezra 4
correctness 7, 13, 14, 32, 37, 38, 40, 54, 55, 58, 62-64, 76-78, 89, 96, 101, 105, 106, 108, 161
Corson, Hiram 12, 18, 157
Crosby, L.A. 43, 141
cultural reading, 100, 101
culture 6, 8-13, 15-17, 27, 53, 59, 65, 69, 81, 92, 94, 100, 102, 104, 105, 108, 110, 111, 112, 113, 119, 130, 137

## D

daily theme (at Harvard) 36, 37, 40
Darbishire, Helen 150
Dartmouth College 21, 115
Darwin, Charles 68
Davidson, Frank 68
democracy 1, 3, 9, 13, 18-20, 92, 125, 126, 129, 130; in education 129
Democratic Party 20
development of English studies 1, 26
Dewey, John 18, 19-20, 126, 130, 161
dialogic 84, 103
diction 7, 36, 41, 62, 64, 85, 144

discipline 3, 4, 15, 25, 31, 44, 45, 58, 59, 66, 84, 119, 131, 132, 134, 141, 157, 162, 163
discussion (role of in thought approach) 20, 21, 27, 33, 36, 46, 47, 55, 68, 70, 75, 77, 79-81, 83, 84, 89, 97, 102, 103, 111, 118, 120, 122, 134-138, 140, 142, 144, 148, 163
Dubois, Charles G. 113

## E

Earle, Samuel Chandler 104, 105
efficiency 13, 27
elective system 4-6, 26, 43, 44, 117, 131, 132, 157, 162
elementary course 109
elementary curriculum 113
elementary students 111, 114
Eliot, William Charles 5, 6-7, 131
Eliot, T.S. 39
Elizabethan scholarship 91
enculturation 100, 101
engineering 4, 5, 10, 15, 25, 27, 55, 84, 91, 94-97, 99-107, 110, 113, 116, 122, 145, 146, 157, 160, 162, 163; education 10, 25, 55, 91, 100, 102, 105
England 2, 10, 40, 46, 47, 92, 118, 120, 142, 145, 146, 163
English A (at Harvard) 5, 30-36, 38, 53, 54, 61, 131, 160, 161
English 2A (at IU) 54, 58, 64-70, 72-75, 83, 87, 88, 91, 99, 145, 159, 163
English 7 (at IU) 62-64, 66, 67, 72, 77
English-History program 5, 115, 134
English literature 5, 15, 16, 47, 48, 50, 55-57, 61, 63, 67, 77, 80, 88, 92, 98, 117, 120, 124, 131-134, 136, 139, 145, 146, 150
English Literature Division at Swarthmore 124, 146
Erskine, John 137
examinations 5, 15, 25, 35, 43-45, 51, 127, 129, 132, 135, 139, 141-144, 149, 150, 152, 155, 160, 162, 163

examinations for honors 141
executives at AT&T 108-111
expression in writing 6, 8, 9, 12, 19, 21, 37, 45, 47, 48, 51, 60, 79, 82, 93, 98, 99, 101, 103, 104, 114, 116, 139, 147-149, 155, 161, 163
expressive rhetoric 83

# F

Firth, C.H. 49, 50, 51, 133
Fisher, Henry C. 115
Fisher, Dorothy Canfield 137, 138
Fite, Warner 124
Flexner, Abraham 42, 151, 154, 160
Foerster, Norman 16, 75-77, 80, 89
football 19, 30, 37, 41, 127
form 3, 7, 8, 10, 19, 25, 26, 29, 32, 35, 36, 38-40, 45, 54-58, 62, 63, 65, 71, 72, 74, 76, 81-83, 85, 86, 89, 93, 94, 103, 108, 110, 112, 121, 131, 132, 137, 140, 143, 149, 160-162
formalism 7, 13, 16, 24, 25, 36, 68, 76, 81, 85, 86, 98, 112, 144
formalist rhetoric 6, 7; methods of 81, 102
Franklin and Marshall College 153
freshman writing program 53
Frost, Harwood 105-106
Fulton, Maurice Garland 79, 80

# G

Gardiner, J. H. 71
Gaston, Charles Robert 84
General Education Board 123, 151, 152
generalist 4, 10, 61, 106
German university 4, 49; as model 10, 61, 106; Ph.D. 10, 15; specialization 10
good writing 8, 13, 24, 50, 60, 64, 83, 101, 163
Goodwin, Thomas G. 98
grading 71, 142
Great Books 132, 136
Greek fraternity system 19
Greek and Roman literature 92
Greek and Latin 14, 15, 161
Green, William 98
Greene, Robert 49, 162
Guggenheim Fellowships 1

# H

Harbinger, S.A. 100
Harris, William T. 42
Harvard 4-7, 10, 13, 14, 16, 24, 25, 29, 30, 32-42, 45, 48-52, 53, 54, 56, 61, 63, 68, 70, 71, 75, 82, 84-86, 89, 98, 103, 105, 106, 112, 131, 144, 151, 155, 159, 161; formalism 13, 16, 24, 68, 82, 85, 86, 112, 144; method of writing instruction 13, 14, 29, 50, 54, 75, 84; reforms 6; rhetoricians 84
Haverford College 123
higher education 1, 2, 4, 15, 18, 21, 26, 126-129, 131, 151, 154, 160, 162
Hill, Adams Sherman 7, 36, 37, 38, 40, 55, 61, 63, 84, 106
Holmes, D.O.W. 22, 23
Holmes, Jesse 136
honors divisions (at Swarthmore) 124, 129, 133, 134
honors education 1, 25, 123, 152, 153, 156, 123, 152, 153, 156, 159; degree 40, 43, 44, 129; program 1, 5, 15, 19, 20, 23-26, 29, 44, 47, 49, 68, 91, 115, 121, 123, 124, 126, 128, 133, 136, 141, 142, 144, 148, 150, 151, 153-157, 162, 163; seminar 20, 25, 133, 135-137, 142, 160, 161, 163; students 5, 11, 18, 43, 124, 129, 133-135, 137, 138, 144, 147-153, 155, 156
honors schools at Oxford 43, 163
Hopkins, Johns 4
Howard University 22
Howe, Will D. 52, 61, 64-65, 72-73, 77
humanistic education 83, 109
humanistic basis of technical communication 2
humanistic enculturation 100
humanities 4, 10, 27, 99, 100, 102, 106, 116, 117, 138, 157
Hunt, Everett 21-22, 125
Huxley, Thomas Henry 16, 69, 79, 93

# I

idea course 16, 19, 27
imitation 13, 55, 56, 63
independent thinking 58, 155

Indiana University (IU) 2, 6, 8, 13, 15, 16, 24, 26, 27, 29-33, 34, 36, 38, 40, 41, 42, 48, 51, 53, 54, 61-64, 66, 72, 73, 89, 93, 96, 99, 100,103, 113, 116, 117 125, 126, 145, 146, 151, 159, 160, 163; English department 31, 61
individual differences 4, 19, 130
industrialization 3, 126
industrialized civilization, 126
infant criticism 70, 71
information (vs. knowledge) 4, 7, 16, 26, 45, 46, 58, 59, 64-69, 71, 81, 83, 87, 88 89, 103, 113, 116, 117, 127, 131, 132, 135, 142, 143, 148, 153
Iowa State University 79

**J**
Jackson, D.C. 92
Jelliffe, R.A. 87
Johns Hopkins University 4, 154

**K**
Kingsbury, N.C. 110-111
Kittredge, George Layman 34, 35
Krapp, George Philip 64, 76-77, 163

**L**
Laird, Stephen 156
Lamont, Hammond 33
land-grant universities 4
Lang, Andrew 46
Latin 3, 14, 15, 34, 42, 161
Latin and Greek 3
leadership 3, 9, 21, 23, 27, 41, 42, 96, 101, 102, 117, 125, 130, 152
Learned, William S. 151
liberal arts 1, 4, 15, 48, 95, 96, 101, 121, 123, 125, 126, 130, 131, 133, 135, 145, 152, 154, 152, 154, 157, 160; courses 15, 131
liberal education 9, 10, 48, 76, 93, 94, 101, 131, 156
liberal knowledge 58, 69, 94-96, 108, 115
liberal culturalists 8-15, 18, 34, 157
liberal culture 8, 15, 25, 29, 31, 49, 81, 93, 137
liberal studies 3, 94
Lincoln, Abraham 4

*Literae Humaniores* 43, 92, 117, 119, 161
literature 2, 5, 9-17, 19, 24, 29-32, 34-36, 40, 41, 43, 44, 47-51, 54-67, 69-73, 77, 79, 80, 84, 88, 91-102, 109, 110, 113, 114, 116-122, 124, 131-134, 136, 137, 139, 140, 143-146, 150, 160, 161, 163; and history 49, 50, 61, 96; and science 79, 97; and writing 2, 10, 29, 60, 66, 160, 163
Logan, Floyd L. 23
Lounsbury, Thomas R. 13, 64

**M**
Maclaurin, Richard Cockburn 91-93, 94, 96, 107, 109, 115, 116, 117, 118, 119
managerial rhetoric 7, 98
Manchester, Frederick A. 75, 77, 80
Mann, C.R. 55, 107, 114, 117
Manning, Frederick 148, 149
mass education (problems with)126, 127, 152
Massachusetts Institute of Technology 2, 5, 11, 13, 15, 16, 25-27, 29, 87-89, 91, 93, 94, 96-99, 101, 106-10, 113-121, 125, 126, 145, 160, 163; Corporation 117; English department 63, 96; English-History program 134
mechanical correctness 7, 8, 13, 14, 29, 30, 32, 36, 62, 64, 65, 72, 76, 87, 149
mediocrity in education 1, 15, 127, 159
Meiklejohn, Alexander 9, 18, 76
mental discipline 3, 4
Merrill, William A. 9
Michener, James A. 147, 155
Milton, John 33, 67, 69, 163
Modern Greats (at Oxford) 133, 161
modes of discourse 7, 8, 12, 13, 16, 25-27, 30, 32, 33, 36, 38, 56, 63, 85, 86, 105
Moore, Paul Elmer 75
More, Thomas 139
Morrill Act 4
Mt. Holyoke College 85
Murphy, Carl 22, 23

## N

Nason, John 24, 91, 152
National Council of Teachers of English 81, 84
Nelson, J. Raleigh 106
new humanist group 75
*New Oxonian* 40
New Zealand 96
New York Public Library 114
New Humanism 75
Newman, John Henry 16, 33, 58-59, 65, 66, 68, 69, 79, 80, 93, 94, 113, 131, 132

## O

Oberlin College 86
Oderman, John F. 110
old college in the U.S. 3, 4, 6, 100
old curriculum 4, 30
Open Scholarship 21
oral examination (at Swarthmore) 142-144
Osgood, Charles G. 14, 136
outside examiners 135, 142-144, 153
Oxford 2, 5, 8, 11, 15, 16, 18, 20, 24-27, 29, 30, 39-52, 53-55, 57, 58, 61-63, 65, 66, 68, 71, 73, 74, 76, 77, 80, 82-88, 91, 92, 99, 102, 103, 114, 115, 117-119, 123, 125, 129, 130, 133-136, 138, 141, 149, 150, 157; conversation 46, 103; educational system 2, 15, 43-45, 51, 114, 133, 138, 141, 157, 161, 163; honors schools 15, 129, 133, 141; traditions 66, 77 tutorials 39, 71, 84, 102

## P

Palmer, Glenn E. 13
pamphlet literature 11, 49
paper assignments 139
papers 7, 20, 25, 30, 32, 39, 45, 49, 50, 52, 61, 68, 70, 71, 104, 106, 110, 111, 127, 129, 134, 136, 138-141, 143-150, 154-157, 160, 161, 163
Park, Clyde W. 100, 104
pass degree 15, 41-43, 162
Pearson, Henry G. 93, 97, 98, 115, 117, 119, 120, 121
Perry, Bliss 10-11, 15, 18, 34, 35, 37, 38
Phelps, William Lyon 34-35, 37, 38, 39
philologists 10, 31, 47, 57
philology 10, 11, 31, 34, 35, 41, 48, 75, 93
Pillsbury, J.S. 4
Plato 82, 83, 140
Platonic rhetoric 82, 83
Pope, Alexander 48, 67, 69
Princeton University 8-10, 13, 14, 124, 136, 137; Institute of Advanced Study 159
professional education and training 9, 10, 93, 94
Prothero, George W. 51

## Q

Quakenbos, G.P. 55
Quakers 21, 124
Queen Elizabeth 40
quizzes and examinations 135, 139

## R

racism 21, 23, 24
Raleigh, Walter 5, 40, 41, 47-51, 52, 82, 83, 106, 133, 161, 162
reading 9, 11-17, 20, 25-27, 32, 33, 35, 36, 38, 44, 45, 47, 49, 51, 54, 57, 59-61, 63, 65-67, 69-72, 76, 78-80, 83, 84, 92, 93, 97, 100-105, 113, 114, 120, 123, 124, 129, 132-140, 142-144, 146-148, 150, 153, 155, 156, 160-163
recitation 3, 6, 68, 84
responses to the Honors Program 151
rhetoric 3, 6-9, 12, 18, 20, 24-26, 31, 32, 34, 36, 55, 56, 63, 77, 78, 82-87, 89, 98, 99, 106, 112, 140, 141, 148
rhetorical principles 25, 32, 56, 81, 84, 86, 87
rhetorical situation 45, 141
Rhodes scholarship 1, 40, 43, 46, 51, 73, 88, 121, 129, 152, 159
Rhodes Will 41
Rhodes, Cecil John 59, 92
Rice, Richard Ashley 73, 77-79

Rickard, T.A. 106
Rideout, H.M. 36, 38
Ristine, Frank 80
Rogers, Robert E. 119
Romantics 69
rule-of-thumb engineering 95

**S**

Sampson, Martin W. 31-32, 33
Sarah Lawrence 20
scholarship 1, 11, 12, 15, 19, 21, 22, 29, 33, 35, 40-43, 47, 49, 53, 73, 88, 91, 121, 124, 129, 137, 151, 159, 160
science 3-6, 10, 19, 30, 33, 48, 58, 69, 79, 80, 92-95, 97, 100, 102, 107, 113, 116, 118, 120, 131, 133-36, 148, 157, 161; and culture 94; and literature 69, 79, 93, 102
Seaver, Henry Latimer 96
sedulous ape 56
seminars 5, 13, 19, 20, 25, 27, 51, 61, 129, 132, 134-139, 141, 142, 144, 147, 148, 152, 154, 157, 160, 162, 163
Shakespeare 33-35, 47, 49, 60, 67, 69, 139, 140, 163
Sherman, L.A. 12
Sidney Sir Phillip 69, 140
Snell, Edna L.F. 85-86
social justice 17, 21, 125
social life (at college) 43, 46, 100, 123, 125, 153, 154, 162
Socrates 82, 84, 103, 149
Socratic method 83, 84, 103
Southwestern College 153
specialists (vs. generalists) 4, 10, 11, 25, 42, 61, 94, 95, 118, 142
specialization 96, 106
Spiller, Robert E. 127
spiritual ideals 113
standard college curriculum 127, 129
Steeves, Harrison viii, 75, 80
Stevenson, Robert Louis 55-56, 57, 113
student-centered curriculum 19
style 7, 14, 16, 25, 35, 36, 39, 40, 47, 50, 51, 55, 56, 60, 62, 82, 86, 89, 96, 101, 106, 147, 150

superficiality of American education 67
Swain, Joseph 33, 42
Swarthmore College 22, 25, 26, 29, 123-158; endowment 152; English Department 127, 146; honors seminars 136-141; reforms 18; sorority system 19, 154; students 22, 49, 132, 137, 154, 155; typical humanities seminar 138
Swarthmore College Faculty 128, 130, 133, 137, 138, 141-144, 147

**T**

teachers 3, 7, 8, 11, 14, 20, 24, 31, 32, 34, 37, 38, 55, 57, 63, 64, 66-68, 70, 71, 74-76, 78, 81, 84-87, 102-104, 119, 133, 136, 142, 160
technical communication and writing 2, 15, 25, 27, 99, 108, 115, 159, 163
technical knowledge 96, 99
technique in writing 24-26, 36, 56, 60, 63, 65, 78, 87, 97, 101, 106, 131, 137, 156
The Greats (at Oxford) 15, 43, 161
Thomas, Joseph M. 16, 18, 106
thoroughness 2, 15, 44, 78, 79, 141
thought 7-9, 11-14, 16-21, 23-27, 29-33, 35, 36, 38-42, 44, 46-49, 52, 53-61, 64, 65, 68, 70, 71, 73-89, 92, 93, 95-99, 101-108, 112, 113, 115-118, 120-122, 124-127, 129-131, 134, 137, 143-146, 148, 149, 154-156, 160-163
thought course 16, 25, 27, 54, 76, 81, 88, 106, 124, 125, 145, 146, 163
thought approach 7, 8, 11-13, 16-20, 24-27, 29-31, 35, 47, 48, 53-55, 57, 68, 70, 74-76, 79-81, 84, 98, 99, 102, 105-108, 112, 115, 118, 120, 121, 160, 161, 163
Thing, Charles Franklin 14, 15
traditional instruction 127
translation 14, 15, 36, 37, 42
tutorial system 2, 44, 51, 115, 134, 135, 160
tutorials 15, 20, 30, 39, 44, 45, 51, 71, 84, 86, 134, 149, 152, 163

tutors 25, 42, 44, 45, 61, 85, 102, 157, 161, 162

**U**

undergraduate education 15, 40, 48, 133, 159, 163
unity, coherence, and emphasis 7
University of Virginia 42
University of Pennsylvania 19
University of Wisconsin 75
utilitarian writing 27, 97, 98, 163
utility/culture 105

**V**

Valentine, Robert Grosenver 98
Van Dyke, Henry 10, 12
Victorian essayists 16, 33, 65, 69, 77, 113
Victorians 16, 79
Vinal, A.C. 107, 108, 110, 111, 113, 114

**W**

War Department 115, 117
weak students 25, 72
weaknesses of thought approach 24, 37, 47, 92, 129
Wellesley College 150
Wells College 153
Wendell, Barrett 7, 32, 34, 36, 37, 55, 61, 63, 84
Wenley, R.M. 10, 11
white minorities 24
Wilson, Woodrow 136
Woolley, Edwin C. 62, 63
Wordsworth 47, 67-69, 77, 163
work-place writing 106
World War I 91, 107, 108
writing and literature 54, 62, 66
writing 2-10, 12-15, 20, 24-27, 29-32, 34, 36-40, 42, 43, 45, 47, 49-52, 53-56, 58, 60-67, 69-72, 75, 77-79, 81-84, 86, 87, 89, 91, 96-111, 113, 115, 120-122, 123-126, 131, 135-139, 141, 143-151, 153, 155-157, 160, 161, 163
writing instruction 6-9, 12, 14, 24, 27, 34, 40, 29, 32, 43, 45, 47, 51, 54, 61, 70, 75, 84, 97, 98, 124, 144, 146, 147, 161
written English 86, 151
written discourse 6, 32, 86, 92
written examinations 143

**Y**

Yale 8, 13, 14, 33, 35, 38, 56, 148
Yale's Sheffield School 13, 77
Yoder, Fred R. 123
Young, Karl 75-76, 77, 80

# About the Author

Michael G. Moran is an Associate Professor of English at the University of Georgia where he has directed the First-year Composition Program and coordinated the Graduate Program. His teaching and research interests include freshman and advanced composition, 18$^{th}$-century British literature, rhetorical theory, the history of composition and rhetoric, and the history of technical communication. He has co-edited three major bibliographies: *Research in Composition and Rhetoric* (with Ronald F. Lunsford), *Research in Technical Communication* (with Debra Journet), and *Research in Basic Writing* (with Matin J. Jacobi). The second won an NCTE Award. His more recent work has been in the history of rhetoric and technical communication, and he has edited and co-edited the following books: *Eighteenth-century British and American Rhetorics and Rhetoricians*, *Three Keys to the Past: The History of Technical Communication* (with Teresa Kynell Hunt), *Twentieth-century Rhetorics and Rhetoricians*, and *Classical Rhetorics and Rhetoricians* (the last two with Michelle Ballif). He lives in Athens with his wife, Molly Hurley Moran, and has a daughter, Alison Emily Moran.

www.ingramcontent.com/pod-product-compliance
Lightning Source LLC
Chambersburg PA
CBHW030112010526
44116CB00005B/212